# Teaching in the Lifelong Learning Sector

# Teaching in the Lifelong Learning Sector

Second edition

*Peter Scales*
with
*Kelly Briddon and Lynn Senior*

Open University Press

Open University Press
McGraw-Hill Education
McGraw-Hill House
Shoppenhangers Road
Maidenhead
Berkshire
England
SL6 2QL

email: enquiries@openup.co.uk
world wide web: www.openup.co.uk

and Two Penn Plaza, New York, NY 10121–2289, USA

First published 2008
Reprinted 2009, 2010, 2011
First published in this second edition 2013

A catalogue record of this book is available from the British Library

ISBN-13: 978-0-33-524653-3 (pb)
ISBN-10: 0-33-524653-2 (pb)
eISBN: 978-0-33-524654-0

*Library of Congress Cataloging-in-Publication Data*
CIP data applied for

Typesetting and e-book compilations by
RefineCatch Limited, Bungay, Suffolk
Printed in Great Britain by CPI Antony Rowe, Chippenham, Wiltshire

"*The new edition contains some really useful additional material. It signposts to key policies and is brought up to date in identifying current influences and debates within the HE and FE sector. There is reference to views on the curriculum. More attention is given to Functional Skills. I liked the positive emphasis placed on classroom management as Behaviour for Learning. New developments and inclusions are well judged. It remains an accessible and sufficiently detailed book for all those who are on teacher education programmes.*"

*Victoria Wright, Senior Lecturer in Post Compulsory Education,*
*University of Wolverhampton, UK*

"*This is a valuable resource that can be used by both trainee and recently qualified teachers, who are considering a career in the Further Education sector. It contains a mixture of both theory and practical activities which have been mapped to the LLUK standards. The contents key at the beginning of each chapter means it can be used for reference purposes. The text is easily readable and, therefore accessible to all.*"

*Cheryl Hine, Lecturer on Teacher Training, Leeds City College, UK*

Once again, to Vanessa, and also to the memory of my mother Evelyn Rose Scales, who made it possible for me to do my education again.

# Contents

# Acknowledgements

The author and publishers would like to thank MICA Management Resources (UK) Inc. for permission to reproduce the figure from Edward de Bono's *The Greatest Thinkers* and The Plain English Campaign for permission to reproduce material from their website.

I would like to thank my students for the past 32 years, from whom I have learned so much. In particular I want to thank Martyn Watson, Russell Godber, Lisa Adamiec, Jasvir Girn, Becca Wildey, Zaheera Sidat and Terry Doherty for permission to reproduce extracts from their journals. Thanks to Barrie Leahy for his behaviour case study. Thank you to Maggie Harnew of Skills Workshop for her advice on functional skills and Skills for Life.

Special thanks to my colleagues at the University of Derby for their advice and support: Lynn Senior; Kelly Briddon; Jo Pickering; Peter Tunnicliffe (who corrected my 'behaviour'); Kath Headley; Patsy Garner; Helen Boulton; Angela Davey; Laura-Lee Marriott.

My sincere thanks go to Fiona Richman and Laura Givans of McGraw-Hill for their patience and support. Thanks also to our copy editor, Penelope Allport, for her diligence and patience.

# Abbreviations

| | |
|---|---|
| ADHD | attention deficit hyperactivity disorder |
| AfL | assessment for learning |
| ALC | Advanced Learning Coach |
| ALI | Adult Learning Inspectorate |
| AoC | Association of Colleges |
| APEL | Accreditation of Prior and Experiential Learning |
| APL | Accreditation of Prior Learning |
| ATLS | Associate Teacher Learning and Skills |
| Becta | British Educational and Communications and Technology Agency (now defunct) |
| BEI | British Education Index |
| BIS | Department for Business, Innovation and Skills |
| BTEC | Business and Technology Education Council |
| CASE | Cognitive Acceleration through Science Education |
| CBT | Cognitive behavioural therapy |
| CERI | Centre for Educational Research and Innovation |
| Cert. Ed. | Certificate in Education |
| CETTS | Centres of Training in Teacher Excellence |
| CPD | Continuing Professional Development |
| CTLLS | Certificate in Teaching in the Lifelong Learning Sector |
| DfES | Department for Education and Skills |
| DTLLS | Diploma in Teaching in the Lifelong Learning Sector |
| EBD | emotional and behavioural difficulties |
| EHRC | Equality and Human Rights Commission |
| ERIC | Educational Resource Information Centre |
| ESOL | English for Speakers of Other Languages |
| E2E | Entry to Employment |
| FE | further education |
| FENTO | Further Education National Training Organisation (now defunct) |
| FLT | Foundation Learning Tier |
| fMRI | Functional magnetic resource imaging |

| | |
|---|---|
| GCSE | General Certificate of Secondary Education |
| GNVQ | general national Vocational Qualification |
| HEI | higher education instution |
| ICT | information and communication technology |
| IfL | Institute for Learning |
| ILP | individual learning plan |
| ILT | information and learning technology |
| INSET | in-service education and training |
| IQ | intelligence quotient |
| IT | information technology |
| LAN | local area network |
| LLN | language, literacy and numeracy |
| LLS | Lifelong learning sector |
| LLUK | Lifelong Learning UK |
| LSC | Learning and Skills Council (now defunct) |
| LSIS | Learning and Skills Improvement Service |
| NCVQ | National Council for Vocational Qualifications |
| NIACE | National Institute for Adult and Continuing Education |
| NQF | National Qualifications Framework |
| NRDC | National Research Development Centre for Adult Literacy and Numeracy |
| NVC | non-verbal communication |
| NVQ | national vocational qualification |
| OCN | Open College Network |
| Ofsted | Office for Standards in Education |
| OHP | overhead projector |
| OHT | overhead transparency |
| PBL | problem-based learning |
| PCET | post-compulsory education and training |
| PDJ | personal development journal |
| PGCEFE | Postgraduate Certificate in Education |
| PGCHE | Postgraduate Certificate in Higher Education |
| PLTS | personal, learning and thinking skills |
| PTLLS | Preparing to Teach in the Lifelong Learning Sector |
| QCA | Qualifications and Curriculum Authority (now defunct) |
| QTLS | Qualified Teacher Learning and Skills |
| QTS | Qualified Teacher Status |
| RPL | Recognised Prior Learning |
| SATs | Standardised Assessment Tasks |
| SfL | Skills for Life |
| SLC | Subject Learning Coach |
| SpLD | Specific learning difficulties |
| STEM | Science, Technology, Engineering and Maths |
| TLRP | Teaching and Learning Research Project |
| UCAS | Universities and Colleges Admissions Service |
| UKCES | UK Commission on Employability and Skills |
| VLE | virtual learning environment |

WEA       Workers Educational Association
ZPD       zone of proximal development

The University and Colleges Union (UCU) provides an online *A–Z of FE and HE*. This comprehensive dictionary of acronyms, abbreviations and terminology, with links to websites, is available at www.ucu.org.uk/media/pdf/i/o/a-z_fehe.pdf.

# Introduction

## Who is this book for?

The lifelong learning workforce includes those in further education; adult and community learning; work-based learning and offender learning. In addition, the public services, the armed services and the health service all have considerable numbers of people involved in training and continuing professional development. This book is designed for all these, and more, including:

- Any pre-service or in-service trainee teachers taking courses leading to:
    - Preparing to Teach in the Lifelong Learning Sector (PTLLS)
    - Certificate in Teaching in the Lifelong Learning Sector (CTLLS)
    - Diploma in Teaching in the Lifelong Learning Sector (DTLLS)
- Teachers in colleges working with 14–16 year olds
- Teachers in sixth forms and sixth-form colleges
- Trainers in private training providers
- Teachers of higher education in further education colleges
- This book might also be useful to lecturers in higher education, including those undertaking Postgraduate Certificate in Higher Education (PGCHE) programmes, who want to develop new ideas and new methods.

The book is not only for those of you who are training to teach but also as a guide and resource during your professional career as a teacher and as support for your continuing professional development (CPD) and in maintaining your licence to practise through the Institute for Learning (IfL).

## Why 'lifelong learning'?

In this part of the introduction I want briefly to put forward some arguments in favour of lifelong learning because I think that people in the sector should be able to debate the issues and to argue for the importance of lifelong learning. These are only a few of the arguments – I'm sure you can think of many more.

Traditional forms of learning have been heavily reliant on learners being able to correctly recall a fairly arbitrary body of knowledge (chosen by educators and politicians) in a formal assessment, generally an examination. One of the underlying assumptions of this system was that people were genetically endowed with fixed levels of intelligence – some were 'bright', some 'less 'bright'; some 'academic', some 'vocational' – and that the job of education was to identify and select these different performers and assign them to the appropriate institutions where they would meet others very much like themselves to be taught by teachers who were habituated to teaching only those kinds of pupils. Education was designed on an industrial model to suit the needs of an industrial society – with a standardised body of learning (the curriculum), a limited range of teaching and learning methods (pedagogy) and a standardised product (assessment and qualifications) used to grade learners and to slot them into a job at the appropriate level of the economy. All of this was delivered in formal, hierarchical settings governed by the clock – just like a factory.

The 'industrial model' of education may have been appropriate for an industrial age; unfortunately we don't live in an industrial age any longer. This may be a matter of regret for many, but that's just the way it is; others might regard it as liberation. In a post-industrial age there is no longer a job for life, probably not even in times of full employment. People will have different jobs, even a 'portfolio' of several jobs at the same time. There will be a need for learning and relearning throughout our lives. Non-standard jobs will increasingly require non-standard and non-uniform learning. People will probably need skills more than knowledge. And all this will happen within a globalised economy in which people will work in many different places – real or virtual.

We are said to be living in a 'knowledge economy' or in an 'age of information'. It could be argued that knowledge and information in themselves are not particularly useful. Real education has never been about just passing on parcels of knowledge from one generation to the next. Knowledge has to be used, interpreted, changed, developed, discarded, become the building blocks for something new. At school, I learned the currency of pounds, shillings and pence – no longer required. As an adult, I learned to programme my VHS recorder – now irrelevant. As the philosopher and mathematician A. N. Whitehead wrote in 1932: 'Knowledge does not keep any better than fish' (p. 147). In the 'information age' knowledge will rapidly become outdated and new learning will be required. We will need to learn how to learn.

This need for lifelong learning, individually, economically and socially, is central to the discussion by Gorard and Rees (2002) of a 'learning society'. While they acknowledge that lifelong learning is a combination of initial and adult education, they suggest that most expenditure on education is 'front-loaded', being spent on schools, colleges and universities. They argue that a learning society will need greater investment throughout people's lives and that a learning society 'deals more effectively with the problem of obsolete knowledge than an educational system that is front-loaded' (Gorard and Rees 2002: 3).

The disproportionate amount spent on formal, front-loaded education is picked up in the National Institute for Adult Continuing Education (NIACE) report on lifelong learning which recommends a slight, in percentage terms, shift of funding towards lifelong learning (Schuller and Watson 2010). As this report suggests, the allocation of funds is 'heavily skewed' towards those in compulsory education and those aged 18 to 25, a situation which probably reflects an assumption that education only really happens in formal settings. From another perspective, we might regard as strange a situation in which the majority of people spend the majority of their lives not in formal education but, according to NIACE, 86 per cent of the total spending on learning and education is directed to those under 25.

Another set of arguments for lifelong learning can be found in brain research. There is much neurological evidence to support the benefits of learning throughout life and the ways in which our brains develop at different stages of our lives. Brain 'plasticity' refers to the brain's ability to mould and shape itself to the demands of its environment. It now seems clear that this plasticity continues much further through the lifespan than was previously thought.

> The demands made on the individual and his or her learning are the key to plasticity – the more you learn, the more you can learn. Far from supporting ageist notions that education is best concentrated on the young – the powerful learning capacity of young people notwithstanding – neuroscience has shown *that learning is a lifelong activity and that the more it continues the more effective it is.*
> (CERI 2007: 153, original emphasis)

Lifelong learning is central to social and economic inclusion. We know that education has failed many people and left them disadvantaged in many ways – emotionally, psychologically, economically and socially. Inclusive learning and widening participation go hand in hand. It is the job of lifelong learning to reach out to people and bring them in and provide learning that meets their needs. Older people need to be brought back into the habit of lifelong learning; younger people not to lose it in the first place.

Many of the arguments supporting lifelong learning are economic – this is undeniably important. Ultimately, however, the best arguments come from the perspectives of fairness, equity and social justice and for giving everyone opportunities to learn and make better lives for themselves. This is admirably expressed by the following quote:

> Adults young and old can change. The way people are today is not how they must be for the rest of their days. The conditions in which people live, and which shape their values and attitudes today, do not have to stay as they are forever.
> (Field 2011: 25)

Some might argue that, particularly in times of economic crisis, extra expenditure on lifelong learning is a luxury we can't afford, but, as somebody once said, 'If you think education is expensive, try ignorance.'

## Importance of expert teachers and expert learners

It could be argued that talk of 'learners' rather than 'students' and of student autonomy and 'learning to learn' is undermining the role and importance of expert teachers.

Whether learners are taking A-level English or GCSE Maths or on programmes of learning for nail technology or plumbing, they need to be taught by experts who are knowledgeable and up to date. People will learn from these experts because, initially, they know more than their students. The need for expert teachers is central to the idea of the 'dual professional' as an expert subject specialist and expert teacher.

These experts who taught you can't, unfortunately, accompany you throughout your life and work. You will need to become your own 'expert', continually able to update your skills and knowledge, find information, think for yourself and solve problems. You will become an expert in your field – eventually you may wish to return to education as an expert teacher.

## Teachers are lifelong learners

The Lifelong Learning UK (LLUK) standards for teachers, tutors and trainers in the lifelong learning sector put reflection and continual improvement at the heart of professional practice. Lifelong learning makes considerable demands on teachers because they have to update both their subject-specific skills and their teaching and learning methods. As Norman Longworth says:

> For teachers, lifelong learning enforces a double whammy. It changes not only the content, but also the methodology of their profession. They become transformed into organisers of all the considerable educational and human resources at their disposal in the interests of actively stimulating learning.
>
> (Longworth 2003: 29)

There's an old adage which goes something like this: 'If you really want to learn about something, write a book about it.' Having worked in post-compulsory education for more than 25 years, I thought I knew pretty well everything about teaching and learning in the sector. However, I've learned a great deal more by writing, and rewriting, this book. In fact it's been an excellent piece of continuing professional development. The point I wish to make is that all good teachers are good learners – indeed, lifelong learners. If you're not learning, you're not teaching very well. Not only will you lack up-to-date skills and knowledge, but you will also have little to enthuse or excite you and, consequently, your learners.

## What does all this mean for teaching and learning?

In a nutshell, it means that learning will be different from what it was in the past. The emphasis is moving away from *teaching* towards *learning*; away from students being filled up with knowledge and tested. Educational discourse has become saturated with references to 'delivering' learning. Pizzas and babies can be delivered: learning can't. Learning is something that individual learners do. Good teaching stimulates good learning. The delivery metaphor is unsuited to the educational, social and economic needs of the future and, as Davison points out: 'A delivered curriculum does not imply the need for a thinking teacher who is developing critical thinking in pupils [learners]' (Davison 2008: 31).

This book is about *active learning*. Precisely what this means will become more apparent as you read, but essentially it describes the kind of learning where individuals are actively involved in creating meaning, knowledge and skills; the kind of learning which encourages questioning, discovery and exploration; the kind of learning which uses assessment as a means of continual improvement rather than as a way of ascertaining at what point people will fail; the kind of learning which believes everyone can continually develop and achieve.

## How to use this book

The simplest way to use this book is just to read it. However, it might a good idea to read the first three chapters on being a professional, reflective practice and communication because these provide the foundations of good practice on which everything else is built. I have tried as far as possible to arrange the chapters in a logical order which will take you from theories of learning through planning, preparation and assessment to evaluation and continuing professional development.

## The LLUK standards

Lifelong Learning UK is no longer in existence but the standards it introduced are still in use and underpin all teaching in the lifelong learning sector. The work of LLUK has been taken over by the Learning and Skills Improvement Service (LSIS). You should download a copy of the 'New overarching standards for teachers, tutors and trainers in the lifelong learning sector' from the LSIS Excellence Gateway website (www.excellencegateway.org.uk/). To provide an overview, the standards are divided into six main domains. These are:

Domain A   Professional values and practice
Domain B   Learning and teaching
Domain C   Specialist learning and teaching
Domain D   Planning for learning
Domain E   Assessment for learning
Domain F   Access and progression

Each domain has a series of competence statements detailing scope, knowledge and practice:

- *S = Scope.* These statements provide an overview of the domain and the underpinning values. For example, BS1 'Maintaining an inclusive, equitable and motivating learning environment'.
- *K = Knowledge.* These statements are derived from the scope statement and describe what a teacher in the lifelong learning sector should know and understand. For example, BK1.1 'Ways to maintain a learning environment in which learners feel safe and supported'.
- *P = Practice.* These statements are also derived from the scope statement and describe the professional practice of teachers in the lifelong learning sector. For

example, BP1.1 'Establish a purposeful learning environment where learners feel safe, secure, confident and valued'.

Each chapter in the book indicates the standards covered. However, you should remember that not all the standards will be met by reading a book; the standards are as much about what you do as what bits of evidence you collect. The standards are based on a competence system that breaks the teacher's job down into a series of competences which should be common to all. You will be asked to provide evidence of how you meet the standards as part of your teacher training. However, all jobs, especially the teacher, are more than the sum of the individual parts. Teaching is a holistic activity that brings together a range of elements – planning; methods; assessment – to work together in concert. The final chapter of this book encourages you to make connections and see the big picture beyond the separate elements.

## Terminology

Throughout this book I have used the term *learner* to include, at least, the following: student, trainee, apprentice. Occasionally, I use the word *student* when I got fed up with writing *learner*. *Teacher* is used to indicate teacher, lecturer, trainer and tutor. I have generally used the term *lifelong learning sector* to include, at least: further education; post-compulsory education and training (PCET); colleges; work-based learning; adult and community learning, and offender learning.

## Further reading

Armitage, A., Evershed, J., Hayes, D., Hudson, A., Kent, J., Lawes, S., Poma, S. and Renwick, M. (2012) *Teaching and Training in Lifelong Learning*. Maidenhead: Open University Press.
Duckworth, V. and Tummons, J. (2010) *Contemporary Issues in Lifelong Learning*. Maidenhead: Open University Press.
Schuller, T. and Watson, D. (2010) *Learning Through Life: Inquiry into the Future for Lifelong Learning*. Leicester: National Institute of Adult and Continuing Education (NIACE).

## Websites

Institute for Learning (IfL) www.ifl.ac.uk
LSIS (Learning and Skills Excellence Gateway) www.excellencegateway.org.uk/

# 1

# The lifelong learning sector
## Kelly Briddon

---

**What this chapter is about**

- Key policies, documents and legislation in the development of the sector
- The role of the Institute for Learning (IfL)
- Associate Teacher Learning and Skills (ATLS) and Qualified Teacher Learning and Skills (QTLS)
- Teacher training qualifications for the sector
- The Learning and Skills Improvement Service (LSIS)
- Being a professional teacher

---

**LLUK standards**

This chapter covers, at least, the following standards:
AS 2; AK 2.1; AP 2.1; AK 2.2; AS 6; AK 6.1; AP 6.1

---

### The lifelong learning sector – an overview

The following overview of the sector's development provides a brief introduction to the key documents, policies and legislation that have shaped the current lifelong learning sector. The sector has experienced significant changes that have impacted on the way it is classified, managed and experienced by learners, staff, employers and governments. These reports reflect the perceptions and intentions of a range of stakeholders and have moulded the evolution of the sector. In education, as in so many areas of public life, change appears to be the only constant and it will be interesting, in the light of the Wolf Report and the coalition government's new Reform Plan, to see what shape (and name) the sector will take in the next five years.

## Green Paper 'The Learning Age' 1998

This set out the importance of lifelong learning for personal, social and economic success and identified the need for teachers to be qualified to national standards. It was the first policy paper that outlined the need to develop education skills from post-school to post-retirement. This key passage captures the essence of the report: 'Learning throughout life can build human capital by encouraging creativity, skill and imagination. The fostering of an enquiring mind and the love of learning are essential for our future success.'

## White Paper 'Learning to Succeed' 1999

This introduced Learning and Skills Councils (LSCs) to provide funding for an expansion of learners within the growing sector. It also introduced a new inspection regime, Adult Learning Inspectorate (ALI), for learners 19 and over and in work-based learning. The 16-19 sector would be inspected by Ofsted, which took over the functions of ALI in 2007. It also established more links between schools and colleges and introduced Connexions to support learners in their choices and mentioned the creation of city academies

## Further Education National Training Organisation (FENTO) Standards 2001

This introduced a set of professional standards for further education (FE) teachers. Previously, it was not a requirement for teachers in FE to possess a teaching qualification. This was mainly due to the recognition that the staff in FE had come from vocational backgrounds and not through the academic route undertaken by primary and secondary teachers. This was invaluable to the growth of the lifelong learning sector (LLS); experts were needed in the skills areas that were required to grow the economy. However, these standards were not received well and were heavily criticised by Ofsted.

## 'Success For All: Reforming Further Education and Training – Our Vision for the Future' (DfES) 2002

This was a reform strategy from the then Department for Education and Skills (DfES) intended to improve the quality and effectiveness of post-16 education and training. It identified the need to work with employers and the importance of high quality teaching and learning. It also recognised the importance of using information communication technology (ICT) in teaching and learning.

## Green Paper 'Every Child Matters' 2003

This emphasised the need for key agencies to work together to protect and nurture young people in all that they do. Five key themes were to be incorporated into lesson planning and are still relevant today: being healthy; staying safe; enjoying and achieving; making a positive contribution; and economic well-being.

## 'The Initial Training of Further Education Teachers' (Ofsted) 2003

This report stated: 'The current system of FE teacher training does not provide a satisfactory foundation of professional development for FE teachers at the start of their careers. . . . While the FENTO standards provide a useful outline of the capabilities required of experienced FE teachers, they do not clearly define the standards required of new teachers' (Ofsted 2003: 5). This report led to the government's proposals for teacher training: *Equipping Our Teachers for the Future.*

## 'Equipping our Teachers for the Future' (DfES) 2004

This identified the need for a new teacher training reform in response to the damning Ofsted report. It proposed the confirmation of Qualified Teacher Learning and Skills (QTLS) to be awarded by the new professional body, the Institute for Learning (IfL), and that trainee teachers would need to complete a passport to teaching initially before completing a full qualification. This would later be referred to as Preparing to Teach in the Lifelong Learning Sector (PTLLS). The date given for implementation was September 2007.

## White Paper '14–19 Education and Skills' (DfES) 2005

This was a key document because it brought compulsory learning into the lifelong learning sector. The White Paper which finalised the work conducted by Mike Tomlinson on 14–19 reform introduced specialised vocational diplomas as an alternative to national curriculum study. It identified the need for Functional Skills in Maths, English and ICT. It provided a link with employer needs for the varying sectors in relation to the needs of the economy. It recognised the need for a more work-based learning route and the importance of engaging disaffected learners with the introduction of Entry to Employment programmes (E2E). It also meant that teachers in the LLS had to now deliver to a different age group, 14–16 year olds.

## The Foster Report 'Realising the Potential: A Review of the Future Role of Further Education Colleges' 2005

This report referred to FE as 'the middle child of education', saying that it lacked a clear focus and purpose. It emphasised the importance of competing globally with other countries in terms of skills development and stressed the need to have a 'core focus on skills and employability' (Foster 2005: 2). This marked a change in focus and direction for both teachers and learners within the lifelong learning sector. There was a significant drive in the importance of ensuring that learners were skilled to work in specific areas which would aid the economy and compete globally.

## White Paper 'Raising Skills, Improving Life Chances' (DfES) 2006

The findings of the Foster Report were further highlighted in the DfES (2006) White Paper 'Raising Skills, Improving Life Chances' which emphasised the need for high class skills development and also the first mention of the importance of Continuing Professional Development (CPD) for teachers. The paper set out the vision for 2020 that all skill levels would be increased for working adults by double. This included basic maths and English, working to Levels 2, 3 and 4 with a focus on sharing responsibility between employers, individuals and the government. The emphasis was on economically valuable and demand-led skills.

### Leitch review of skills 'Prosperity for All in the Global Economy' (2006)

Leitch identified the demand for economically valuable skills, particularly in relation to how far behind we were in the global market. Once again the impact on the LLS was the drive for upskilling the workforce and providing the necessary skills to compete globally.

### Further Education Teachers' Qualifications (England) Regulations 2007

This legislation outlined the new framework and requirements for teacher training currently in place today. It identified two distinct teaching roles: Associate Teacher and Full Teacher and their corresponding teacher training qualifications: Certificate in Teaching in the Lifelong Learning Sector (CTLLS) or Diploma in Teaching in the Lifelong Learning Sector (DTLLS) respectively; both qualifications must include PTLLS which was the 'passport' alluded to in 'Equipping Teachers for the Future' (2004). Associate Teacher of Learning and Skills (ATLS) and Qualified Teacher of Learning and Skills (QTLS) would be conferred by the IfL on completion of the appropriate endorsed qualifications. It was also at this point that the sector was officially referred to as the lifelong learning sector.

### Education and Skills Act 2008

In response to Leitch's recommendations, the Act declared that education and training should be compulsory until the age of 18. This will be in full effect by 2015. Learners will have to stay in full-time education, undertake work-based learning such as an apprenticeship, or part-time education or training if they are employed, self-employed or volunteering until they are 18.

### Review of Vocational Education, 'The Wolf Report' (DfE) 2011

Professor Alison Wolf reviewed vocational education in this country and found it lacking in a number of key areas. This is an influential report that could again see changes in the way in which vocational education and also English and Maths are delivered, funded and supported in the lifelong learning sector. A key recommendation of the report is that teachers holding QTLS should be considered employable on equal footing with school teachers if they possess the knowledge, skills and experience that may be lacking in the school sector to deliver 14–16 vocational subjects. This has been an ongoing sector argument since QTLS was introduced and one of the aims of the professionalisation of the sector was to earn parity with Qualified Teacher

Status (QTS) holders. The government responded positively to this recommendation and agreed that this would happen, but would require a change in the law. At the
time of writing, this has not yet occurred.

### 'New Challenges, New Chances: Further Education and Skills System Reform Plan' (BIS, Department for Business, Innovation and Skills) 2011

This policy paper outlines the new coalition government's plans to reform the Further
Education and Skills system. (It is interesting to speculate if this might be the
coalition's preferred title of the sector.) The emphasis again is on the importance of
developing the right skills to compete and support national and global needs and
goals. It further develops the government agenda outlined in 'Skills for Sustainable
Growth', stating that: 'This Government's purpose is to return the economy to
sustainable growth, extend social inclusion and social mobility and build the
"Big Society". Underpinning every aspect of this purpose is the improvement of
skills' (BIS 2011: 3). It also outlines the proposal to independently review
'professionalism in the FE and Skills Sector' (BIS 2011: 13) with an aim of changing
and/or improving the current system of ITT. There is an emphasis on 'vocational
pedagogy', which has been a national concern in teacher training within the lifelong
learning sector for a long time. This is mainly drawn from comparisons with
teachers in the compulsory sector, who are trained to teach their subject on initial
teacher training. However, this is almost impossible in lifelong learning because the
range of subjects is vast and often specialised. It will be interesting to see what the
outcome is.

### Role of the IfL

The need for a professional body for teachers and trainers in further education was
proposed by FENTO in 2001. The IfL's status as an independent professional body
was confirmed in January 2002. It was, and still is, member led. At its inception,
membership was voluntary. The role of the IfL took on new relevance after the
Department for Education and Skills (DfES) published *Success for All* (2002);
*Equipping Our Teachers* (2004); the Foster Report (2005); the FE White Paper
(2006), which collectively contributed to the need for the teachers within the
sector to be registered and to undertake regular CPD. Following the 2007 reforms
(see above), the IfL became a key player in the sector responsible for registering
teachers and monitoring professional development. The body began accepting
members from August 2007 and by the end of January 2009 it had more than 180,000
members.

The IfL is currently identified as the 'professional body for teachers, tutors,
trainers and student teachers in the further education (FE) and skills sector' and its
role is to 'to support professional development and excellence in order to deliver the
best possible teaching experience to millions of learners' (www.ifl.ac.uk/about-ifl/
what-we-do). The IfL registers all FE teachers and trainers in skills; oversees the
CPD requirement from all registered members; and confers ATLS and QTLS via a
Professional Formation process on the completion of an appropriate initial teacher

training qualification. The institute also provides a Code of Professional Practice to regulate professional behaviour. The Ifl includes in its description of providers within the lifelong learning sector:

- adult and community learning
- emergency and public services
- FE colleges
- the armed services
- sixth-form colleges
- the voluntary sector
- work-based learning.

This description demonstrates the breadth and diversity of the lifelong learning sector. However, the Ifl's main remit is the further education sector (in line with the FE Qualifications Act).

There are other areas that are counted within the sector, but are not bound by Ifl regulations:

- offender learning
- higher education
- libraries, archives and information services
- the third sector – voluntary and community groups including charities
- careers guidance.

**Activity**

*IfL*
What do you think are the advantages of having a nationally recognised body representing the lifelong learning sector?

Can you think of any disadvantages?

Have a look at the IfL website at www.ifl.ac.uk and familiarise yourself with, for example, the vision and strategy, membership benefits, latest sector news.

## ATLS and QTLS

It was recognised that prior to the introduction of the new standards there were different roles for teachers and trainers within the lifelong learning sector. With this in mind, two different teaching roles were defined, initially by Lifelong Learning UK (LLUK) when they published the standards. The two roles, as defined in the Further Education Teachers' Qualifications (England) Regulations 2007, are associate teaching role and full teaching role.

## Associate teaching role

This 'means a teaching role that carries significantly less than the full range of teaching responsibilities ordinarily carried out in a full teaching role (whether on a full-time, part-time, fractional, fixed term, temporary or agency basis) and does not require the teacher to demonstrate an extensive range of knowledge, understanding and application of curriculum development, curriculum innovation or curriculum delivery strategies'.

## Full teaching role

This 'means a teaching role that carries the full range of teaching responsibilities (whether on a full-time, part-time, fractional, fixed term, temporary or agency basis) and requires the teacher to demonstrate an extensive range of knowledge, under-standing and application of curriculum development, curriculum innovation or curriculum delivery strategies'.

Identifying the role that you undertake within the sector is important in determining the teaching qualification you embark on. Prior to the introduction of the teacher training standards, there was no requirement for teachers within the sector to possess a teaching qualification and teachers and trainers chose different routes of teacher training, usually on a voluntary basis. The main teaching routes were the City & Guilds 7307 and 7306 awards and also the higher education institute (HEI) routes of Certificate in Education (Cert. Ed.) and Postgraduate Certificate in Education (PGCEFE) for graduates. The introduction of the FENTO standards in 2001 meant a significant change to the existing system with implications for trainees and teacher trainers. All the FENTO standards were at Level 4 and, essentially, first year undergraduate level. This caused some challenges with new entrants to the profession who were not only starting a new job or career but also had to complete an academic level qualification concurrently.

## Teaching training qualifications for lifelong learning

The FENTO standards were very detailed and prescriptive and many people in the sector felt that teacher training programmes based on them were over-assessed and too theoretical and not always appropriate for new teachers in the sector. The teachers that I trained during this period would probably agree with me, but they would also say that it was a very useful and worthwhile process in the end. When the FENTO standards were replaced by the LLUK standards in 2007, a new suite of qualifica-tions was introduced. Some of the criticism of the FENTO standards was taken on board and PTLLS/CTLLS and DTLLS were the result.

## PTLLS

This is the introductory teaching award for teachers entering or wanting to enter the LLS. Everyone involved in teaching or training within the sector has to complete this 12-credit award.

## CTLLS

The Certificate in Teaching in the Lifelong Learning Sector is for Associate Teachers who can then qualify for ATLS.

## DTLLS

This is the qualification for Full Teachers who can qualify for QTLS. This is usually offered up to Level 5 but some HEIs offer them up to Level 6 for graduates. These qualifications are delivered by awarding bodies and HEIs across the country, but the introduction of the legislation in 2007 means there is now a standard and uniformity regarding how our teachers are trained.

### Recent changes to the qualifications

In 2011 it was decided that LLUK as the sector skills council for lifelong learning would not be recommisioned and its roles and responsibilities would be divided between the IfL and Learning and Skills Improvement Service (LSIS). Their final act before they were dissolved on 31 March 2011 was to conduct a nationwide review of current teacher training qualifications in the sector and to consider their fitness for purpose. The main outcome of this review was to extend the PTLLS to a minimum of 12 credits and for it to be taught independently before any continuation on to CTLLS and DTLLS. Following criticism from work-based learning providers, changes were made to the options available for CTLLS and DTLLS to embrace the wider sector, not just the FE.

The content of the PTLLS/CTLLS/DTLLS will stay the same in essence but there are some structural changes and more flexibility to teach content beyond the FE sector. The review recognises the need to train our teachers for the wider context of the lifelong learning sector including, for example, training related to apprenticeships, work-based learning and careers guidance. There will also be clear 'stop-off' points after PTLLS and CTLLS and Year 1 DTLLS which will enable trainee teachers only to complete the awards they need and also provide suitable Recognised Prior Learning (RPL) for those whose role changes and developments throughout their teaching career.

## Are you a PTLLS, CTLLS or DTLLS?

### Case study 1

*Barbara is a qualified nurse and has taken early retirement. She is interested in gene-alogy and has pursued it as a hobby for a number of years. She wants to be able to design a beginner's course on genealogy to put on a website but doesn't know where to start in terms of the technicalities of planning lessons and courses. She contacts a local teacher training provider and discusses her needs. She is advised to complete a PTLLS course and, because she is not currently teaching or training, this is the only option open to her. She completes the course and learns the basics of teaching and learning which enables her to consider planning and delivery and the importance of meeting individual learner's needs. The course gives her the confidence to set up her introductory course.*

### Case study 2

*Paul is a radiographer. He is not required to teach trainees on a full-time basis but he does train new radiographers in health and safety on an ad hoc basis. Paul's employer believes that a CTLLS course would benefit him and prepare him more technically in planning and delivery of sessions and also supporting trainee radiographers on a one-to-one basis. On completing the CTLLS course, Paul feels more equipped and qualified to conduct this role and is considering moving into full-time training so he can then complete his DTLLS qualification.*

### Case study 3

*Amir has been a plumber for 20 years. He has decided that he would like a career change and applies for a job at a local FE college as a lecturer in plumbing. He is accepted for the post but is told that he will need to complete his DTLLS. Amir has no teaching experience so he relies on his vast experience as a plumber to be a subject expert in the classroom. He realises that there is more to teaching than just knowing the subject. As he progresses through his DTLLS qualification, his confidence increases in terms of planning, delivery, assessment and all of the wider issues that encompass teaching in the lifelong learning sector. On completion of the DTLLS, he went through professional formation and was conferred by the IfL for QTLS status.*

FE colleges and training agencies mainly run awarding body provision of PTLLS/CTLLS and DTLLS which can be completed at Level, 3 or 4 (PTLLS and CTLLS) or at Level 5 for DTLLS. However, if you are a graduate, you can complete a higher level qualification at an HEI that can offer the awards at Level 6 and, possibly, optional units at Level 7.

## Being a professional teacher

**Activity**

- What is a 'profession'?
- What does it mean to be a 'professional'?
- Are you a professional?
- What is it that makes you professional – is it education, experience, values or attitudes?

The meanings and expectations of 'profession' and 'professionalism' are somewhat fluid. Traditionally, the notion of the 'professional' carried with it some powerful but unspoken associations. These included the idea of 'entry' to the professions being dependent on specialist knowledge and skills, professional autonomy, authority and altruism. Professionalism also implied virtuous behaviour. The professions, and entry to them, were strictly regulated by professional bodies, organised and run by members of that profession. Those discovered to have behaved inappropriately were liable to be 'struck off'. Lea et al. (2003: 60) state:

> Textbook definitions of professional usually include a combination of the following characteristics; long training programmes in specialist knowledge; an ethic of altruism; autonomous work practices and the presence of a professional body.

Furlong (1998) echoes this, arguing that traditionally the foundations of professionalism have been based on the three themes of *information, autonomy* and *responsibility*. The information theme suggests that becoming a professional involves extended periods of study, for example, studying for a degree or higher qualification, leading to substantial specialist knowledge and understanding. Typical examples of this would be the study and subsequent training undertaken by doctors, accountants, lawyers and teachers. This definition assumes that people who have not completed this level of study could never gain or demonstrate the necessary knowledge to call themselves professionals. Once this knowledge has been gained, professionals are granted autonomy by the government and, more widely, by society to practise their professions. The third theme is responsibility. A doctor, for example, demonstrates responsibility by acting within a set of appropriate professional values, based on professional judgement. Importantly, they always act impartially and independently, not on behalf of a third party such as a government. Furlong (1998) now argues that in the FE and LLS arena, these three themes that once defined a professional are now being gradually eroded by bureaucracy, reduced funding and an agenda of targets, control and accountability.

If we accept the above as the defining characteristics of professionalism, to what extent can we apply them to teachers in the lifelong learning sector? How relevant is the notion of 'extended study' today? Does a two-year, part-time diploma course equate to a period of extended study? Gleeson and James (2007) offer an alternative to the traditional notion of professionalism, suggesting that specifically in FE people are becoming 'learning professionals' who work in both academic and vocational settings where the environment is more complex but where the period of extended study is substituted for more practical 'on the job' experience.

---

**Activity**

Randle and Brady (1997: 231) suggest that professionalism in education includes the following:

- The primary importance of student learning and the teaching process
- Maintaining loyalty to students and colleagues
- Expressing concern for academic standards
- Recognition of teachers as experts
- Resources for education being made available on the basis of educational need
- Some elements of autonomy being essential
- Quality being assessed on the basis of inputs and processes
- Maintaining a spirit of collegiality.

To what extent do you agree with these characteristics? Do you they reflect your own perceptions of yourself as a professional?

---

## Professional rights and responsibilities

The notion of rights having concomitant responsibilities is a key theme in social and political ideas. We have become, according to some commentators, a society that expects to have rights but is less keen to accept the responsibilities which come with them; this applies to us as professionals in the lifelong learning sector. It might be helpful to break this down a little further into an evaluation of our rights and responsibilities as teachers. Table 2.1 outlines some of the rights and responsibilities that could be associated with teaching in the lifelong learning sector. You must also read the professional values underpinning the LLUK standards for teachers in the sector.

## New role of the LSIS

On 1 April 2011, the LSIS acquired the standards and qualifications aspect of LLUK as part of their remit. The LSIS defines itself as 'the sector-owned body that aims to accelerate the drive for excellence in the learning and skills sector, building the sector's own capacity to design, commission and deliver improvement and strategic change' (LSIS 2011). The standards and qualifications for the lifelong learning sector are

**Table 1.1** Professional rights and responsibilities in the lifelong learning sector.

| Rights | Responsibilities |
|---|---|
| Respect as a professional in our chosen field. | Engagement with scholarly activity relating to either pedagogy or subject specialism. |
| Autonomy to prepare, plan and deliver teaching sessions. | Provision of relevant and timely CPD. |
| Commensurate pay and conditions. | Display appropriate conduct and behaviour towards students and colleagues. |
| A voice at local and national level. | Engagement with relevant industry and educational bodies including the IfL. |
| Status in the eyes of a community and wider society. | Commitment to an appropriate level of qualification. |
| Support from colleagues, managers and government. | |

conducted by the LSIS's Qualifications and Skills Team which has the responsibility for the standards, qualifications and strategic oversight of the further education and skills workforce in England.

One of the most useful aspects that has transferred from LLUK to LSIS is the Information and Advice Service. This allows anyone with questions concerning qualifications in the sector to contact a member of LSIS who will reply to any query. In my experience, this has always been a very useful point of contact, no matter what your role is in the sector. The contact address is lluk.advice@lsis.org.uk.

LSIS has also recently relaunched the Excellence Gateway which is a comprehensive source of information and resources for lifelong learning teachers and anyone connected to it. It provides a wealth of information and resources on all aspects of teaching and learning, support, news and research. I would advise it to be a favourite in any teacher's bookmark list!

## Further reading

Avis, J., Fisher, R. and Thompson, R. (eds) (2010) *Teaching in Lifelong Learning*. Maidenhead: Open University Press. See particularly Chapters 2 and 3.

Department for Business, Innovation and Skills (BIS, 2011) *New Challenges, New Chances; Further Education and Skills System Reform Plan*. London: BIS. www.bis.gov.uk/assets/biscore/ further-education-skills/docs/f/11-1380-further-education-skills-system-reform-plan.pdf.

Robson, J. (2006) *Teacher Professionalism in Further and Higher Education*. London: Routledge.

## Websites

Institute for Learning (IfL) www.ifl.ac.uk.
LSIS (Learning and Skills Excellence Gateway) www.excellencegateway.org.uk/

# 2

# The reflective teacher

The most distinctive characteristic of these very good teachers is that their practice is the result of careful reflection. . . . They themselves learn lessons each time they teach, evaluating what they do and using these self-critical evaluations to adjust what they do next time.

(Ofsted 2004b: 8)

**What this chapter is about:**

- Reflective practice – what is it? Why and how should we do it?
- Reflection 'in' and 'on' action
- Some models of reflective practice
- Using reflection as a basis for improving learning and teaching
- Writing your personal development journal (PDJ)
- Your individual learning plan (ILP)
- What makes a good teacher in lifelong learning?

**LLUK standards**

This chapter covers, at least, the following standards:
AS 4; AK 4.2; AP 4.2; AK 4.3; AP 4.3
CK 1.1; CP 1.1; CK 4.1; CP 4.1
DS 3; DK 3.1

## What is reflective practice?

The Lifelong Learning (UK)(LLUK) Professional Standards for teachers, tutors and trainers in the lifelong learning sector (LLS) state that those working in the sector should value: 'Reflection and evaluation of their own practice and their continuing professional development as teachers' (AS 4). In addition, their professional knowledge and understanding includes: 'Ways to reflect, evaluate and use research to develop own practice and to share good practice with others.' As part of their professional practice, they should: 'Share good practice with others and engage in continuing professional development through reflection, evaluation and the appropriate use of research.'

Qualified Teacher Learning and Skills (QTLS) status requires trainees to begin the practice of continuing professional development (CPD) right from the start of their training by keeping a development journal. This practice continues after completion of training. All teachers in lifelong learning are required to provide evidence of a minimum of 30 hours CPD each year in order to maintain their licence to practise.

There is one quality above all that makes a good teacher – the ability to reflect on what we do; why and how we do things and to adapt and develop our practice within lifelong learning. Reflection is the key to successful learning for teachers and for learners. As the LLUK standards make clear, reflection is an underpinning value; it is the key to becoming a professional teacher and the foundation of continuing professional development.

A common-sense view of reflection is that it involves just thinking about things. Perhaps thinking about the structure of the universe or why you disagreed with your partner last night could be regarded as reflection – others might consider it nothing more than idle and self-indulgent speculation. Most of us spend some time thinking about what we do and the effects we have on others, but we don't always take it a step further and reflect on our actions and make plans to do things differently. In a professional setting, reflection is:

- deliberate
- purposeful
- structured
- about linking theory and practice
- to do with learning
- about change and development.

Jenny Moon suggests:

> Reflection is a form of mental processing that we use to fulfil a purpose or to achieve some anticipated outcome. It is applied to gain a better understanding of relatively complicated or unstructured ideas and is largely based on the reprocessing of knowledge, understanding and, possibly, emotions that we already possess.

> (Moon 2005: 1)

## From 'help!' to 'second nature'

The process of reflection helps us to monitor our own development from raw beginner to experienced professional. Reynolds' (1965) model of developing competence in

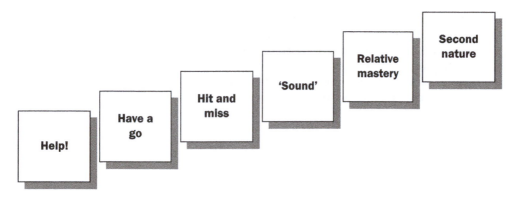

**Figure 2.1** Reynolds' (1965) model of developing competence.

social work suggests six stages (Figure 2.1). Those of you who recall learning to drive will recognise these stages. Mastering, for example, clutch control is a deliberate practice of trying, sometimes failing, trying again, becoming confident, until eventually it becomes an unconscious process. Our teaching careers follow a similar process. Early fears about the timing of activities or the use of information technology (IT) are initially difficult, even frightening, but eventually become second nature.

Another, uncredited, model suggests a movement through the stages of:

- *Unconscious incompetence* – in which we are unaware of what we can't do or don't know.
- *Conscious incompetence* – in which we become aware of our development needs and start to do something about them.
- *Conscious competence* – where we are using our new skills and knowledge, but watching and monitoring ourselves.
- *Unconscious competence* – the skills become naturalised. This is like Reynolds' notion of 'second nature'.

Many of our skills, our knowledge and competences will become, like driving a car, second nature. However, we must ensure that 'second nature' doesn't become complacency. Success in teaching requires us always to challenge and develop our practice by regular reflection and review.

David Berliner (2001) outlines the stages of teacher development as going from the novice – the raw recruit who is learning the basics and is relatively inflexible – to the expert, who is very much like the racing driver or the professional footballer who is completely at one with their art, performing effortlessly and naturally. Experience and length of service do not, however, necessarily make an expert; experience needs reflection if we are to become expert teachers. Rollett (2001) describes what it means to be an expert teacher. This is a very useful model and is worth quoting at length:

> Experts rely on a large repertoire of strategies and skills that they can call on automatically, leaving them free to deal with unique or unexpected events. . . . The wealth of knowledge and routines that they employ, in fact, is so automatic that they often do not realise why they preferred a certain plan of action over another. However, when questioned, they are able to reconstruct the reasons for their decisions and behaviour.
>
> (Rollett 2001: 27)

## Reflection – some theory

### John Dewey

Dewey was a leading educational philosopher of the late nineteenth and early twentieth centuries whose ideas are still influential. He believed that traditional education, as then practised in his native America, was rigid, static and inadequate for the rapidly developing society and economy of the time (the same criticism is frequently made of education today.) Dewey advocated child-centred learning and stressed the importance of each individual's lived experience as a starting point for learning. Key to Dewey's philosophy was the development of thinking, particularly, reflective thinking. In *How We Think*, he states:

> Thought affords the sole method of escape from purely impulsive or purely routine action. A being without capacity for thought is moved only by instincts and appetites, as these are called forth by outward conditions and the inner state of the organism. A being thus moved is, as it were, pushed from behind.
>
> (Dewey 1933: 15)

In other words, such a person is not in control. They are dragged along by events, unable to understand or change them. To use more recent terminology, such a person is merely reactive, rather than active or proactive – things happen to them, they don't make things happen. We must, as Dewey says, move from routine action to reflective action which is characterised by ongoing self-appraisal and development.

Dewey believed that reflection begins in a state of doubt or perplexity which, for teachers, is most likely to be encountered when working with learners, particularly new or unfamiliar learners. When we are faced with difficulties and uncertainties in practice, when things don't go according to plan or don't fit with the theory, we may feel powerless and unable to resolve the situation. For Dewey, however, these are key moments for learning; we can reflect on these problems to solve the perplexity and learn from it.

### Donald Schon

Schon (1983) developed the notions of *reflection in action* and *reflection on action*. For the purposes of this book I will explain these two concepts very simply as *reflecting while you're doing it* and *reflecting after you've done it*. When delivering the learning you have so carefully planned and prepared, you need to be constantly aware and monitoring the session as it develops. This awareness allows you to make changes as the situation demands, to be able to 'think on your feet'. When the session is complete you can reflect on, analyse and evaluate the learning and teaching. This post-action reflection then informs your subsequent planning and preparation, leading to a cycle of continuing improvement. We can represent the process as shown in Figure 2.2.

A further development in Schon's work is the distinction between *technical rationality* and *tacit knowledge*. This distinction could be characterised more simply as the 'theory–practice gap'. Like Dewey, Schon believed that reflection begins in working practice, particularly those areas of practice where professionals are confronted with unique and confusing situations; 'the swampy lowlands of practice' as Schon calls them. Teachers may have acquired the theoretical knowledge (technical rationality) of their subject or of the practice of teaching and learning, but while this might explain their classroom practice as it should be, it might not explain it as it

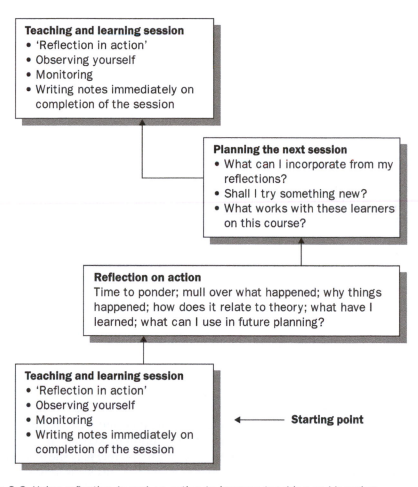

**Figure 2.2** Using reflection *in* and *on* action to improve teaching and learning.

actually is. From these real-life experiences teachers can develop tacit knowledge – a synthesis of theory and practice which they have developed for themselves. It is vital that these learning experiences are recorded in journals and discussed with mentors and fellow trainees.

Trainee teachers might express the opinion that 'this theory stuff is all very well, but it doesn't work in the real world'. Teacher trainers may be offended by such rejections of theory, but their trainees may have a point – theory is only of any use when it is applied and developed in practice. The real teaching environment is where theory is applied, tested and evaluated. Theory is never used rigidly, nor does it provide all the answers to the problems which teachers encounter. It is, however, the starting point for developing teaching and learning in practice. Reflection in and on action allows teachers to continually improve their practice and even to the development of *practice-based theory*.

During your training and professional development, and as a result of reading this book, you will acquire a body of theoretical knowledge related to teaching and learning which you will want to apply in your learning sessions. For example, humanist theories of teaching and learning stress the development of the whole person and the creation of a non-threatening, positive learning environment. In practice, this might not be as easy as the theory suggests. However, this does not invalidate the theory, but it does mean you will need to adapt and experiment with it in practice. Schon calls this application and development of theory in the real world *theory-in-use*.

## David Kolb and Graham Gibbs

The notion of reflection linking theory and practice underlies the work of Kolb and Gibbs. The models of learning and reflection they developed are sometimes called 'iterative' because they are based on a repeating but continually evolving and improving cycle of learning. Kolb's (1984) experiential learning theory shows a four-stage cycle of activity. These four elements are:

- Concrete experience
- Reflection
- Abstract conceptualisation
- Active experimentation.

The learner, in this case the teacher, can begin the cycle at any point but must follow each step in order.

Consider, for example, a trainee teacher who uses role play in a session (concrete experience). The role play is only partially successful. The teacher reflects on the use of this learning method and considers how it could be improved and made more effective (reflection). She reads up on the use of role play and talks to more experienced colleagues and, as a result, formulates an improved version of the activity (abstract conceptualisation). The next time she plans to use role play she incorporates her new ideas into the planning (active experimentation). This leads a new concrete experience and the repetition of the cycle.

**Activity**

Consider a recent example from your own teaching when you have tried a new method or resource. Using Kolb's four stages, consider the development of the technique in practice.

Several writers on reflective practice have emphasised the importance of the teacher's feelings as part of the reflective process. We may experience a wide range of feelings during and after our teaching – elation, confusion, anger, helplessness, blaming the learners – and it is important to recognise and reflect on them. Gibbs (1988) adds feelings to his model of 'learning by doing'. The stages of learning in his model are shown in Figure 2.3. Gibbs' model provides key points in development, especially description, evaluation, analysis and action, which we will consider further in the section on methods of reflection. Before then we need to examine the reasons for reflective practice.

## Jack Mezirow – transformative learning

The notion of transformative learning develops mainly from the work of Mezirow (1991) whereby a dilemma can lead to a reflection and transformation not only of content but also of ourselves as teachers. It's about challenging our assumptions and presuppositions and changing our perspectives. This is reinforced by Moon (2004) who says that reflective practice is about having the capability and skills to facilitate

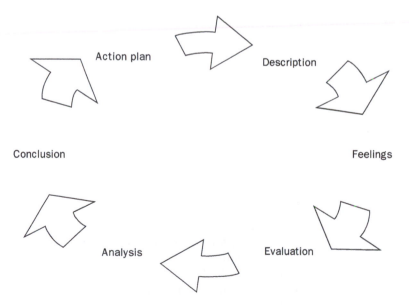

**Figure 2.3** Gibbs' model of 'learning by doing'.

the taking of a critical stance in relation to problem solving and development. Reflective practice, in this formulation, involves moving out of our comfort zones and taking some possibly life-changing risks.

## Reflective practice – why should we do it?

Reflective practice is a professional requirement and we have to provide evidence of it, usually in a journal or log. This requirement brings teachers in the lifelong learning sector up to date with other professionals such as nurses, social workers and human resource professionals. Just as we wouldn't want to be cared for by a nurse who wasn't familiar with the latest techniques, we probably won't want to be taught by someone who doesn't know their subject or the best ways of teaching and learning.

Another reason for reflective practice is because it encourages us to understand our learners and their needs and abilities. Every learner is different and there are likely to be varying interpretations of what we say and do within any group of learners. There are 'different worlds' within our classrooms and skilled teachers will try to see themselves as their students see them. Stephen Brookfield believes: 'Of all the pedagogic tasks teachers face, getting inside students' heads is one of the trickiest. It is also the most crucial' (Brookfield 1995: 92).

This book is based on the principle that active learning is preferable to passive learning and that active learning requires reflection. Reflective teachers are more likely to develop reflective learners. If we practise reflection we can more effectively encourage learners to reflect on, analyse, evaluate and improve their own learning. These are key skills in active learning and the development of independent learners. Reflection can also help us to develop our emotional intelligence, particularly if we include a consideration of feelings as part of our reflections. The concept of emotional intelligence, developed by Daniel Goleman (1995, 1998), encourages the development of self-awareness of feelings and the recognition and management of emotions.

Finally, and most importantly, reflective practice is the key to improvement. If we don't think about, analyse and evaluate our professional practice we cannot improve.

## Activity

Empathy (see Chapter 3) is important in developing your reflective practice, particularly the ability to imagine what it would be like to be a learner in your own class.

I can well recall a staff development session in which a colleague talked to us for more than an hour. At the end of it I was extremely annoyed at just being a passive object. It was a salutary experience and made me realise what it would be like to a student in a passive, non-stimulating environment. When you're teaching you have considerable freedom of movement and activity – you can stand up, sit down, walk around and generally direct operations. This is not usually the case for learners.

Next time you're in 'learner mode', at a conference or staff development session, think about how you feel. Do you feel stimulated, interested, engaged, or restless and fidgety? Would you like to move around a bit, stand up for a while, say something, do something?

## Reflective practice – how to do it

Reflection is a process and an activity that teachers undertake, primarily for themselves and the benefit of their learners. It is not about the production of mountains of paper evidence at the behest of teacher trainers or managers – such 'other-directed' activity becomes a chore for trainees and teachers from which they will derive little value. Reflection will, however, lead to a product-diary, log, personal development journal – that will contribute to assessment and, subsequently, be used as evidence of CPD.

### The right mental attitude

We should remember that reflection is not an end in itself; it is the starting point of becoming a reflective practitioner. For Jenny Moon, reflection is used 'with the sense of saying something not so much about what a person does as what they are' (Moon 1999: 36).

The basis of all reflection is a willingness to undertake the process and to value it as a means of improvement and development. Reflection can be difficult, even threatening, because it forces us to be honest with ourselves and recognise not only our successes but also areas where we need to improve. It makes us take responsibility for our teaching and learning. Being a reflective practitioner is like being your own observer and your own critical friend. We can refer to this willingness to reflect and develop as the 'right mental attitude', without which the whole process of reflection is pointless.

### PDJ

There are many forms of reflection and occasions on which you will reflect, but as a trainee teacher the main form of reflection will be through your reflective journal, commonly referred to as the PDJ.

Your PDJ is a written record of your experiences of and feelings about planning, preparing and delivering teaching and learning. It will contain general accounts of learning sessions but, more importantly, will identify critical incidents which can be the basis for learning and CPD.

The PDJ is subjective; it is written by you and for you and provides an opportunity to conduct a dialogue with yourself. You must remember, however, that as a trainee your tutors and mentors will see the journal, so it pays not to be indiscreet or make personal comments. The journal is also a place where you can relate theory to practice. We have already established that theory is only useful if it is used, tested and evaluated in your teaching and learning.

Success or otherwise in teaching is not just a matter of luck. It results from thorough planning and preparation, knowing your students and reflection on and evaluation of your practice. You will experience the wonderful feeling you get after a class has gone well; the learners, and you, have enjoyed themselves and above all learned. You will also experience the depths of despair following a session which just hasn't worked, where the learners don't seem to want to learn and you just long for the end of it all. The reflective teacher uses both extremes to learn and develop. If it went well, are there general conclusions you can draw to try with other learners? Are there specific points you can use with this group again – remember each group of learners is unique and reflection helps you to get to know them and work effectively with them. After the dreadful session, you might be chastising yourself (or worse, your learners) for the failure. Neither course is appropriate. You must reflect analyse, evaluate, learn and change.

One of the most valuable functions of your PDJ is to help you identify development points for action planning. You should review your journal regularly to see if there any recurring themes which you need to pick up on for your training and development. It will be useful to summarise your journal at the end of your course. This summary can have two functions: first, you can see how far you have come since you started your training; second, you can use it as the basis for your continuing professional development. Remember, evidence of CPD is a requirement in getting QTLS and maintaining your licence to practise.

## Writing your PDJ

Many trainee teachers in post-compulsory education and training (PCET) worry about writing their journals – what form should it take typed or handwritten; how much; how often; is it right? The main message is – don't worry. When it comes to journals, you can't do them wrong! There are, however, guidelines and advice to help you make them more useful and more effective.

### Writing and written style

Writing is a very effective way to make sense of experience – to organise, evaluate and learn from it. Creative writing is often used as a form of therapy through which people can work things out and find solutions for problems. Cognitive behavioural therapy (CBT) requires clients to recognise and write down examples of mistaken thinking and to imagine more positive scenarios – in other words to reflect, analyse, evaluate and, most importantly, change.

It is important to get into the habit of writing and to do it as soon as possible after the event. It's a good idea to include a reflection box at the end of your session plans in which to record some immediate thoughts which will form the basis of your journal entry. When you start writing, don't spend too much time thinking about it. Let the writing flow and try to capture the experience and some critical incidents. Once you've recalled the events, then you can start to learn from them. Little and often is a good rule, particularly in the early days of journal writing. You should always be regular in your journal writing habits. You might find it useful to track a particular group of learners, or perhaps to compare groups. Your course tutors will advise you regarding how much you should write and what period of time your journal should cover.

As for writing style, you should be free, spontaneous and informal. There's no need for the impersonal, academic style; some of the best journals I've seen are quirky and idiosyncratic. You must, however, avoid inappropriate language or too much slang or colloquialisms and never make personal comments about teachers or colleagues – unless, of course, you are referring to their good practice. There will be times when you are frustrated and annoyed in your training or in your work. You can use your journal to get some of this out of your system, it can even be therapeutic, but you must use it as a basis for learning and development – extended moaning is not acceptable.

In keeping with the spontaneous and informal approach you will probably write your journal by hand, but it's best to check if your tutors have any preferences regarding written or word-processed documents. Some of you will prefer to type your reflections straight on to your computer, possibly using a template you have designed to suit your needs. When you are reviewing your journal it's useful to highlight key points for your summary, for action plans, or as discussion points for tutorials.

I have known trainees who recorded their journals on to dictation machines (digital rather than tape). This can increase the spontaneity but obviously necessitates transcription into written form – if you've got voice-activated software this is less of a problem. Increasingly, trainees are experimenting with using blogs for their reflective journals. This provides some interesting opportunities for sharing ideas with a whole range of people and even the development of 'communities of practice'. Again, you must check with your tutors regarding the acceptability of this format.

'Communities of practice' don't have to be online. You can share your reflections with fellow trainees in taught sessions or group tutorials. It can be very helpful to find that colleagues are experiencing the same uncertainties or difficulties as you and, hopefully, enjoying successes. Sharing ideas and developing strategies together is an extremely valuable collaborative activity. You may even wish to build in presentations to colleagues on particular issues.

Many teachers, like many learners, will want to include diagrams, drawings or any other visual modes. I always encourage this, particularly as visuals can help you get the big picture and explore relationships between ideas. One of my former students who taught art produced a wonderful journal full of written entries, pictures, sketches, quotes and jokes – quite a work of art in itself. Personalise your journal by all means, but remember you will need to share it with your tutors and possibly submit it for assessment, so be prepared to summarise and translate as necessary.

### More than just description

The most inadequate reflections are those that merely describe what happened in a teaching and learning session. On its own, this is of no value, but it is a start. To the *description* (what happened), you need to add *analysis* (how, why), *evaluation* (how effective was it?) and *conclusions* (suggestions for future practice). Driscoll and Teh (2001), working in nursing and clinical practice, provide a simple but very useful framework for reflection based on three questions:

- *What?*        Description of the event
- *So what?*     Analysis of the event
- *Now what?*    Proposed actions following the event

They also provide a range of 'trigger questions' for each stage, for example:

## WHAT?

- What happened?
- What did I see/do?

## SO WHAT?

- How did I feel at the time?
- What were the effects of what I did (or did not do)?

## NOW WHAT?

- What are the implications of what I have described and analysed?
- How can I modify my practice?

Perhaps the most complete model of reflection is provided by Gibbs (1988). His model makes explicit the need for conclusions and action plans. The trigger questions he suggests are shown below:

| | |
|---|---|
| *Description:* | What happened? Don't make judgements yet or try to draw conclusions, simply describe. |
| *Feelings:* | What were your reactions and feelings? Again, don't move on to analysing these yet. |
| *Evaluation:* | What was good or bad about the experience? Make value judgements. |
| *Analysis:* | What sense can you make of the situation? Bring in ideas from outside the experience to help you. What was really going on? Were different people's experiences similar or different in important ways? |
| *Conclusions (general):* | What can be concluded, in a general sense, from these experiences and the analyses you have undertaken? |
| *Conclusions (specific):* | What can be concluded about your own specific, unique, personal situation or way of working? |
| *Personal action plans:* | What are you going to do differently in this type of situation next time? What steps are you going to take on the basis of what you have learned? |

## Critical incidents

Critical incidents are specific occurrences within teaching and learning sessions which you consider significant or important. Critical incidents may be positive or negative. They can be moments in which you suddenly become aware of a problem, or a solution to a problem; when you realise that you have a particular development need or a particular strength. They could be described as 'light-bulb' moments when there is a particular incident or a sudden realisation. For example, as a young and naïve teacher I made what I considered to be a humorous comment about a student's name. His strong negative reaction was a critical and memorable incident for me when I realised that people's names are precious to them and should be respected.

You will have many critical incidents in your training and during your working life as a teacher; they are all occasions for learning. You might, for example, be faced with behavioural difficulties with learners or a refusal by one or all of a group to engage. You might suddenly realise that you have talked for too long and the answer is to provide a change of activity. Critical incidents will often lead to generalisable ideas and solutions which are transferable to other groups and learning situations.

**Layout and form of your PDJ**

PDJs can take many forms – notebook, a ring-binder with loose-leaf pages, a file on your computer, whatever is easiest for you. Again, you should check with your course tutors to see if they have any preferences, although generally teacher trainers avoid giving too many guidelines for PDJs for fear of producing uniformity and stifling the student's own approach. If you use a notebook, an A4 size with perforated and hole-punched pages will be the easiest. You can design your own template for use with word-processing, perhaps under categories such as:

*   Description
*   Analysis and evaluation
*   Conclusions for future practice.

I favour just a straightforward written narrative without too much preconceived structure which might detract from the spontaneity.

A useful device has been developed by Heath (1998) which involves a split-page or two-page approach, using the left-hand side to record the description of the events and the right-hand side for reflection.

| *Left-hand page* | *Right-hand page* |
| --- | --- |
| Time/date/contextual details | Reflection |
| Description of the session | Analysis and evaluation |
| Describe critical incidents | Reference to theory (if appropriate) |
| Initial feelings | Thoughts added during review or tutorials |

**ILPs**

In your work or on your teaching placements you will very likely have negotiated and used individual learning plans with your learners and you will be expected to do the same as a trainee on a course leading to QTLS. Your ILP can be considered as the starting point of reflection and of your CPD. It can take the form of an audit of your existing knowledge, skills, attitudes and personal qualities; to identify your strengths and to highlight any uncertainties you have about becoming a teacher in the lifelong learning sector. It is most likely that your course tutors will provide an ILP format which you will be expected to use as an initial audit, but also as a document to refer to during tutorials and as a measure of the distance you have travelled at the end of your course. The important point is to use the ILP to kick-start your personal and professional development, not merely something you produce because you've been asked to.

If you haven't been provided with an ILP pro-forma, here are a few areas you might wish to consider for your development. You can develop a rating scale for these so that you can see your starting point and the distance travelled. What do you know about or how confident are you about the following:

- the roles and responsibilities of a teacher
- planning a course
- planning a session
- how people learn
- functional skills
- communication skills
- presentation skills
- demonstration skills
- questioning and explaining
- using a range of teaching and learning methods
- designing and using resources
- using information and communication technology (ICT)
- health and safety
- assessing learning
- reflection
- equality, inclusion and diversity
- subject knowledge and skills
    - how up to date you are
    - latest ideas in teaching and learning
    - sources of information
    - subject specialist professional development.

### An 'autobiographical' approach to your ILP
Stephen Brookfield (1995) suggests we have four 'critically reflective lenses' through which we can reflect on our teaching. These are:

- our autobiographies as learners and teachers
- our students' eyes

- our colleagues' experiences
- theoretical literature.

We will concentrate here on the first of these lenses – our autobiographies as teachers and learners.

Without reflection, there is a danger that we will teach in the ways we ourselves like to be taught. For example, if your school experience was of didactic, teacher-centred lessons or of formal lectures at university, these could become your dominant mode of teaching. If you have happy memories of making discoveries in science or researching a project for history, you will probably want to incorporate such methods into your teaching. Many people have bad memories of school and how these affected their learning. Maths for me was just an alternative spelling of the word 'fear'; answers were either right or wrong and wrong meant trouble. No one told me that maths could be interesting and useful, even fun. So, a useful starting point on your critically reflective journey might be to recall and discuss some of your experiences of being a student and of being taught.

## What makes a good teacher?

When you start teaching it's useful to have some sort of guidelines or role models of good teachers to provide something to aim at, especially when you're starting your ILP.

### 'Good teachers are born not made'

You might have heard this old maxim and thought yourself not suited to be a teacher. The main problem with this saying is that it's wrong. True, there are those who exhibit confidence and an ability to inspire and motivate groups of people. Such people, however, are not necessarily good teachers. They may struggle to plan classes, to explain properly, to assess, and are deficient in a whole range of other necessary skills. They might occasionally provide a stimulating session – but they fly by the seat of their pants. This is no way to teach. Teaching in lifelong learning is a profession and requires you to behave like a professional by learning and developing the necessary skills and practice.

**Activity**

*Best and worst teachers*

1  Think back to your days at school, college or university. Think of someone who was a particularly good teacher.
2  List the top five personal qualities, skills or attitudes which made them so good.

> 3  Think of your worst teacher.
> 4  List the top five personal qualities, skills or attitudes which made them so bad.
> 5  As a group, identify any recurring themes.
> 6  Produce a top five for the group.

The introductory statement to the LLUK Standards states:

Teachers in the lifelong learning sector value all learners individually and equally. They are committed to lifelong learning and professional development and strive for continuous improvement through reflective practice. The key purpose of the teacher, tutor or trainer is to create effective and stimulating opportunities for learning through high quality teaching that enables the development and progression of all learners.

(LLUK 2006:1)

Lifelong learning is a diverse sector with millions of learners in a wide range of settings. You will need a variety of teaching and learning methods in your toolbox if you wish to be successful. In addition, you will need to know about your learners and what elements of good practice will develop effective learning. Fortunately, there is plenty of research to help you. Rosenshine (1971) developed the following list of effective teaching behaviours. This research is over 30 years old now and is based on teaching in schools, but it is still relevant today to both the compulsory and post-compulsory sectors. According to Rosenshine, good teachers show these characteristics:

1  Introducing (structuring) topics or activities clearly.
2  Explaining clearly with examples and illustrative materials.
3  Systematic and business-like organisation of lessons.
4  Variety of teaching materials and methods.
5  Use of questions, especially higher order questions.
6  Use of praise and other reinforcement (verbal and non-verbal).
7  Encouraging learner participation.
8  Making use of learner's ideas, clarifying and developing them further.
9  Warmth, rapport and enthusiasm, mainly shown non-verbally.

A simpler and more reliable guide to teacher skills and qualities is provided by the publication *Mentoring Towards Excellence* (AOC/FENTO 2001). As a part of the project 700 learners were asked what they thought makes for good teachers and teaching. The top five professional characteristics were:

- understanding and supportive
- committed, dedicated and hardworking
- fair with an inclusive and respectful approach
- warm
- humorous.

The top five teaching skills were:

- clear instruction and presentation
- strong communication and active listening
- patience
- motivation and encouragement
- organisation and classroom management.

The top five favourite teacher qualities were:

- sound subject knowledge
- understanding and gives good advice
- creative, interesting and imaginative
- warm and cheery
- clear instruction and presentation.

Above all, teachers need to understand their learners, their characteristics, needs and motivations. They need to be able to adapt and adjust content and style to suit the needs of groups and individuals. Most importantly, they must be good communicators – this takes us neatly to the next chapter.

---

**For your journal**

If you are just starting your career in lifelong learning, the important thing is just to get yourself a notebook or set up a document on your computer and begin writing.

You can begin by reflecting on your feelings of meeting learners for the first time. It's easy to be negative and just concentrate on what you feel went wrong, but try to consider the positives as well. If the learners became more attentive or responsive, try to work out what you did that made the difference. Start reading and researching your subject and general texts on teaching and learning. Talk to colleagues and students. Get some feedback.

> **Journal extract: Martyn, training to teach popular music**
>
> My journal ... records not just the disconsolate musings that follow an unsuccessful session but also episodes of naïve joy and moments of sudden enlightenment that the Japanese call 'satori'. Each evening at 8:00 pm my mobile phone alerts me to the need to complete my PDJ and it is in this *regularity* that I find most reward as it determines that *all* of the emotional ebb and flow of 'learning to teach and teaching to learn' is recorded. The mixed media format of my journal reflects not just an abiding passion for collage but also the cut and paste/record and overdub nature of 'pop'. My PDJ is a 'visual representation of (my) values, opinions and philosophy' and a working document to which I constantly refer. It is not simply a diary of critical incidents but something to read, question, amend and augment.

## Further reading

Atherton J. S. (2011) *Learning and Teaching; Reflection and Reflective Practice.* www.learningan-dteaching.info/learning/reflecti.htm (accessed 15 October 2011).

McGregor, D. and Cartwright, L. (2011) *Developing Reflective Practice: A Guide for Beginning Teachers.* Maidenhead: Open University Press.

Moon, J. (2004) *A Handbook of Reflective and Experiential Learning: Theory and Practice.* London: Routledge.

Rushton, I. and Suter, M. (2012) *Reflective Practice for Teaching in Lifelong Learning.* Maidenhead: Open University Press.

Scales, P., Pickering, J., Senior, L., Headley, K., Garner, P. and Boulton, H. (2011) *Continuing Professional Development in the Lifelong Learning Sector.* Maidenhead: Open University Press.

## Websites

REfLECT is an online personal learning space that enables IfL members to plan, record and assess the impact of CPD on their practice. You can access REfLECT and a wide range of support materials at www.ifl.ac.uk/cpd/reflect.

# 3

# Communication and the teacher

It is important that the training of teachers incorporates knowledge of the processes of interpersonal communication that lie at the heart of effective learning and teaching. . . . Is it not surprising that professional communicators should not be trained to communicate?

(Harkin *et al.*, 2001: 72)

---

**What this chapter is about**

- What is communication?
- Communication theory for teachers
- Barriers to communication
- How learners construct meaning
- Communication skills, including: non-verbal communication; listening; speaking; empathy; giving and receiving feedback
- Communication 'climate'

---

**LLUK standards**

This chapter covers, at least, the following standards:
AK 5.1; AP 5.1: AK 5.2; AP 5.2
BS 3; BK 1.1; BP1.1; BK 1.3; BP 1.3; BK 3.1; BP 3.1; BK 3.2; BP 3.2; BK 3.3
BP 3.3; BK 3.4; BP 3.4

---

The LLUK standards state that all teachers in the lifelong learning sector (LLS) should know and understand the 'effective and appropriate use of different forms of communication informed by relevant theories and principles' (BK3.1). This chapter is intended to support your progress in meeting this standard.

## What is communication?

Effective communication is the foundation of all successful and inclusive teaching and learning. It's easy to assume that communication and communication skills cannot be taught; that communication is something you are either good at or not. But there are many successful courses and therapeutic procedures which can and do improve people's communication skills. We could argue that communication is the most important element of teacher training and that becoming a successful teacher entails identifying, evaluating and developing your communication skills. It has frequently been said that 'One cannot not communicate'. Therefore, as reflective teachers, we need to be aware that everything we do is communicative and will have an impact on the success and effectiveness of our teaching and our students' learning.

Communication is such a fundamental part of being human that we tend to take it for granted. Communication is the 'glue' that holds people together; it makes connections and interactions between people possible. It is the start and end point of all human activity and interaction and it makes possible everything we want to do. We communicate to achieve particular needs and purposes – to make friends, to persuade, to form relationships, to teach and to learn. Many introductory teacher training texts include a brief section on communication, almost as an afterthought, but it is important to remember that communication is what makes it all possible. As teachers our primary function is to communicate; our purpose is teach and to facilitate learning.

The study of communication basically comprises two schools of thought. The first sees communication as a process involving the transmission of messages from senders to receivers. The second sees communication as a social activity in which people create and exchange meaning. We do not need to concern ourselves here with the debates between these two schools; we can learn something from both of them.

Contrary to popular opinion, communication does not involve the transmission of thoughts and this simple principle underlies all communication theory. You can prove this by a simple experiment. Think of something and focus all your attention on that thought. Now turn to the person next to you and without speaking or moving or any form of physical action transfer this thought to that person. I can fairly safely predict that the thought remained in your head and stubbornly refused to cross to the mind of your colleague.

So, if we can't exchange thoughts, how is communication possible? Whenever we need to communicate we have to find a way of encoding this need into a form that can be transmitted – spoken or written words, a gesture, a facial expression. This message is then sent to and received by someone who decodes it and, hopefully, understands it. This, put simply, is the process school of communication. However, we can immediately see some problems with this explanation of communication as a process when someone says 'I don't understand what you mean.' The sender of the message, in this case the teacher, could easily blame the receiver (learner) for not paying sufficient attention or not being sufficiently intelligent; it's all too easy to blame learners for not understanding. Alternatively, the teacher might assume there is a problem in the process of transmission which can be solved, perhaps, by speaking more slowly or clearly; using a different explanation, or making handouts more readable. However, a third explanation is possible – the learner just doesn't understand because they have no previous experience or concepts that they can connect to the new information and ideas. Learners can't just be given meanings by their teachers; they have to create them for themselves and fit them into the things they already know. This is the essence of the school of communication which sees communication as the creation of meaning.

Part of the teacher's job is to help learners create meanings by connecting with their existing knowledge and understanding. As we shall see in subsequent chapters, this relates to the ideas of constructivism and meaningful learning. Equally, however, the teacher's role is to create the best conditions for learning and the most effective ways of communicating.

## Some communication theory

Theory is really only useful for teachers if they test it out in practice and make use of it to improve and develop. The theoretical models of communication shown here are intended to help you analyse, evaluate and develop your communication skills.

### Sender–receiver model

This simple model, developed from the work of Shannon and Weaver (1949), shows communication as a process and is sometimes known as the sender–receiver model (see Figure 3.1). We can apply this model to analyse a real-life situation with the

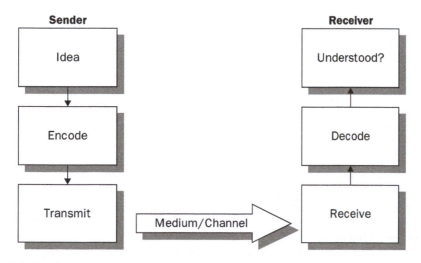

**Figure 3.1** Sender–receiver model of communication.

example of a teacher using a Powerpoint presentation to explain behaviourism in a psychology class. The process goes something like this:

1   The teacher needs to explain behaviourism in a psychology class because the subject specifications demand it and, therefore, the learners have to know it.
2   The information is encoded in written language and visual images on the Powerpoint slides with the teacher's spoken commentary.
3   The information is transmitted using the medium of the Powerpoint presentation via the visual and auditory channels.
4   The message is received by the learners.
5   The message is decoded by the learners.
6   The message is understood – or not.

We can use this model as an analytical tool to identify barriers and to improve the process of communication and learning. A communication barrier is anything which prevents a message from a communicator reaching the receiver – from teachers to learners. When Shannon and Weaver developed their model, they identified three categories of barriers which could interfere with effective communication: physical or mechanical barriers; semantic barriers; psychological barriers. Using the model and these three types of barriers we can consider stages at which communication might be problematic and some of the possible causes.

### Physical or mechanical barriers
These barriers concern the physical transmission and reception of the message. Examples could be the readability of handouts or the focus of the data projector, the volume of the teacher's voice, or noise inside or outside the teaching room. Students who are uncomfortable because of excessive heat, cold or thirst will find it difficult to concentrate. You might have learners who have hearing or sight difficulties for whom you need to adapt materials and presentations.

### Semantic barriers
Semantic barriers are essentially to do with meaning and the extent to which meanings are successfully generated and shared. At one level this could be to do with spoken or written language – possibly the use of jargon or technical language of a subject or profession which is not yet understood by the learners. For example, students doing a simple research project at Level 2 will be mystified by discussions of epistemology or ontology. Problems with meaning can also occur at a non-verbal level, for example, if teachers or learners use unfamiliar or culturally specific gestures, such as the thumb and first finger forming a ring. In America and many western countries this means 'A-OK'. In some cultures it says 'You're worth nothing.' In yet other cultures, the meaning of this gesture is far too offensive even to discuss here.

### Psychological barriers
The ways in which we perceive other people affect how we approach them and com-municate with them, but our perceptions are influenced by our experiences, beliefs,

values and attitudes. The attitudes we have towards individuals and groups can be positive or negative – even the most well-intentioned and sensitive of us will have some element of prejudice which will affect our perceptions of our learners. These kinds of prejudice can lead us to make assumptions about learners, which, if we don't subsequently adjust them as we get to know people, will affect our communication with them. At their worst these types of barriers can lead to sexism and racism and assumptions that those of particular race, gender or social class will be less, or more able and intelligent than others. Psychological barriers can lead to teachers taking contributions from some learners more favourably than others or treating some learners with less respect than others. Similarly, insensitivity or uncertainty can lead us to make assumptions about the disabilities and abilities of learners.

## Applying the sender–receiver model

Using this model and its associated barriers we can consider how and at what points in the process the teacher's communication could go wrong.

### Motivation for teaching and learning

This is the first step in our example of the psychology teacher explaining behaviourism. If even unconsciously you give the impression that you are only doing this because the specifications demand it, then students will regard it as little more than drudgery. You must always explain why a particular topic is important, relevant and, above all, something learners can connect to their own experience and make meaningful: for example, students who are not interested in statistics can suddenly become enthused if they are encouraged to apply them to their favourite sport.

### The idea

The idea or the content might not be fully realised or organised in the teacher's mind. Teachers need to be clear about the ideas they are communicating.

### Encoding

There may be problems with using jargon or inappropriate technical language, particularly if learners are new to this area of work. Encoding and decoding will only be successful if teachers and learners share, as far as possible, the same concepts and reference points.

### Encoding and transmission

Effective encoding and transmission of the message can give learners an excellent concise, visual overview of the new concept. Conversely, if it is the third PowerPoint presentation they've seen that day they could be less receptive to the message.

### Transmission

The transmission of the message can be ineffective in many ways, for example: the pace and volume of the teacher's voice; the visibility of visual aids; the size and layout of the room; the ability of all learners to see in a demonstration. It should be an easy job for teachers to check these things but, unfortunately, they are often overlooked.

## Transmission of messages

Thought given to transmission will aid the reception of the message. However, we need to ensure that we create an environment in which students are willing to receive messages. Even the most attentive adults can only listen and concentrate for relatively short periods of time – excessive teacher talk will eventually lead to inattentive learners. Consider the tone, pace and variability of your voice and keep teacher input lively. Learners are less likely to concentrate and attend to you if it's too hot or cold, if the session is too long, if they are thirsty or uncomfortable. Most importantly, learners will not be receptive to learning if they feel that the learning environment is not emotionally safe – if they are likely to be humiliated, ignored or not valued.

## Decoding and encoding

These are two sides of the same coin. Teachers have a responsibility to check learning and understanding. This is not done effectively by saying 'Is that all right?' or 'Does everybody understand?' or, worse still, simply 'OK.' Many learners, particularly younger ones, will find it too easy not to put their heads above the parapet and admit that they don't understand. Checking understanding can be done much more effectively by, for example, using open questions to get students to discuss and explore their learning.

---

**Activity**

Think of a recent learning session you have organised and delivered.

Use the sender–receiver model and associated barriers to analyse the process of communication in the session.

What specific conclusions can you draw to improve your future practice?

Can you record these in your reflective journal or use them as a basis for discussion in tutorial sessions?

---

## Who? What? To whom? How? Why?

Harold Lasswell, an American political scientist concerned with researching propaganda techniques, developed his general model of communication in 1948. It is a deceptively simple yet powerful tool which can be used to analyse virtually any communication event. Lasswell's original five questions were: *Who? Says what? In which channel? To whom? With what effect?* (Lasswell 1948). I have adapted the questions as follows (see Figure 3.2):

- Who?
- Says what?

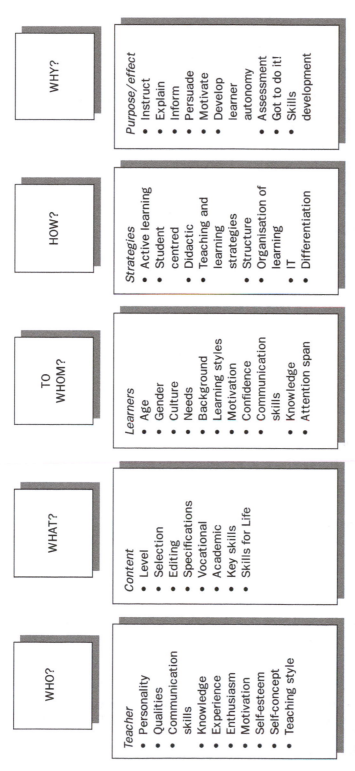

**WHO?**

*Teacher*
- Personality
- Qualities
- Communication skills
- Knowledge
- Experience
- Enthusiasm
- Motivation
- Self-esteem
- Self-concept
- Teaching style

**WHAT?**

*Content*
- Level
- Selection
- Editing
- Specifications
- Vocational
- Academic
- Key skills
- Skills for Life

**TO WHOM?**

*Learners*
- Age
- Gender
- Culture
- Needs
- Background
- Learning styles
- Motivation
- Confidence
- Communication skills
- Knowledge
- Attention span

**HOW?**

*Strategies*
- Active learning
- Student centred
- Didactic
- Teaching and learning strategies
- Structure
- Organisation of learning
- IT
- Differentiation

**WHY?**

*Purpose/effect*
- Instruct
- Explain
- Inform
- Persuade
- Motivate
- Develop learner autonomy
- Assessment
- Got to do it!
- Skills development

Each box contains a range of factors which a teacher should consider in their planning, preparation and delivery of teaching and learning. In each case the list is not exhaustive – add others you think appropriate.

**Figure 3.2** Lasswell's model of communication (modified).

- To whom?
- How?
- Why?

To help you understand this model, I'll begin with a personal anecdote. When I rediscovered education as a mature student, I studied O Level sociology. Our first teacher was extremely erudite and knowledgeable sociologist with a real passion for his subject. Unfortunately, he didn't know how to adjust his teaching to suit a group of students keen to learn but with little or no sociological grounding. He wasn't able to consider how he would select what we needed to know from what he knew, and how to present it in a way that would gradually bring us into the subject and give us confidence. His approach just frightened off some of my fellow students. We are all experts in something but it can be all too easy to forget that our audience, our students, do not yet share our knowledge and skills.

### Who?
The starting point of any effective communication is to consider yourself, the communicator, in this case the teacher. You may be highly qualified and knowledgeable in your subject but you must consider how you will select from your knowledge the necessary content for your learners at this stage in their learning. For example, a teacher with a Masters in English will not need to discuss Bernstein's theories of restricted and elaborated code with GCSE English language students.

You should also consider your personal style, your motivation for teaching, and your experience – how similar to or different from your learners are you? Equally importantly, you need to consider your experience as a learner, for example, did you like to be involved and questioning or did you like to listen and take notes. If you did have a preference, you need to take care that this doesn't become your main style of teaching. Just because you liked lectures, for example, this doesn't mean your learners will.

### Says what?
This develops from the point above. What are the elements of content, skills, knowledge and understanding that your learners need at this time? This may be related to the level (entry, foundation, intermediate or advanced) or the requirements of the specification. What must you include and what can you omit at present and return to when learners have the big picture. There will be many instances, particularly in adult and community education, where you will be able to negotiate content with your learners. Rogers (2001) outlines the concepts of *action learning* and *self-managed learning* by which learners can take some responsibility for what they learn and how they learn it.

### To whom?
A key question for all lifelong learning teachers is 'Who are your learners?' The LLUK standards stress the importance of teachers knowing their learners and their needs. You need to consider, for example: what is the age and gender composition of the group? What is the cultural mix of the group? What is their previous experience

and what existing knowledge and skills do they have? One of your first tasks when you meet a new group of learners is to find out about them and what they already know and can do. As this book emphasises on many occasions, effective teaching and learning starts with what people already know.

## How?

This includes, for example, what teaching and learning methods you will choose for this group and for this purpose. We will consider teaching strategies later but you will need to develop a wide range of different methods to suit different learners. There will be times when you need concentrated teacher input but others where you will want to develop more active or discovery learning strategies. When planning your teaching, you will have to consider how you can differentiate the learning for different members of the group.

## Why?

A very basic question we may frequently overlook is, 'Why am I doing this?' Why am I teaching this class or why am I using this particular strategy? The answers will be many and varied. It might be because you've got to – because the specifications say you should. It could be that you wish to change the learners' attitudes or behaviour. It might be to develop particular skills in your learners. If you want to be an effective teacher you will need to enthuse and motivate your learners.

**Activity**

All the key questions of Lasswell's model will be explored in subsequent chapters. However it might be useful to start to apply it now and reflect on it in your journal.

1   If you're already teaching, see if you can answer each question (Who? What? To whom? How? Why?) and use them as reflective questions to improve your teaching.
2   Effective learning is about making connections and developing thinking skills. Work out ways in which each question impacts on the others. For example, in what ways does To whom? affect What? What's the relationship between How? and Why?
3   Use this model to analyse the planning, delivery and effectiveness of a session you have recently delivered. Start with To whom? and How?

## The problem of meaning

Wells (1986: 218) takes issue with the notion of teaching as the 'transmission' of knowledge. He asserts that 'it is not possible, simply by telling, to cause students to come to have the knowledge that is in the mind of the teacher. Knowledge cannot be transmitted. It has to be constructed afresh by each individual.'

Let's start with a controversial statement – words have no meanings. You might initially be shocked by this statement, but a moment's reflection suggests that it must be true. If words contained their own meanings then we wouldn't have to learn languages – foreign, technical, occupational, or others – we would simply listen and unpack the meaning. Teachers wouldn't have to teach – they would simply tell people things and they would then know the meaning. David Berlo (1960) makes a series of statements about meaning:

- Communication does not consist of the transmission of meanings, but of the transmission of messages.
- Words do not mean, only people mean.
- People can have similar meanings only to the extent that they have had, or can anticipate having, similar experiences.
- Meanings are never fixed: as experience changes, so meanings change.
- No two people can have exactly the same meaning for anything.

This last statement could seem particularly hopeless for teachers. If we can't share meanings, what's the point? Things are not this bad; we can and do share meanings and teachers do help learners to understand and create meaning. However, we must remember that merely transmitting messages doesn't necessarily mean that we have communicated meaning. Many of our communication problems result from the assumption that my message means the same to you as it does to me.

How does this seemingly obscure discussion relate to teaching and learning? First, it relates to constructivist theories of learning which suggest that learners have to actively create meaning – they can't just be given it. Second, it reminds us that successful teaching and learning rely on identifying those areas of shared experience which teachers and learners can use as a common pool from which to develop further learning. To illustrate this Wilbur Schramm (1973) devised a simple model to demonstrate this (see Figure 3.3).

To encourage successful communication and learning we need to find areas where the circles overlap and where there are shared areas of experience and understanding. For example, someone teaching *Romeo and Juliet* to 16 year olds may find the language of Shakespeare a barrier to understanding the story and the plight of the 'star-crossed lovers'. However, a shared reference point might be a comparison with a similarly doomed love affair in a film or soap opera. Purists might regard this as 'dumbing down', but it's a starting point for increasing learners' understanding of the

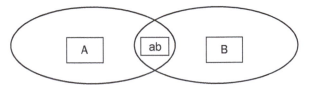

**Figure 3.3** Wilbur Schramm's model of communication (1973). A = the teacher, B = the learners. The area ab represents the area of shared knowledge or experience.

play and, subsequently, with the language and themes of the play. Similarly, ESOL teachers can overcome cultural differences by finding common ground with their learners, perhaps through examples from music, food or sport.

## Communication skills

A communication skill is an ability to encode or decode messages effectively. In the case of encoding, this means trying to understand and relate to your audience (the learners) and to consider their needs and motivations. We encode using a range of different forms of communication, including speech, body language, written or visual elements. Such skills are frequently taken for granted. We might, for example, observe an expeienced teacher who can enthuse, motivate and engage learners and assume that they are naturally gifted communicators; this is rarely true. The social psychologist Michael Argyle has written extensively on communication and interpersonal skills. He compares them to physical and motor skills and suggests: 'In each case the performer seeks certain goals, makes skilled moves which are intended to further them, observes what effect he is having and takes corrective action as a result of feedback' (Argyle 1994: 117). In other words, we watch what we're doing while we're doing it, evaluate its effectiveness and try new strategies to achieve our goals. There is a very clear connection here with theories of reflective practice, especially Schon's 'reflection in action'.

There are several components of communication skills. The following are the most relevant to teaching and learning (the first, reflection, has been covered in the first chapter):

- reflection
- non-verbal communication
- listening
- speaking
- empathy
- feedback
- written communication.

## Non-verbal communication (NVC)

**Activity**

Think about meeting a group of learners for the first time.

- Even before much has been said, what do you notice most about the group and the individuals in it?
- How do you get information about their feelings, attitudes and behaviour?
- How is this information shown?
- To what extent do you think they will notice the same things about you?

Non-verbal communication refers to all the bodily signals we send, deliberately or unconsciously, when we are communicating with others. NVC includes the following:

- eye movement and eye contact
- gestures
- posture
- proximity and orientation
- facial expressions.

These elements are commonly referred to as body language, but NVC also includes:

- Vocal elements of speech (sometimes called 'paralanguage'). This comprises stress, pitch, tone, volume and speed of speech, as well other sounds such as sighs, grunts and gasps. We will consider this further when we look at speaking.
- Appearance – including fixed elements such as your size and stature, and relatively fixed elements including hairstyle and colour, clothing and bodily adornments such tattoos and body piercing.

Despite the claims of some popular psychologists and tabloid newspapers, non-verbal communication is not an exact science. Folded arms *can* mean that a person is being defensive or feeling vulnerable; it is also possible that the person is happy and relaxed but just like folding their arms. Non-verbal communication signals cannot reliably be read in isolation. We need to consider the total package of what we see and hear before we can make judgements and react appropriately.

Unlike verbal communication we cannot cease non-verbal communication; it is a constant stream, occasionally accompanied by speech. Communication specialists refer to the 'primacy of NVC', which means that the content of messages, especially emotional content, is transmitted primarily by NVC (including vocal elements) rather than by the verbal elements of speech. If we encounter a learner frowning and looking mystified during an introduction to a new topic, her muttered reassurance that 'everything's OK' is likely to be contradicted by her facial expression and the sound of her voice.

**Activity**

Recall a teacher from your own educational experience – school, college, trainers, university.

What were their most noticeable and annoying non-verbal habits?

Why were they so annoying?

Did they affect your learning?

## Eye contact and eye movement

Eye contact and eye movements are probably the most expressive elements of our non-verbal repertoire. They enable us to react to other people and to influence and change their behaviour in various ways. We are frequently nervous of eye contact, especially when prolonged, because it can be too intimate. We may have the feeling that eyes are 'the window of the soul' and that when we look at people too intensely they will know what we are thinking. Eye movements have a number of functions in social interaction, particularly in teaching, including the following:

1   *Opening and controlling channels of communication.* Making eye contact with particular learners is a way of opening a channel of communication to them. If you want someone to answer a question or offer a contribution to the session, looking at them invites them in. Similarly, when that person's contribution is finished you will switch eye contact to another contributor to open the channel of communication. Eye contact makes connections between people, indicating liking, interest, or sometimes threat.

    Eye contact shows attention and interest. You may have experienced a teacher or lecturer who doesn't look the learners in the eyes, perhaps tending to look down or speak over people's heads. You may also know how this made you feel – inferior, not valued, just a member of another group to be taught. We should remember, however, the proviso that non-verbal communication is not an exact science. Much of our school experience will suggest that not looking at the teacher, doodling, or gazing out of the window are signs that the learner is not paying attention, but there is evidence to suggest that such behaviours can actually increase concentration and help to visualise and internalise what they are hearing. During interaction, participants will look at each other between 25 and 75 percent of the time; listeners will look more than speakers. For teachers, particularly in a classroom setting, it is important to include all the learners by distributing eye contact around everyone in the group. It is especially important to include those at the periphery. Individual eye contact will normally be between 5 and 15 seconds; to each individual in a group it is usually between 4 and 5 seconds. Don't, even unconsciously, pick favourites in the group who always return your eye contact – include everyone.

2   *To give and receive feedback.* When we are speaking we like to know that people are listening. When teachers look at their learners, they make connections with them. Learners feel that the teacher is taking an interest in them and are also likely to feel that the speaker is more confident and more believable. Avoiding eye contact looks shifty and is often associated with lying. Learners, generally, look while they are listening to teachers to get extra visual information to supplement the words and to gauge their feelings and emotions.

3   *To affect and control behaviour.* Eye contact can be a very powerful signal in behaviour and motivation. If you have a small group of people who talk while you are talking or interrupt others, a slightly longer than usual gaze, combined with a serious facial expression, is almost guaranteed to induce quiet, even if only for a short period of time. Eye contact can indicate authority, as well as cooperation and friendliness.

## Gestures

Gestures are physical actions which signal meaning, deliberately or unconsciously, to those who are watching. Unfortunately, we all have some habitual and unconscious gestures which are distracting or annoying. Such gestures may be more prevalent when we are nervous or meeting a new group for the first time. Excessive hand and arm movements might suggest confidence and exuberance, but can easily become more fascinating to the learners than the content of the teacher's input. It's a good idea to video yourself to identify any idiosyncratic movements or gestures, or even ask your learners. Conversely, a teacher or trainer who stands or sits still can be uninspiring, to say the least. Gestures and body movement indicate excitement and enthusiasm, which hopefully will transfer to your students. Certain hand gestures, known as 'baton gestures', are particularly important in supporting and reinforcing key points or punctuating speech. Baton gestures include a raised finger, a sweep of the hand or a hand-chop, but don't use threatening gestures such as pointing.

## Posture

Posture refers to the way in which we arrange our bodies when we stand, sit or walk. Much of our posture is unconscious. We may not be aware that our shoulders are drooped, our heads down, or we have a generally slumped appearance. But as teachers we need to be aware of our posture and adjust it to suit the circumstances and purposes of the session.

Posture is a key indicator of our feelings and emotions and as such communicates a great deal to our learners and helps to set the tone for the session. We might wish to be authoritative for a group of young learners who need a structured environment, but more relaxed for a group of adults with whom we are working on a more collaborative basis. An effective posture for most teachers is one which is poised yet relaxed with the body upright, weight spread evenly on both feet, shoulders not slumped and the chin level. This posture suggests a quiet, businesslike authority combined with approachability. A bad posture, hunched shoulders, clasped hands and feet pointing inwards sends messages which could be interpreted as vulnerability or lacking confidence. An erect posture, extending yourself to your full height, not only makes you appear more confident, but also makes you feel physically better. You will breathe more efficiently, which will bring more oxygen to the brain, and you will speak more clearly and project your voice better. Try leaning forward – a seated person leaning forward towards individuals or groups of learners gives the impression of being more interested in the participants and the topic under discussion than a person leaning backwards or away from their audience.

The posture of your learners can also provide valuable feedback regarding their understanding and the progress of the session. This kind of awareness becomes natural to experienced teachers and is central to the ways in which they manage learning and behaviour. You might also want to encourage appropriate postures as part of your behaviour management routines. Without wishing to return to a rigid school-style atmosphere with students sitting bolt upright, try to discourage over-relaxed postures – students will feel better and work more effectively when they are comfortable. Balancing on the back of two legs of chairs is not desirable, even if only for health and safety reasons.

## Proximity and orientation

Proximity refers to the distance between people who are communicating and in teaching sends very powerful messages concerning relationships, status, attitude and emotions. We frequently refer to our personal space, particularly the invasion of it by others. There are personal and cultural differences in our use of personal space, but there are some guidelines we can use in estimating what is appropriate in various settings. Edward T. Hall (1966) divided space into four zones:

- *intimate* – 0–50 cm – generally inappropriate in teaching and learning!
- *personal distance* – about 50 cm to 1.2 m. Most English people will talk in the street about 1–1.5 m apart. For teachers this distance might be appropriate when working one to one or with a small group.
- *social distance* – About 1.2 to 3.5 m. This is the distance at which most transactions, including classroom-based teaching, takes place.
- *public distance* – 3.5 m and upwards. University lecturers addressing large groups of students in lecture theatres will tend to inhabit this zone.

Your perceptions and use of space will vary according to the situation and purpose. Moving closer to individuals and groups, especially when sitting, can create a relaxed and collaborative atmosphere. Standing over a seated learner can suggest authority and control. As with all other aspects of communication, reflection and sensitivity should guide the use of space.

Orientation refers to the spatial positions that people adopt in interaction. This is most apparent in classroom layouts and even experienced teachers sometimes pay too little attention to the way in which chairs, tables and equipment are set out in learning spaces. I have frequently observed small numbers of learners spread out all over a classroom set up for 20 or 30 learners. While you are using a room you can organise it however you want, provided you remember to put things back as you found them. The physical environment is just one of the many elements a skilled teacher can manipulate to create a feeling of positive learning. If you've got a small group, try making a small island of desks around which you and the learners can sit. You will notice an immediate difference in the feel and atmosphere. If you feel the need to be more 'traditional' in style and presentation, stand up and move away from the learners.

You should remember to adjust the room layout to suit the activities you have planned for the session. A horseshoe shaped layout is best for general activity and provides the best view for you and your learners. If you are using small group activities you should arrange desks and chairs in small islands to facilitate this. Some occasions, perhaps student presentations, will require an open space. A very useful class set-up tool is provided by scholastic.com (see details at the end of this chapter).

While we're on the subject of rooms – keep them tidy. Scruffy rooms with desks and chairs all over the place don't send messages of professionalism and a business-like attitude to teaching and learning. The appearance is even more depressing when empty drinks bottles, crisp packets and piles of unclaimed handouts are strewn around.

**Activity**

Consider the following room layouts and discuss how they might positively or negatively affect the learning environment.

- desks and chairs set out in rows – school style
- a horseshoe or three-sided arrangement
- an island of desks
- several islands of desks round the room.
- a circle of chairs, including the teacher, with no desks
- all the desks and chairs cleared to the edges to make an open space.

For your journal – reflect on your use of space and arrangement of furniture. In what ways does it affect the 'atmosphere' and the learning?

Finally, you should consider your movement and position around the learning space. A teacher seated behind a desk at the front of the room can appear imposing and authoritative, and in some situations you might feel this is appropriate. At other times, however, try moving your desk out of the way completely and avoid any physical barriers between you and your learners. Moving around the class creates added visual interest and allows you to involve all the learners yet move easily to a position where you can work at close quarters with individuals or small groups.

**Journal extract: Terry, trained to teach in the Ambulance Service**

We have just opened up a small off-site classroom. The furniture had just been placed in the room in no particular arrangement. Our normal classroom layout is very much the horseshoe with the projector taking centre stage.

For a change I decided I would not use that format but rather keep the tables together in a block formation in the centre of the room. My thoughts were that this particular course was extremely difficult for the students and with everyone sitting around the same set of tables it would help to bond the group of nine students. Obviously on the odd occasion I used the projector some movement was required to ensure everybody could fully see the screen.

This arrangement was to last for the first week. The subsequent week I was accompanied by another teacher who is less open to change. It became obvious he was not comfortable with this arrangement. And by the end of Week 2 he had achieved his aim of returning the room to what he perceived as being the correct layout, namely the horseshoe.

Trying not to show friction between the teachers I went along with this arrangement but mainly because I would be leaving the course in a couple of days to take up other duties. It was interesting to note the indirect comments passed by students about how they had liked the original classroom layout.

Did it work? Yes, I feel it did, right from the outset there was a terrific feeling of belonging, being part of a team. Students were more willing to be involved by contributing to the lesson, nobody seemed to be left out on the wings. I felt there was a sense of ownership. There was a feeling that everyone was of equal value. Obviously this could have been associated with us being off site in a remote location thus creating a much more relaxed atmosphere.

From a practical point of view it was considerably easier to influence and direct the group when in the block formation. All the students very quickly got to know each other and started using individual's names.

## Facial expression

In communication terms, the face is the most important source of information and people focus attention on it for verbal cues which support or contradict spoken messages. Facial expressions are also the most complex and difficult channel of non-verbal communication to interpret. One reason for this is that facial expressions change rapidly, providing a continuous commentary while we are speaking or listening. As teachers we can and should consciously control our facial expressions, particularly to send messages of support, encouragement and interest. It is equally true, however, that our faces often flash indications of our 'true' feelings – sometimes contradicting our spoken words – and even the slightest expression of disapproval can discourage learners. Social psychologists call this phenomenon 'leakage'.

## Listening

We spend more time listening than we do speaking, writing or reading, but we rarely have any training in listening. Listening is considered a passive activity, something we just do. It is rarely considered a skill, still less a skill which we can develop and improve. Many surveys of learners at all ages suggest that what they dislike most is not being listened to. In a survey of adult learners' perceptions of teachers' communication skills, listening was ranked highest (Wolvin 1984).

Hearing is not the same as listening. If we go back to our sender–receiver model of communication, it's easy to see that hearing is equivalent to the reception of the message; listening is about decoding the message. There are many barriers to listening, including the following:

- Being distracted by another task or by thoughts and personal concerns.
- Being put off by the speaker and/or what they are saying.
- Making assumptions about speakers and allowing prejudice and stereotypes to affect our perceptions of what they are saying.

- Thinking about how we will respond before we've heard everything the speaker says.
- 'Pseudo-listening' – the face and body language suggest an attentive listener, but they're not taking any notice.
- 'Hogging the limelight' – these people don't listen attentively because they'd prefer to be talking.
- Selective listening – just listening for and attending to those things that interest you.

Effective listening requires that we 'forget' ourselves to some extent so that we can make space for the experiences of our learners. Alan Mortiboys, writing about teaching and emotional intelligence, points out:

> Sometimes your readiness to jump in with your own analysis or wealth of anecdotes and experiences can take away from what the learner is actually saying. You can fail to truly value the learners' experience and sometimes not even hear correctly what they have said because of your rush to contribute.
>
> (2005: 70)

Listening well is hard work and we need to make conscious efforts to listen closely and to show that we are listening. We don't just listen with our ears. We use our eyes, face and body to show others that we are listening to them. This applies whether we are in a one-to-one situation, such as a support or tutorial session, or with a group of learners. Willingness to listen actively is likely to encourage learners to offer their ideas and join in discussion. Active listening is a key element of active learning. Hargie and Dickson state:

> Research has shown that speakers want listeners to *respond appropriately* to what they are saying rather than just listen. In other words, they desire active listening in the form of both verbal and nonverbal behaviours. Although verbal responses are the main indicators of successful listening, if accompanying nonverbal behaviours are not displayed it is usually assumed that the individual is not paying attention, and *ipso facto* not listening.
>
> (Hargie and Dickson 2004: 194)

### Tips for effective listening

1  *Avoid distractions.* No matter how busy you are, stop what you're doing and listen to the speaker. Carrying out any physical activity will be interpreted as not listening. Attention will fade quite quickly and you need to be aware when this is happening.

2  *Remember body language.* Your posture will show that you are actively attending. Sitting more forward or inclining yourself towards the speaker will show interest.

3  *Keep an open mind.* You might hear things you don't agree with or contradict your ideas and beliefs but you still need to listen. Try to avoid making assumptions about people based on their appearance or their personal style.

4  *Listen for the main ideas.* These are likely to come at the beginning, middle and end of the speaker's message. Try to summarise the main points in your mind, then check them with the speaker.

5  *Let the speaker finish.* Be sure that the person has finished speaking before you begin. Even a pause does not necessarily mean that they have said all they wanted to say.

6  *Try to avoid thinking of your response while you're still listening.* Concentrate on what the person is saying.

7  *Give feedback while the person is speaking.* Listener responses show that you are listening. Occasional head nods and smiles all assure the speaker that you are attending to them.

8  *Reflecting back.* Training in counselling skills encourages listeners to 'reflect back' to the speaker. This generally means summarising or paraphrasing what the person has said in a way that reflects both the feelings and thoughts of the speaker. This can be useful for checking and for showing empathy, but if overused can sound contrived and unsympathetic.

## Speaking

Just as we have an obligation to be good listeners, as teachers we also have a duty to ensure that we speak in ways which encourage listening and understanding. The major components of effective speaking are:

*   structure
*   clarity and use of language
*   voice qualities.

### Structure
Learning requires clearly structured oral presentations that are logically organised, which help learners to follow the teacher's input and grasp the main points. Effective lesson planning will contribute significantly to this end, but even unplanned discussions which occur during a session need to be managed in order to ensure that all learners are able to see their structure.

### Clarity and use of language
To be a good teacher you need to be able to express yourself clearly and to help people learn, understand and develop. It is a teacher's job to enlighten, not to impress people by how much they know or by using long words and convoluted phrases. All spheres of human interest – occupational or educational – have their own particular language. Teachers will discuss SATs, spiral curricula and constructivism; bricklayers talk about 'compo' and Flemish bonds; solicitors know about habeas corpus and ultra vires, ABH and GBH. Used appropriately, this kind of language represents effective communication because it is shared by the users and represents a kind of verbal shorthand to refer to complex ideas. When such language is used with an audience

that is unfamiliar with it, this is ineffective and inconsiderate communication. All disciplines require specialised language and no teaching and learning materials can be jargon free. Becoming a doctor, for example, is to a great extent about acquiring medical language and concepts but, like a foreign language it has to be learned; it is part of the training. Education, particularly post-compulsory education and training has become littered with initialisations and acronyms which are frequently used as if understood by all (for example, LSIS, BIS, Ofsted, ILP, APL). Trainee teachers will find glossaries of such terms invaluable.

**Activity**

Identify some words or phrases peculiar to your area of work; an interest or hobby.

Try to explain these to others in your group.

Did you try to find any areas of shared knowledge/experience to explain?

**For your journal**

Have you experienced any occasions in your teaching when you and/or your learners used unexplained acronyms or specialist language? What was the effect?

## Voice qualities

Every voice is unique and makes a certain impression on those hearing it. Our voices reflect our personality and our self-esteem. Assertive and emotionally expressive people tend to have loud voices; shy people tend to have soft voices. We should recognise our unique vocal qualities but also remember that, like all aspects of communication, we can change and develop them.

**Activity**

- Think of how many different ways you can say 'I love you'. How do you make it sound convincing?
- Try saying 'Hello' to express surprise, pleasure, annoyance, boredom, seduction.
- Say the words *import* and *export* as verbs. Now say them as nouns. How do you make the difference?

From the above activity you should have been able to deduce that voice qualities include: stress, pitch, volume and speed of speech. We can also mention the 'ums' and 'ers' of hesitation and a variety of sounds including gasps, grunts and sighs. In teaching, vital messages of support, encouragement, enthusiasm or disapproval are conveyed largely by vocal qualities. Use of voice should be carefully monitored for, as Michael Argyle (1994: 33) points out: 'the voice is "leakier" than the face; that is, true emotions which are being concealed tend to show through'. Consider the following voice qualities:

1    *Intonation.* We don't have to be Laurence Olivier reciting Shakespeare to arouse and interest our learners, but we need to ensure that we avoid a monotonous tone when speaking. Intonation, or tone, is the rise and fall of the voice and variations will add to interest and emphasis.

2    *Pitch.* This indicates the use of a high voice or a low voice. When speakers are nervous they speak in a higher voice, which listeners quite easily interpret as nervousness. Anxiety means that your vocal chords are stretched tightly and you are not relaxed, which will eventually affect your voice.

3    *Volume* is easier to control than pitch. Teachers need to be able to adjust the volume of their speaking according to the size of the venue; the number of people and to signal their intentions clearly. Learning to project your voice is crucial and is clearly linked to posture and confidence. Voice is part of a repertoire of non-verbal elements by which we indicate; for example, confidence; knowledge; authority, as well as support and encouragement.

4    *Speed.* When teachers, particularly trainees, are nervous or feel under-prepared, they tend to speak rapidly, basically because they want to get the whole thing done and leave as quickly as possible. The main problem, of course, is that learners won't be able to hear what you are saying or keep up with you. Another problem with speaking too quickly is that there are no gaps in which your learners can seek clarification or ask questions. In your early days of teaching you will need to slow right down to what might seem feel a ridiculously slow pace, but you will adjust and find your natural level. Don't forget that silence can be effective. Leave gaps and scan the faces of learners for feedback. The keys to avoiding hurried and nervous delivery are thorough preparation, confidence that you are an expert in your subject, and relaxation.

## Empathy

Empathy is not the same as sympathy. To sympathise is to feel for somebody, often to feel sorry for them. Empathy goes a stage further. It is a particular kind of perception by which we can 'tune in' to the feelings of others and communicate more sensitively. Those who lack empathy find relationships and communication difficult, even to the point of being dysfunctional. Unable to understand or recognise their own feelings, people who lack empathy find it hard to recognise and understand the feelings of others. Egocentric people have problems because empathy requires a genuine interest in others and their feelings, be they joy, pain, anger or happiness.

Empathy grows from self-awareness. The more we can recognise and manage our own feelings, the better we can understand others, particularly our learners. Empathy requires the ability to recognise and interpret non-verbal signals. Daniel Goleman, a leading figure in emotional intelligence, says that 'just as the mode of rational mind is words, the mode of the emotions is non-verbal' (Goleman 1995: 97). The non-verbal signals discussed above provide vital information for teachers to gauge the feelings and attitudes of their learners. Without the ability to recognise such signals we are unable to adjust and adapt our teaching.

## Feedback

Feedback in teaching and learning is generally understood as written or spoken comments provided as part of assessment. Feedback has a more general meaning in the communication process. Gill and Adams (1998: 74) define it as, . . . 'a response from the receiver which gives the communicator an idea of how the message is being received and whether it needs to be modified'. Good teachers look for and seek feedback from their learners, particularly whether the messages been received and understood. It may be that the form of communication does not suit everyone. For example, many learners will struggle to understand a spoken or written explanation, but will see the point, quite literally, when a visual representation is used or an appropriate example or analogy given.

Feedback is clearly linked to empathy in that it requires you to notice non-verbal feedback from your learners, interpret it and respond accordingly. Good teachers notice and respond to feedback and make efforts to obtain it; bad teachers carry on regardless of or even fail to notice feedback.

**Activity**

In what ways, non-verbal and verbal, do your learners give you feedback?

How do learners indicate they are: interested, attentive, bored, distracted?

Does all feedback have to be responded to by the teacher?

## Written communication

Writing is frequently overlooked in advice on effective communication. Like all other forms of communication, writing must be produced with the audience and purpose in mind; writing is usually for other people to read and, hopefully understand. This does not mean 'dumbing down', but it does mean writing clearly, concisely and effectively.

Writing that does not consider the needs, level and experience of the learners or, worse still, is designed to impress rather than inform is bad writing. Some academics seem to be scared to write plainly. Clearly there are the necessary conventions of academic writing – objectivity, being impersonal, referencing sources – but these requirements should not hinder readability and understanding. Michael McCarthy (2006), in an article on academic writing, believes: 'Texts are for readers, not for their writers, and we should respect our readers by choosing our grammar appropriately, so that it helps, not hinders, the processing of the specialist vocabulary and concepts.'

Jargon, as we discussed earlier, is the language of particular groups of people in specific occupations or disciplines. It is a useful shorthand between these people but is often used, consciously or unconsciously, to exclude others. Some of the most valuable advice on writing clearly and avoiding jargon is available from the Plain English Campaign. The Plain English Campaign does 'exactly what it says on the tin', that is to identify and publicise bad uses of language and to persuade anyone who issues written documents to consider their readers by writing simply and directly. In addition, they publish examples of jargon and cliché on their website for amusement and as anti-role models. Here's are an example from their 'before and after' section:

Before:
High quality learning environments are a necessary precondition for facilitation and enhancement of the ongoing learning process.

After:
Children need good schools if they are to learn properly.

(© Plain English Campaign)

## Communication climate and emotional intelligence

I want to conclude this chapter by discussing two concepts that bring together the various elements of communication. The first comes from Adler et al. (1998) who refer to *communication climate*. The second element is the more recent concept of *emotional intelligence*, developed mainly by Daniel Goleman (1995).

In teaching, as in so many areas of human activity, the most obvious things are frequently overlooked, even ignored. Emotions and the understanding their effects have had no real place in mainstream education. Some people have traced this back to the French philosopher René Descartes and his separation of mind and body, emotion and reason, head and heart. The life of the mind became superior; emotions, human weaknesses to be overcome or ignored. Most of us, however, will be able to recall times when emotions got in the way of our learning and, in many instances, negative emotions were induced by the learning environment. Nobody ever learned effectively or meaningfully by being bored, frightened, humiliated or anxious. Recently, I have heard stories of teachers who physically or emotionally separate school pupils they consider to be achievers and non-achievers. Clearly, such acts will produce negative emotional states which will impede learning. Learners perceived as failing and labelled as such are more likely to fail – this is often referred to as a 'self-fulfilling prophecy'.

Successful teaching and learning requires the creation of a positive emotional environment. Adler et al. (1998: 327) define communication climate as: '. . . the social/psychological tone of a relationship. A climate doesn't involve specific activities as much as the way people feel about each other as they carry out those activities.' They go on to suggest that a positive communication climate is one in which people feel valued. Feeling valued comes from communication between learners and teachers. Simple things such as knowing and using learners' names, listening, congratulating achievement, using eye contact are referred to by these authors as *confirming responses*. Responses and teacher behaviour that result in a negative communication climate are *disconfirming responses*.

**Activity**

Bearing in mind the elements of communication discussed in this chapter, give examples of behaviour, particularly non-verbal, which are likely to be:

*   confirming
*   disconfirming

Remember, this could include unexpected elements such as the tone and the style of a written handout.

**For your journal**

Consider times when you have been aware of a negative communication climate. How did you try to change it?

The essence of emotional intelligence, particularly as propounded by Goleman, is that it is at least as important as IQ. The area of our brains which deals with emotions is, in evolutionary terms, older than the neocortex which deals with cognitive aspects such as logic and reasoning. Because emotions and feelings are more fundamental than intellect and reasoning, if they are not recognised and managed by teachers and learners then effective learning cannot occur. As Goleman says: 'emotions enrich; a model of mind which leaves them out is impoverished' (1995: 41).

Learners bring many things to our sessions – some of which we don't know about – that can positively or negatively affect their learning. They bring their needs, their life experiences, their fears and uncertainties, their hopes and aspirations, their prejudices and assumptions, their happy or unhappy homes. We are not therapists and we cannot and should not try to uncover these feelings, but neither should we expect students simply to put them aside and concentrate on learning. Awareness of emotional intelligence helps us to create a positive learning state in which learners feel 'valued, curious, safe, relaxed, connected and motivated' (Mortiboys 2005: 29).

## Developing communication skills

### The back-to-back exercise
This is designed to develop understanding of communication as a process and to identify barriers to communication and learning.

### Process
Group members split into pairs and sit back to back. One is nominated the sender, the other is the receiver.

The sender is given an A4 sheet which has between five and eight different shapes or objects drawn on it. The sender's job is to describe these to the receiver so that he can reproduce them as accurately as possible. This is done twice – once without any communication from the receiver; the second time the receiver can seek as much clarification as he wishes.

At the end of the exercise, the results are compared and conclusions drawn.

### Using video
It can be instructive to make a recording of yourself teaching. This will allow you to analyse and evaluate your communication skills. If you are brave enough, share and discuss it with colleagues.

## For your journal

### A communications skills audit

The following questions can be used as the basis for an audit and evaluation of your communication skills in teaching and learning. Some of the conclusions might inform your personal development journal. You can adapt and add to these questions in any way you wish, possibly by adding a rating scale. You might want to use them to get feedback from your learners.

1  I use eye contact to include all learners.
2  I am aware of my posture when sitting or standing.
3  My posture communicates, for example confidence, authority, approachability.
4  I move around the room and get amongst my learners.
5  I adjust the room layout to suit the number of learners, purpose and communication climate.
6  My students can hear me clearly.
7  I am aware of my voice and adjust speed, pause, pitch, volume and stress to suit learners and purpose.
8  I am a good listener.

9   I let learners finish speaking before I reply.

10  I know learners' names.

11  I avoid unnecessary use of jargon/specific language and ensure that learners understand new words and phrases.

12  I consciously try to reduce mechanical/physical barriers to communication.

13  I am aware of the effects of emotions on teaching and learning.

14  I try to create a safe and positive communication climate conducive to learning.

15  I recognise that I might make assumptions about learners.

16  I notice feedback from learners.

17  I am prepared to adjust how and what I am teaching in response to learners' feedback

18  I consider carefully the structure and clarity of written material.

---

**Journal extract: Jane, training to teach childcare**

This was my first session with the childcare group and I felt very nervous, even though I was very well prepared. When I walked into the room I felt all eyes were on me and scrutinising me. Looking back, I'm aware that I was probably looking a bit apologetic for being there; I think I was hunched and avoiding eye contact.

My first questions to the group were met with silence, even a few sniggers – this made me feel even worse. As the session developed I began to relax and take my time. I started to look at the learners and the responses began, gradually, to improve.

## Further reading

Appleyard, N. and Appleyard, K. (2010) *Communicating with Learners in the Lifelong Learning Sector*. Exeter: Learning Matters.

Burton, G. and Dimbleby, R. (2007) *Between Ourselves: An Introduction to Interpersonal Communication* (4th edn). London: Arnold.

Goleman, D. (1995) *Emotional Intelligence*. London: Bloomsbury.

Stanton, N. (2009) *Mastering Communication* (5th edn). Basingstoke: Palgrave Macmillan.

## Websites

Plain English Campaign. Download free guides on 'How to Write in Plain English' and 'The A-Z of Alternative Words'. www.plainenglish.co.uk.

Scholastic.com is a web tool providing a wide range of resources. For an interactive class set-up tool see www.scholastic.com/tools/class_set up/.

# 4

# A curriculum for inclusive learning

**What this chapter is about**

- Defining the curriculum
- Process, product and praxis views of the curriculum
- The 'hidden' curriculum
- What is inclusion?
- Inclusive learning
- Widening participation
- Equality Act 2010
- Specific learning difficulties (SpLD) e.g. dyslexia

**LLUK standards**

This chapter covers, at least, the following standards:
AS 1; AK 1.1; AP 1.1; AS 2; AK 2.1; AP 2.1; AS 3; AK 3.1; AP 3.1
BS 1; BK 1.1; BP 1.1; BS 2; BK 2.5; BP 2.5
DS 1; DK 1.1; DP 1.1; DK 1.3; DP 1.3; DS 2; DK 2.1; DP 2.1; DK 2.2; DP 2.2

**Activity**

Perhaps we simply assume that what is taught in colleges, learning providers and schools is 'natural'. Critical and reflective practice requires us to challenge these 'taken for granted' assumptions.

Discuss the following in relation to what you teach and/or what you have learned as a student or school pupil:

- What is taught?
- Why is it taught?
- Who is it learned by?
- Who decides what the content of the learning should be?
- How is it taught?
- How is it learned?

## What is a curriculum?

Your discussions about the questions in this activity are essentially discussions about the 'curriculum'. So, what do we mean by curriculum? Some understand curriculum to mean the content of a course; others might regard it as the total offer of learning programmes provided by one institution or the range of provision at a national level, as in the National Curriculum or the Adult Basic Skills Curriculum.

The content of a particular course or programme is called a 'syllabus' or the 'specifications'. A list of programmes available in a particular institution is not a curriculum – it is a prospectus or a directory. The term 'curriculum', in its fullest sense, includes not only the content of what is learned but also how it is learned; how it is assessed; the wider personal, intellectual, learning and social skills it aims to develop; the values of the learning provider and, in the case of the lifelong learning sector (LLS), the values which underpin the LLUK standards for teachers. Above all, a fully realised curriculum will have, even if only implicitly, a clear philosophy and a rationale which all those teaching on it can explain and discuss. Further education colleges frequently refer to 'student learning' and the 'student experience' – a comprehensive definition of curriculum includes both. Kelly (2009: 9) states: '. . . We will understand by the term 'curriculum' the overall rationale for any educational programme . . . the prime concern must be with the totality.'

Your discussions from the activity will probably have brought up issues relating to who learns what and the extent to which learners are selected or guided towards particular programmes of learning and places of learning. Any discussions of curricula are, almost inevitably, also discussions about inclusion and inclusive learning.

## Product view of the curriculum

In the 'product' view of the curriculum, education is seen as the transmission of content. The key point is who defines and selects the content and for what purpose. The majority of education in our system is based on an 'accepted' body of subjects whose content and methods are relatively certain and can be prescribed in the form of specifications and examinations by awarding bodies. The range of subjects studied in schools, colleges and universities will be familiar to most of us – English, maths, sciences, history, geography, religious studies, etc. These subjects are generally the ones considered to have the most status and credibility, whereas recent arrivals such as media studies are considered less favourably.

This view of the curriculum also holds that one of the main functions of education is to transmit the culture of society. This, we could argue, is essential to the continuity of society, but again begs a question – whose culture is to be transmitted? The notion of 'multiculturalism' has been the subject of considerable debate but it is undeniable that we live in a diverse society in terms of, for example, religion, ethnicity, social class, gender and disability. There is a political dimension here and a clear link to inclusion. If the mainstream culture is based, as some suggest, on a predominantly white, middle-class, 'middle England' worldview, then people of different cultures or different life experiences may feel excluded or unable to participate fully in the education system as it is. These concerns are apparent whenever politicians and teachers make competing claims about what should be taught in the school history curriculum or in English literature.

The product view of curriculum also derives in part from the aims and objective approach to education associated with Ralph Tyler (1949) and subsequently developed in Benjamin Bloom's *Taxonomy of Educational Objectives* (Bloom 1956). These ideas were based on a more 'scientific' approach to education, the key idea being that if the aims and objectives were clearly defined then the educational 'outcomes' could be more accurately and reliably assessed and reported. This 'reporting' is an important consideration:

> . . . Such approaches are highly valued because they can be evaluated in ways which are valued by managers and government ministers . . . it is a simple exercise to evaluate an objectives-driven curriculum: they have either been met or they have not.
>
> (Tummons 2010: 24)

## Process view of the curriculum

The product view of the curriculum is concerned, mainly, with *what* students learn. The 'process' model, in contrast, is concerned with *how* learners learn and with their growth and development as human beings. In this view, learners are seen as active participants in the construction of knowledge and development of understanding rather than as passive recipients of knowledge. It is, therefore, associated with cognitive and constructivist theories of learning and with notions of active learning and deep learning. This approach to learning is more likely to develop learner autonomy and a propensity to lifelong learning.

This approach to the curriculum and to learning has a long tradition. John Dewey (1938) emphasised the importance of experience in education. Whitehead (1932) suggested that 'the curriculum is to be thought of in terms of activity and experience rather than of knowledge to acquired rather than facts stored.' (quoted in Kelly 2009: 100).

The most frequently cited reference to the process curriculum is Lawrence Stenhouse's *An Introduction to Curriculum Research and Development* (1975) in which he sets out his arguments against behavioural objectives as the basis for the curriculum and proposes an inquiry-based approach to learning. While Stenhouse does not deny the importance of passing on the knowledge base of a subject, he emphasises the importance of inquiry and discovery in the development of learners' understanding and allowing for the emergence of 'unintended learning outcomes' which might not be specified in the objectives and not necessarily assessed. Rather than the use of aims and objectives to prescribe the content and structure of learning, Stenhouse's scheme advocates the use of loosely framed objectives in which learners can explore and discover within the subject or area of study.

## Why not process *and* product?

Education is beset with arguments concerning the desirability or efficacy of one theory or idea over another. Politicians, academics, teachers and cultural commentators fiercely defend their own point of view and lobby for it to become accepted practice. At the time of writing there is a 'discussion' around the relative merits of teaching 'facts' and of 'student-centred' learning and policies are likely to be developed on the basis of who wins the argument and can garner the most convincing evidence to support their beliefs.

The underlying themes of this book, you might rightly conclude, are towards a student-centred, process view of the curriculum and of learning. Other views, however, are available and they are not necessarily mutually exclusive. The curriculum doesn't have to be, and probably can't be, either process or product. Unlike Charles Dickens', fictional Mr Gradgrind, to whom facts were the only things necessary and everything else was to be ruthlessly expunged, even the most ardent proponents of the product view of the curriculum would struggle to deny that learners' development and growth are an important part of what they do. Those who tend to the process view are often criticised because they put the development of the individual before, or even instead of, subject knowledge.

John Dewey's contrast between *traditional* and *progressive* education is mirrored by the contrast between the product and the process views of curriculum. In *Experience and Education* he cautions against the imposition of one extreme and the rejection of the other and asserts:

> Because the older education imposed the knowledge, methods and the rules of conduct of the mature person upon the young, it does not follow, except on the basis of the extreme *Either–Or* philosophy, that the knowledge and skill of the mature person has no directive value for the experience of the immature.
>
> (Dewey 1997: 21)

It seems appropriate to suggest that when you are designing your curriculum or a programme within it you should seek to develop both process and product approaches in a mutually beneficial combination. The development of understanding is a desirable aim of education but it has to be an understanding of *something* – usually a subject or a vocational area. Whether we like it or not, the content of subjects is to a greater or lesser extent prescribed. Maths teachers can't reject the syllabus in favour of a radical programme based on their own particular interests. What they can do is to consider not only the 'what' of the subject but also the 'how' it is taught and learned. Swan (2006) has carried out research into maths teaching and concluded that learners who struggle with maths can benefit from methods which include discussion to enhance their understanding.

## Praxis view of curriculum

Praxis essentially refers to the two dimensions of human activity – theory and practice, thought and action – and recognises that one is not complete without the other. A rigid, preplanned curriculum specifies the ends to be achieved and the knowledge or skills to be acquired. These ends are usually prescribed – by teachers, awarding bodies or the government – and taken for granted as appropriate to all learners in all situations. The praxis approach to curriculum doesn't necessarily begin with the ends to be achieved but with the lived experience of the learners, and is based on continual dialogue, action and reflection. A praxis curriculum is not prescribed; it is negotiated and constantly adapted. As Smith says:

> As we think about what we might want to achieve, we alter the way we might achieve that. As we think about the way we might go about something, we change what we might aim at. There is a continual interplay between ends and means . . . between thought and action.
>
> (Smith 2011: 4)

Freire (1972) referred to the 'banking concept' of education in which 'deposits' of knowledge are placed in the learners' heads with no reference to their lives or their situation. In this model the only knowledge that is worthwhile is the teacher's knowledge, which learners receive passively. Flanagan (2006: 188) suggests that this kind of education 'robs students of the responsibility of thinking and acting for themselves'. The process model of the curriculum is more student-centred and is based on developing learners' abilities to construct and interpret meanings, but doesn't necessarily consider whose interests are being served; for example, the school system, the social system or the economic system. A praxis approach goes beyond this by encouraging students to think about their learning and to examine, evaluate and change their situations for the better.

If we take the example of young people without jobs, we can see that previous initiatives imply that these young people are deficient in some way and that if they can be 'fixed' by improving their social and life skills and basic skills, they will be able to get jobs. In reality the main cause of joblessness is not inadequate young people but a lack of jobs. Similarly a 'medical model' of disability implies that disabled people themselves have problems rather than the problems being located in society's attitudes towards them; the implication being that disabled people have to 'fit in' rather than society changing to accept and value them as they are.

The praxis approach involves a commitment to action and change and the improvement of the learners' life situations. As Grundy (1987: 102) points out, a praxis approach 'means acting with, not upon, others'. As such it is a political action and many in the lifelong learning sector may feel unable, or possibly not allowed, to take such action.

## The 'hidden' curriculum

The planned curriculum provides an 'official' statement of the content of what is to be taught. This might include not only the subject content but also describe the skills and behaviours which learners will be expected to develop within their courses and within the places of learning. The 'hidden' curriculum is a concept developed from educational sociology and refers to the unplanned, unintentional and possibly unconscious consequences of the curriculum as it is experienced by the learners. It refers to the values, attitudes and ways of behaving which are, or might be, learned in educational institutions. These 'messages' are subtle and implicit and transmitted through what happens in classrooms and workshops and throughout the ethos of the organisation. The hidden curriculum is often understood negatively as being a subtle and oppressive form of social control but there may also be positive aspects. An organisational ethos which prescribes and expects certain kinds of behaviour – punctuality, respect for authority, politeness – is not necessarily a 'plot' to stifle individuality and produce unquestioning conformists. It might have the intention of producing people who can live and work successfully in a mutually dependent society.

The curriculum might be hidden from learners but understood, even planned, by teachers. For example, learners might not necessarily be told 'we are going to teach you how to behave', but there will an agreed system of rules and procedures which has been planned and implemented by teachers and managers. The 'curriculum' might be hidden from everybody – learners, teachers, the organisation – because it's so taken for granted as a cultural norm that nobody questions it. In my own secondary education in the 1960s it was accepted that girls did cookery and domestic science while boys did woodwork and metalwork. The implicit message seemed to be that girls would become homemakers and boys would become manual workers.

### Is there a hidden curriculum which makes schools different from the lifelong learning sector?

Prior to the early 1990s a large further education would be likely to provide an academic and vocational curriculum which covered a wide range of programmes from A-levels, possibly even pre-degree foundation courses, to City and Guilds programmes in plumbing and catering as well as BTEC programmes in business or hospitality; many also offered adult and access to higher education courses. The lifelong learning sector has developed to include FE colleges, training providers, offender learning and work-based learning. The prevailing ethos in the sector, however, has now switched to a focus on skills and training. This is not necessarily a bad thing but the hidden curriculum at a national level might well be that schools and universities are for *education* while the lifelong learning sector is for *skills*, with the former perceived by potential learners as 'better' than the latter. Writing on inclusion Cutting (2009: 152) suggests that we now have a 'system based on greater inclusion and participation, but one which is very much based on skills, particularly vocational ones'.

At the time of writing, the government is opening up and increasing competition within the higher education (HE) sector by encouraging outside and new providers, particularly further education (FE) colleges, to offer university level courses. It remains to be seen whether HE provision in FE will have the same status and esteem.

### Conform and succeed?

The most positive message that colleges and schools can give is that success and achievement are important. The hidden curriculum might, however, carry additional messages that only certain kinds of success in certain areas of activity are desirable or have the most prestige. Our education system is, to a great extent, dominated by testing and examination success underpinned by various kinds of selection based on notions of fixed intelligence and ability. Beliefs in fixed ability are used to justify different curricula for different young people, particularly the split between academic and vocational provision. Politicians and educational planners might consider, often quite genuinely, that these different provisions are necessary and appropriate to learners' different aptitudes, but they have never enjoyed parity of esteem (and probably never will). Hart et al. (2004: 37) suggest that the 'less able' are frequently assigned to a repetitive regime of low-level teaching which might well be the opposite of what they need:

> . . . Ideas of fixed ability have been used to justify offering a restricted curriculum to some pupils on the grounds of their presumed ability . . . these ideas have justified selecting priorities for these pupils' learning that deprive them of the very kinds of opportunities that might actually challenge and stimulate them to learn more successfully.

In the lifelong learning sector we sometimes encounter people who have had such experiences and the judgements made about them have stuck and become part of their self-concept. Schools require, understandably, a level of conformity and want students to achieve. Along with this goes an ideal type of what a good student is like – well disciplined, hard working and accepting of the messages of ability and success. Many young people aren't like this. In a classic piece of educational sociology, Nell Keddie suggests that teachers like conformity and in essence favour those students who accept their input and their worldview unquestioningly. This, Keddie (1971: 156) asserts, is the key to their success: 'It would seem to be the failure of high-ability pupils to question what they are taught in schools that contributes in large measure to their educational achievement.' For many, the message of the hidden curriculum could be 'conform and succeed'.

## What is inclusion?

It might be easier to consider inclusion in terms of its opposite – exclusion. There is legislation intended to prevent anyone from being deliberately excluded from learning, but many may feel less welcome, less able to participate or not adequately provided for. The 'excluded' might include, for example, those with disabilities or specific learning difficulties; some ethnic groups; those with mental health problems; travellers; people on low incomes; or those deemed to be 'less able'. All societies are diverse but many institutions and organisations struggle to recognise and cater for this diversity, leading to the development of negative labels and stereotypes which tend to be applied to all members of these groups as if they all have identical needs.

Inclusion means that we value and respect all people equally and provide learning opportunities for them. Ainscow and Booth (2011) provide some useful defining characteristics of inclusion. The references to schools can easily be replaced by references to colleges or learning providers:

- Valuing all students and staff equally.
- Increasing the participation of students in, and reducing their exclusion from, the cultures, the curricula and communities of local schools.
- Restructuring the cultures, policies and practices in schools so that they respond to the diversity of students in the locality.
- Reducing barriers to learning and participation for all students, not only those with impairments or those categorised as 'having special educational needs'.
- Learning to overcome barriers to the access and participation of particular students to make changes for the benefit of students more widely.
- Viewing the difference between students as resources to support learning, rather than problems to be overcome.
- Emphasising the role of schools in building community and developing values, as well as increasing achievement.
- Recognising that inclusion in education is one aspect of inclusion in society.

## Inclusive learning and teaching

Inclusive learning meets the needs, styles, abilities and experiences of all who come into our institutions. We can't just say 'This is how we teach' and expect everyone to fit in with it. We need to find out how people learn and to develop provision, methods and resources to suit them. Inclusive teaching is the responsibility of the whole institution and includes matching the provision to students' needs; recognising diversity; anticipating student needs and incorporating regular reflection, review and improvement as an ongoing project. Two key documents in the journey to inclusive learning are the Tomlinson Report (1996) and the Kennedy Report (1997).

## Inclusive learning

Professor John Tomlinson was asked to research and report on educational provision for learners with learning difficulties and disabilities. The final document, however, had implications for all learners and was a keystone in the development of inclusive education. The Tomlinson Committee moved the focus from those with learning difficulties and disabilities to a more learner-centred approach for all and, in essence, makes clear that all learners are unique individuals with their own particular needs and experience. The report moves away from labelling and asserts that difficulties are not located within the learner; rather it is the duty of educational providers to understand individual learners and to find ways to meet their requirements. The key message of Tomlinson is summed by this statement:

> The aim is not for students to simply take part in further education but to be actively included and fully engaged in their learning. At the heart of our thinking lies the idea of match or fit between how the learner learns best, what they need and want to learn and what is required from the FE sector, the college and teachers for successful learning to take place.

By inclusive learning therefore we mean the greatest degree of match or fit between the individual learners' requirements and the provision that is made for them.

(Tomlinson 1996: 10)

In a later article, Tomlinson (2003) reviews and reaffirms the centrality of inclusive learning. He puts it into a contemporary context and makes clear that it applies right across the lifelong learning sector in work-based learning; adult and community learning, colleges and sixth forms. He reminds us that inclusive learning is not just for those with learning difficulties and disabilities: 'Inclusive learning also applies to all learners, teachers and providers.' Tomlinson recommends an individually designed learning environment as the best way to ensure that provision meets learners' needs. This environment would have, and develop for all, the following components:

- an individual learning programme
- a curriculum which promotes progress in learning
- effective teaching
- counselling, guidance and initial assessment
- opportunities for students to discuss and manage their own learning
- support for learning
- support for learners, such as crèche facilities
- procedures for assessing, recording and accrediting achievement
- learning materials and resources
- technical aids and equipment
- learning technology
- trained staff.

**Activity**

To what extent do you think that your institution meets the criteria for an individually designed learning environment as set out by Tomlinson?

## Widening participation

Widening participation describes the positive attempts made by learning organisations to bring people from across the diversity of the community into learning, particularly those who have experienced difficulty, disadvantage, discrimination and disappointment in their earlier learning. The key document here is *Learning Works: Widening Participation in Further Education* (Kennedy 1997), commonly referred to as the Kennedy Report, which stated the 'irresistible case' for widening participation in education. Recently we have heard a great deal, rightly, about the importance of learning and skills for economic success. Kennedy recognised this but added, perhaps more importantly, the case for learning as a way to develop social unity and lessen social exclusion. Kennedy understands that many people who have failed in their early learning have suffered economic and social disadvantages from which they may not easily recover. Far too many people have come out of school believing that education is over and they never return to it. As Kennedy wryly says: 'If at first you don't succeed . . . you don't succeed.' For the health of society and the economy these people need to be given opportunities to return to and succeed in learning. Kennedy stated:

> We must widen participation not simply increase it. Widening participation means increasing access to learning and providing opportunities for success and progression to a much wider cross-section of the population than now. All those who are not fulfilling their potential or who have underachieved in the past must be drawn in to successful learning. Widening participation in post-16 learning will create a self-perpetuating learning society.
>
> (Kennedy 1997: 15)

In May 2003, following a consultation process, the Learning and Skills Council (LSC) launched its *Successful Participation for All: Widening Adult Participation* strategy. This built on the Tomlinson and Kennedy reports and reflected the LSC's concern that a significant number of adults do not continue in education or training beyond school and the implications of this for individuals and the economy as well as wider social issues including crime, health and community cohesion. The important implication for our practice as teachers is that the strategy brings together two key ideas:

> We cannot separate widening participation from inclusive learning. Widening participation is about seeking to reach under-represented groups and retaining these groups in learning. Inclusive education addresses the learning programmes needed for individuals and groups to succeed in learning.
>
> (LSC 2003: para. 49)

Further, the strategy provides important messages for the ways in which we plan, prepare, deliver and assess learning. It highlights some of the ways in which many people were turned off learning by early negative experiences, including:

- too much teaching and too little learning
- content which had little interest to them or relevance to their lives
- frequent experiences of failure and humiliation.

In considering ways in which learners can be encouraged to return to and remain in learning the report asserts: 'Nothing is more likely to demotivate learners than to feel they are being criticised as failures. Nor are they likely to be willing participants in a process that is "being done to them"' (LSC 2003: para. 50).

**Activity**

Consider the above points.

In what ways can you link these to the theory and practice discussed elsewhere in this book, particularly learning theories; teaching and learning methods; assessment and motivation.

## The Equality Act 2010

The Disability Discrimination Act (DDA) 1995 made it unlawful to discriminate against a disabled person in the provision of employment, services or property. The Special Educational Needs and Disability Act 2001 amended the DDA to make it unlawful for educational providers to discriminate against learners with disabilities. Education providers must make 'reasonable adjustments' to ensure that disabled learners do not suffer a substantial disadvantage in comparison to people who are not disabled. Institutions should also anticipate the likely needs of disabled learners as well as respond to individual needs as they arise. For example, an institution might not previously have had learners who are wheelchair users but provision should still be made. The 2010 Equality Act consolidates and simplifies all previous disability discrimination with all other previous equality legislation into a single Act.

### Protected characteristics

Under previous legislation, six strands of diversity were identified. Under the 2010 Equality Act these six strands are replaced by nine 'protected characteristics' which protect against discrimination on the following grounds:

- age
- disability
- gender reassignment
- marriage and civil partnership
- pregnancy and maternity
- race
- religion or belief
- sex
- sexual orientation.

### Types of discrimination: prohibited conduct

As with the previous legislation, the Equality Act prohibits:

- direct discrimination
- indirect discrimination
- harassment
- victimisation.

### Direct discrimination

Direct discrimination means when a person is treated less favourably than others on the grounds of any of the protected characteristics. For example, this means refusing admission to a course on the basis of a person's disability or gender would be direct discrimination and, therefore, unlawful. In their guidance, the Equality and Human Rights Commission (EHRC) give the example of a man being refused admission to a course in childcare because the college considers it inappropriate for a man to be working with children.

### Indirect discrimination

Indirect discrimination happens when a learning provider applies a provision, criteria or practice in the same way for all students which results in putting students with protected characteristics at a particular disadvantage. Indirect discrimination applies to all the protected characteristics except pregnancy and maternity, although a 'provision', 'practice' or 'criterion' which disadvantages pregnant students or new mothers may be indirect sex discrimination.

### Harassment

There are three types of harassment which are unlawful;

- Harassment related to a protected characteristic. EHRC guidance gives the example of tutor who makes derogatory remarks about a local traveller site when there are members of the traveller community in the learning group who find the tutor's behaviour degrading and offensive.
- Sexual harassment is any unwanted behaviour of a sexual nature which violates a student's dignity or creates an intimidating, hostile, degrading, humiliating or offensive environment for the student.
- Less favourable of treatment of students because they submit to or reject sexual harassment or harassment related to their sex. For example, if a tutor fails an otherwise excellent assignment because the student has rejected their harassment.

### Victimisation

Victimisation means treating less favourably someone who has carried out a 'protected act' which is defined in the Act as follows:

- Making a claim or complaint of discrimination under the Act.
- Giving evidence or information to support another person's claim under the Act.
- Alleging that the learning provider or someone else has breached the Act.
- Doing anything else in connection with the Act.

An example of victimisation would be if a student subjected to sexual harassment makes a complaint and is subsequently treated badly as a result. EHRC guidelines also give the example of a finance department refusing to process a claim from a student who has supported another student's sexual harassment claim.

## Single Equality Duty

Public bodies including learning providers and further education colleges now have a Single Equality Duty which consolidates all the former duties relating to race, gender and disability into a single duty. Private training providers are not included in this requirement but they are covered by the service provider provisions of the Act. Under the Act learning providers have a general equality duty which requires them to:

• eliminate discrimination, harassment and victimisation
• advance equality of opportunity between different groups
• foster good relations between different groups.

In addition, they have specific duties which require them to:

• publish sufficient information to demonstrate their compliance with their general equality duty across all of their functions
• prepare and publish objectives to demonstrate how they will meet one or more of their general equality aims.

## Content and delivery of the curriculum

Learning providers are not allowed to discriminate against students in the provision of education or in their access to any facility, benefit or service. These obligations, however, do not apply to the content of the curriculum. Learning providers and teachers are rightly concerned to meet their equality and diversity obligations, to uphold the law and not to cause offence to, or discriminate against, any groups of people. This can lead to teachers being cautious to avoid controversial content, but as the EHRC guidelines show teachers should have academic freedom and be able to discuss a range of issues:

> ...You are not restricted in the range of issues, ideas and materials you use in your syllabus and will have the academic freedom to expose students to a range of thoughts and ideas, however controversial. Even if the content of the curriculum causes offence to students with certain protected characteristics, this will not make it unlawful unless it is delivered in a way which results in harassment or subjects students to discrimination or other detriment.
>
> (EHRC 2011: 42)

Although the curriculum content can be controversial, teachers must ensure that the delivery and the ways in which the content is taught do not subject students to discrimination. The example is given of a teacher covering the apartheid period in South Africa who repeatedly uses racist language when talking about black people. The discussion of the topic is acceptable but the language is likely to cause offence and is, therefore, likely to be unlawful harassment.

## Learners with learning difficulties and/or disabilities

The Disability Discrimination Act 1995 defines a *disability* as: 'a physical or mental impairment which has a substantial and long-term adverse effect on your ability to carry out normal day-to-day activities'. This can include:

- sensory impairments, e.g. people with visual impairments or who are hard of hearing
- learning difficulties, including specific learning difficulties such as dyslexia
- mental health conditions ('clinically well recognised')
- severe disfigurements
- progressive conditions, such as multiple sclerosis, cancer and HIV
- conditions characterised by a number of cumulative effects such as pain or fatigue
- a past history of disability.

The Learning and Skills Act 2000 states that a disability 'prevents or hinders [a person] from making use of facilities of a kind generally provided by institutions providing post-16 education or training'.

A *learning difficulty* is when someone has greater difficulty in learning than the majority of persons of their own age. A person who has a learning difficulty may also have a disability, for example, a person who has Down's syndrome may have some degree of learning difficulty.

## Medical and social models of disability

The *medical* and *social* models of disability describe different attitudes towards disability and their consequences. The medical model focuses on the person's disability and sees it in terms of what they can and cannot do. There is an implicit assumption in this model that the difficulties which disabled people encounter are the direct result of their disability rather than the fact that society and institutions do not adequately provide for them. This model of disability leads to a labelling approach which takes a narrow view of disabled people and ties them into cultures of dependency.

The social model doesn't view disabled people as having something wrong with them and shifts the focus to society and its institutions and attitudes. The social model takes as its starting point the belief that all disabled people have a right to belong and not be discriminated against. The Disability Equality Duty places an obligation on institutions to 'understand and dismantle barriers before they have an impact on individuals' (Rose and Faraday 2006).

**Activity**

The Learning and Skills Council requires all providers to have a disability statement.

Have you found and read the disability statement for your institution? Is it widely available to all learners in a variety of formats?

## Specific learning difficulties (SpLD)

Specific learning difficulties (SpLD) refers to a range of learning difficulties, including dyslexia, dyspraxia, dyscalculia, ADHD and autistic spectrum disorders. Individually and collectively these conditions have been widely researched and there is a great deal of information in specific texts and websites to support and your learners. The following is a brief overview of specific learning difficulties, some words of advice and references to further reading and websites.

### Dyslexia

About 4 per cent of the population is affected by dyslexia to a significant extent and a further 6 per cent to a lesser degree. We know that until recently dyslexia was not fully understood and many dyslexic children and adults were regarded as stupid or lazy. The percentage of the prison population who are dyslexic is higher, certainly above 10 per cent, and it has been suggested that in some prisons more than 50 per cent of the population is dyslexic. Wright et al. (2006) provide a comprehensive list of symptoms that a dyslexic person may have some or all of:

- Generally disorganised – the student's file is always in a mess with pieces of work missing or 'mislaid'.
- The student is often late or misses appointments.
- He or she may seem 'clumsy', always knocking things over or bumping into objects.
- The student avoids reading aloud in class and always takes a passive role in group discussion.
- The student has difficulty with pronunciation, particularly with multi-syllabic words.
- The student has difficulty with writing essays, although he or she appears to understand the subject during the lessons. Generally he or she is 'good' orally but has not produced much written work and may even avoid it completely.
- The student consistently makes spelling errors, even though he or she has had those errors corrected several times.

- The student's handwriting may be messy and immature.

- The content of the student's work may be inspiring but there is a lack of appropriate punctuation and grammar.

- The student may be a very good artist, hairdresser, musician or mechanic, but struggles to meet deadlines with assignments.

(Wright et al. 2006: 71–72)

It could be argued that dyslexia is more properly referred to as a learning difference rather than a learning difficulty, since dyslexic people can often be innovative and creative thinkers with intuitive problem-solving skills. There are several ways in which you can help dyslexic learners and, fortunately, most of these are good methods for all learners:

- Like most learners dyslexic students benefit from seeing the big picture. Use some form of advance, particularly graphic, organiser such as a concept map or diagram to introduce topics and highlight key points.

- Make learning multi-sensory – looking, listening, saying and doing. Using different materials and objects for writing with. One teacher working with prisoners describes her learners' success when writing in sand or on to a bar of soap.

- Flow charts are good for explaining procedures.

- Spelling – dyslexic learners like to visualise, so look for words within words, e.g *bus* in *business*.

- Keep your boardwork neat and use colour to highlight different elements. Keep essential points grouped together.

- Provide glossaries of abbreviations and jargon.

- Don't use light text on a dark background. Use coloured paper for handouts, off-white or cream is good. Matt paper reduces glare.

- Give clear instructions and avoid long, complicated explanations.

- Assess work positively and provide positive feedback.

- Encourage learners to word-process their work.

This last point is particularly important because research suggests that dyslexic people lack 'automaticity'. For most of us such things as word recognition and multiplication tables become automatic and the retrieved information can be accessed rapidly without the brain having to process individual units of information. For dyslexics these processes are not so automatic and they have to think about them as well as the content and style of what they are writing. Louise Green has carried out research using word-processing with dyslexic learners in schools. In her article 'Freed from the Pen', she concludes:

> So dyslexic pupils find it helpful to write using a keyboard not because they cannot write by hand, are lazy, or want to rely on a computer program to help them spell. It is because the demands on their working memory are reduced when

they are allowed to use a keyboard rather than having to retrieve from memory each time how to form a letter or spell a word. Typing provides far less distraction from expressing what they want to write. Quite simply most dyslexics report that they can 'think better' when they type.

(Green 2007)

Under the Disability Discrimination Act, education providers are obliged to make 'reasonable adjustments' to support learners with dyslexia. This support may take the form of assistive technology, such as voice recognition software; specialist support from a specialist dyslexia tutor to assess and support learners; mentoring; specialist assessment and any necessary changes to the presentation of documents.

## Dyscalculia

Dyscalculia is similar to dyslexia. Learners have difficulty with numbers rather than words. Professor Mahesh Sharma explains that dyscalculia is 'dysfunction in the reception, comprehension, or production of quantitative and spatial information', which results in difficulty 'in conceptualizing numbers, number relationships outcomes of numerical operations and estimation' (Sharma 2003). Teachers can help learners who have dyscalculia in a number of ways:

- Improving understanding and self-esteem by making number work relevant to everyday life; for example, checking change or estimating quantities in specific vocational areas. Clearly such 'situated learning' would have benefits for all learners.
- Using Socratic questioning to structure and scaffold learning.
- Encourage visualisation.
- Get them to read problems out loud. Discuss mathematical problems.
- Repetition and practice.
- Use of technology.

## Dyspraxia

Dyspraxia is a complex neurological condition which can affect many areas of life. The Dyspraxia Foundation estimates that up to 10 per cent of the population is affected, 2 per cent severely. It is characterised by difficulty in planning and carrying out complex movements. Additional difficulties include:

- 'clumsiness' and dropping things
- problems judging distance
- problems distinguishing between left and right
- inability to do two tasks at once
- taking a long time to complete tasks
- poor handwriting.

## Further reading

Booth, T. and Ainscow, M. (2011) *Index for Inclusion: Developing Learning and Participation in Schools*. Bristol: Centre for Studies on Inclusive Education (CSIE).

Equality and Human Rights Commission (2011) *What Equality Law Means for You as an Education Provider – Further and Higher Education*. www.equalityhumanrights.com/advice-and-guidance/new-equality-act-guidance/equality-act-guidance-downloads/.

Fairclough, M. (2008) *Supporting Learners in the Lifelong Learning Sector*. Maidenhead: Open University Press.

Kelly, A.V. (2009) *The Curriculum: Theory and Practice*. London: Sage.

Wright, A.-M., Sina, A.-J., Colquhoun, S., Spear, J. and Partridge, T. (2006) *FE Lecturer's Guide to Diversity and Inclusion*. London: Continuum.

## Websites

ADHD Information Service. www.addiss.co.uk/

Association of Colleges briefing guide on the Equality Act. www.aoc.co.uk/en/briefings/briefings2011/employment/employment-8611—equality-act-specific-duties-what-do-colleges-need-to-know.cfm

BBC Skillwise site that has useful articles on Asperger syndrome, hearing impairments and dyslexia. www.bbc.co.uk/skillswise/tutors/inclusive-learning

British Deaf Association. www.bda.org.uk/

British Dyslexia Association. www.bdadyslexia.org.uk/

Centre for Studies on Inclusive Education. www.csie.org.uk

Dyscalculia – advice for learners and teachers. www.dyscalculia.org.uk/hc3.asp.

Dyspraxia – advice for learners and teachers. www.dyspraxia.org.uk/

Equality and Human Rights Commission. www.equalityhumanrights.com

Excellence Gateway providing comprehensive article on theories of dyslexia and ways to help dyslexic learners. www.excellencegateway.org.uk/page.aspx?o=124856

National Autistic Society. www.autism.org.uk/

Open University site aimed at teaching in higher education, but also has some useful videos. www.open.ac.uk/inclusiveteaching/pages/understanding-and-awareness/

Royal National Institute for Blind People. www.rnib.org

Skill: National Bureau for Students with Disabilities. www.skill.org.uk

# 5

# Learning theories

## What this chapter is about

- What is learning?
- Behaviourism
- Cognitivism
- Constructivism
- Humanism
- Educational neuroscience
- Motivation
- Intelligence
- Adult learning
- Situated learning

## LLUK standards

This chapter covers, at least, the following standards:
AK 4.1; AP 4.1
BK 2.1; BP 2.1; BK 2.2; BP 2.2; BK 2.3; BP 2.3
CK 3.1; CP 3.1

## What is learning?

'Learning' can have a wide variety of meanings which differ according to who is using the word and the circumstances of its use. In behaviourist terms it is 'a change in behaviour and . . . changes in behaviour occur as a response to a stimulus of one kind or another' (Pritchard 2009: 11).

'Change' features in most definitions of learning. This might be in terms of change in behaviour, knowledge, skills, ability and, in the wider sense, changing as a person. When we are planning courses and learning sessions we should consider not only the content of the programme but also the wider elements of how learners can change and what they can become. These might include: becoming independent and lifelong learners; becoming more autonomous; learning to learn, and coping with change.

Marton and Saljo (1976) researched students' conceptions of learning and developed the following categories for understanding different ideas about learning:

1   Learning is an increase in knowledge, acquiring information.

2   Learning is memorising, storing information that can be reproduced.

3   Learning is learning facts, skills and methods to be retained and used as necessary.

4   Learning is making sense or abstracting meaning. Learning involves relating parts of the subject matter to each other and to the real world.

5   Learning is interpreting and understanding reality in a different way. Learning involves comprehending the world by reinterpreting knowledge.

Conceptions 1 to 3 suggest a less complex view of learning in which we acquire or 'possess' knowledge. This kind of learning might result from transmission approaches to teaching and learning in which the teacher dispenses knowledge and the learners attempt to retain it. There is nothing wrong with these conceptions of learning; it is often appropriate for learners to be told things and to memorise, repeat and practise them. Conceptions 4 and 5, however, imply a deeper and personal process of learning which is about individual change and understanding the world differently.

## Why bother with theory?

Everyone learns – this much is undeniable. There is less certainty, however, about what learning is and how it happens and, consequently, we develop theories to explain it and try and understand how it happens. Jordan et al. (2008: 1) suggest that 'consciously or unconsciously, everyone holds theories of learning'. These theories might be personal, 'common-sense' theories based on our own ideas and experiences of learning, or they might be the 'accepted' theories of learning developed by academics through research, experiment and investigation. These theories are vital to our understanding of learning and our professional development. Without some theoretical tools and concepts we will have little on which to base our reflections and to improve our teaching and our students' learning.

Theories are not facts and we should be prepared to criticise, adapt or even reject some as well as use them as frameworks to understand, guide and improve our practice. An understanding of learning theory is essential for teaching in post-compulsory education and training. However, theory is most useful and more readily understood when it is put into practice. This is made clear in the LLUK standards, which state that teachers in the lifelong learning sector (LLS): 'use relevant theories of learning to support the development of practice in learning and teaching' (AP 4.1).

An understanding of theory, then, is one of the keys to improvement of learning and teaching. Biggs and Tang (2007) suggest three levels of thinking about teaching and learning:

1 *What the learner is.* In this level of understanding the responsibility for learning or not is seen to be the learner's. It fits with theories of fixed ability. The teacher's role is to transmit content. Those learners who understand it do so, this model suggests, because they have ability. Those who don't understand it don't have ability. It's a kind of 'blame the student' model.

2 *What the teacher does.* This level of understanding is more positive in that it stresses the role of the teacher in improving their teaching. It's about widening the range of teaching and learning techniques and improving effectiveness in order to 'get the message across' more effectively. This level, however, still lacks a coherent theory of how people learn.

3 *What the learner does.* This level is more student centred and encourages teachers to understand how learners learn and how they can help them. It is based on constructivist theory which suggests that learning cannot merely be transmitted or 'delivered' to learners. They have to create their own understanding and connect it to what they already know.

(Biggs and Tang 2007: 16–19)

The main schools of learning theory we will consider are:

- behaviourism
- cognitivism
- constructivism
- humanist approaches
- adult learning
- situated learning.

We will also briefly review some ideas around intelligence and recent research in educational neuroscience. None of these theories is definitive or provides the 'correct' answer to how people learn. However, there is something for trainee teachers to learn from each of them. Successful teaching and learning is likely to be an amalgam of elements from a range of theories and ideas.

It is important that we avoid a 'common-sense' approach to the question of how people learn and not assume that how we learn best is how everyone will learn best. A simple theory of learning is the one I refer to as the 'empty bucket' theory. You might see this referred to as 'transmission learning'. The basic elements are as follows:

- Teacher knows everything.
- Students know nothing ('empty buckets').
- Teacher's job is to fill the empty buckets with knowledge.

- Students' job is to learn and retain the knowledge.
- Teacher tests students to assess if they have retained the knowledge.
- Students who have retained and can regurgitate the knowledge are successful.
- Students who cannot retain the knowledge are considered 'leaky buckets' who need further teaching or are deemed less intelligent.

You should be able to work out a number of reasons why this approach is flawed (e.g. teachers are experts but they don't know everything) – more criticisms will become apparent by the end of this chapter.

## Behaviourism

Early psychologists were mainly concerned with introspection – that is the interior, mental processes of individuals' thinking. Behaviourists rejected the notion that psychology was basically concerned with individuals' mental processes. They considered such approaches to be unscientific and subjective, arguing that the mind could not be studied objectively. Behaviour, however, was observable and could be studied and measured scientifically. Behaviourism is concerned with observable changes in behaviour and suggests that we learn in response to external stimuli. A stimulus is an internal or external factor which stimulates an organism and causes action; it could be anything – a sound, a hunger pang, a pleasant or unpleasant smell, a colour, a particular classroom. A response is any action or activity generated by a stimulus, for example, picking up your mobile when it rings, or rapid move away from an unpleasant smell.

### Ivan Pavlov – classical conditioning

Pavlov (1849–1936), a Russian physiologist, during his research into the digestive systems of dogs, observed occasions when dogs salivated at the smell of food. This is a natural response which Pavlov described as an 'unconditional response'. In subsequent experiments the arrival of food was preceded by the sound of a bell and eventually the sound of the bell alone caused the dogs to salivate. This is known as a 'conditional (or conditioned) response'. However, once a conditional response has been learned it will not remain indefinitely and will eventually fade away. If Pavlov's dogs repeatedly heard the bell but no food arrived, the salivation would cease. This principle is referred to as 'extinction'.

### B. F. Skinner – operant conditioning

B. F. Skinner (1904–1990) is perhaps the most well-known behaviourist. His chosen animals for experimentation were rats and pigeons and his equipment was called the Skinner Box. Skinner showed that these animals could be trained to carry out increasingly complex tasks. Essentially, an animal would be placed in the Skinner Box and through a process of trial and error would learn to obtain food pellets by pressing a lever.

Skinner's main contributions to behaviourism were the notions of *positive* and *negative reinforcement*. He maintained that positive rewards were far more effective than negative rewards or punishment in developing desired behaviour. Skinner also developed the idea of *behaviour shaping*, that is training humans or animals to carry out new tasks through a series of increasingly complex activities leading to the completion of the desired task. Shaping can be used to help learners who have severe learning difficulties, for example, in the acquisition of language.

## What can we learn from behaviourism?

Behaviourism is frequently criticised for being too simplistic and reducing human behaviour and learning to nothing more than a process of stimulus and response. Pavlov and Skinner may well have produced learning in their animals but we can be fairly certain that it was learning without understanding. Human learning, it is argued, is much more complex and involves thinking, reasoning and social factors. Apart from brief discussions, behaviourism is largely absent from the discourse of learning theory. McLay et al. (2010: 88) assert that behaviourism 'diminishes the richness of learning', although they suggest that we shouldn't dismiss it completely as it offers some insights into how the role of reward, in the form of praise and achievement, can positively benefit learning. Behaviourism can also offer insights into the origins of some learners' fears and anxieties.

Clearly there are instances in early child education where the role of behavioural learning is obvious. Discipline can be reinforced by rewarding appropriate behaviour and punishing inappropriate, although the child might learn to carry out inappropriate behaviour where it cannot be seen. We may, however, find it hard to understand how behaviourism can provide any useful insights into post-compulsory and adult education. The following points summarise some useful aspects of behaviourism:

* Positive rewards and encouragement are more effective than negative responses. For learners in post-compulsory settings, encouraging comments in response to class contributions, for example, are likely to encourage further learner involvement. Constructive and developmental comments on learner's work are preferable to the old-school style 'could do better'.

* For many adults considering a return to learning, memories of authoritarian and rigid schools can act as negative stimulus and affect their willingness to enrol and participate. It is up to us to provide friendly and supportive learning environments.

* There are instances where teacher demonstration followed by student practice and repetition are appropriate, for example, in learning and developing skills such as bricklaying; drawing, or playing a musical instrument. Skills cannot be acquired without frequent practice. Active learning is more effective than passive learning. 'Learning by doing' is important.

* Behaviourist theories suggest that learning is more effective when learners are clear about the objectives. Learning objectives (for example, 'At the end of this session learners will be able to . . .') are frequently referred to as 'behavioural objectives'.

## Cognitivism

Cognitivism is the scientific study of mental processes and the ways in which people receive and process sensations and perceptions; how they organise knowledge, and their learning and memory. Cognitivism differs from behaviourism, which doesn't recognise mental processes, in that it sees humans not simply as organisms which react to stimuli but as processors of knowledge.

One of the key concepts in cognitivism is the *schema*. Schemas are mental models or frameworks which every individual creates to organise and understand the world and to store this in the long-term memory. Each schema consists of discrete pieces of information that are connected together in ways which are meaningful to the individual. Every human has a need to organise and categorise and schemas provide a sort of mental store for this to happen. An adult may have thousands of schemas and although individuals may have similar schemas everyone is unique.

Figure 5.1 shows a diagram of a schema representing the Industrial Revolution in England, a historical period which can be difficult to understand because of the interlinking of so many technological, economic and social elements. This schema will develop and change as new information is acquired, but the key point is that it provides a flexible framework for organising a big idea and its constituent parts.

### Advance organisers

The schema of the Industrial Revolution shows how we can create devices to help learners organise their knowledge and to provide them with advance frameworks for

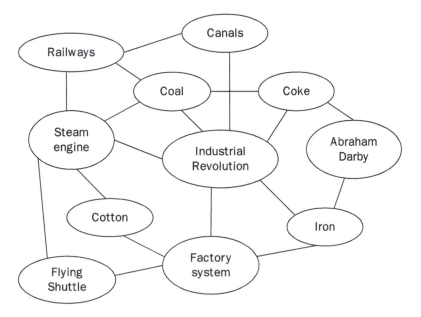

**Figure 5.1** Concept map representing schema of Industrial Revolution.

new learning. The psychologist David Ausubel (1918–2008) developed the concept of 'advance organisers' (Ausubel 1960) which are devices for providing organisational frameworks that teachers present to learners to prepare them for what they are about to learn. They link previous knowledge and learning to the coming topic or provide the 'big picture' for new learning. As well as preparing for learning to come, organisers can be used for revising learning, connecting learning and discovering new ideas and concepts, analysing and thinking. Examples of advanced organisers include:

- concept maps
- flow charts
- diagrams
- written overviews
- charts
- timelines
- maps
- tree diagrams
- bullet points.

What these organisers do most effectively is 'fix' an idea or concept so that new learning can be related to it. In English literature a teacher can fix the structure and characters in a play or novel by a visual representation. Organisation charts help business studies students to see clearly and to analyse the structure of businesses. Advanced organisers which use a visual element are sometimes called 'graphic organisers'. Edward de Bono's book *The Greatest Thinkers* (1976) provides essays outlining the work and ideas of significant thinkers from Moses to Sartre. Each essay is introduced by a diagrammatic overview the ideas. Figure 5.2, from the essay on Charles Darwin, shows a simple visual representation of the prevailing notion that God created all creatures and they remained unchanged. This is contrasted with the model after the publication of the *Theory of the Origin of the Species* which represents evolution as a series of adaptations and changes with some branches dying out and others adapting and surviving.

Advance organisers that use a visual element are sometimes called 'graphic organisers'. Thinking visually can help learners and teachers to become more familiar with the big concepts in a subject and structuring ideas and solving problems. In his book *The Back of the Napkin* Dan Roam (2008) shows how initial thoughts and ideas can be captured and developed using a range of visual techniques. Similarly, concept mapping provides opportunities for teachers and learners to produce the big picture and explore connections. There are several concept mapping tools available which you can buy or sometimes download for free on your computer; MindGenius is a good example.

Sometimes an advance organiser can consist simply of a concise spoken or written introduction to a session which sets out the key issues to be considered or questions to be answered. Margaret Archer, writing about educational systems, begins her article with an admirably simple overview:

'How do educational systems develop and change?' This first question about the characteristics of education can be broken down into three subsidiary ones: 'Who gets it?'; 'What happens to them during it?' and 'Where do they go after it?'

(Archer 2002: 363)

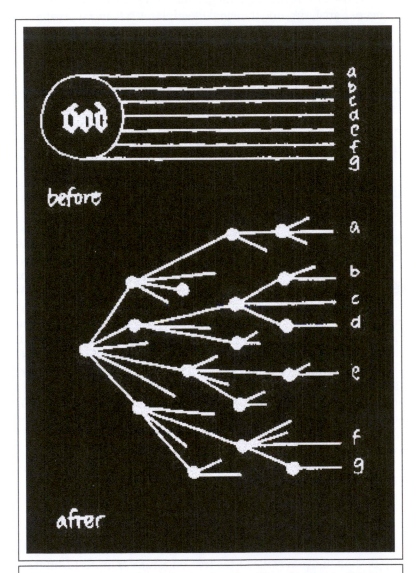

**Figure 5.2** Example of an advanced organiser.

Immediately we know where we're going and what the main issues are.

Ausubel favoured the use of *expository learning*, or direct instruction by the teacher. However, as Legge and Harari (2000: 32) suggest:

> What is interesting about this approach is that although it is presented as completely teacher-led, Ausubel actually argues that it is constructivist because the student is not a passive recipient of information, but actively learns from it.

In other words, the use of advance organisers is not simply a method for organising and processing knowledge but a way in which learners can create meaning. This notion of meaning making takes us to the theory of constructivism.

## Constructivism

Constructivism is based on the idea that learning is a result of mental construction whereby new information is connected to what we already know and our mental frameworks adapt and develop. Constructivist theory suggests that we must provide, and help learners to create, frameworks for learning. (Note the frequent use of construction metaphors in this theory – building, scaffolding, framework.) The most effective learning is active, student-centred learning – the opposite of the 'empty buckets' view outlined earlier. Whereas cognitivism sees learning as *knowledge processing*, constructivism sees learning as active and personal *knowledge construction* or meaning making. This idea of 'meaning making' suggests that:

> We never really understand something until we can create a model or metaphor derived from our own unique personal world. The reality we perceive, feel, see and hear is influenced by the constructive process of the brain as well as by the cues that impinge upon it. It is not the content stored in memory but the activity of constructing it that gets stored . . . Humans don't *get* ideas; they *make* ideas.
>
> Costa (2001: xvi)

As Woolfolk et al. (2008: 411) point out, constructivism draws on the work of a wide variety of philosophers, psychologists and educators as well as the research of the Gestalt psychologists and Piaget, Bruner and Vygotsky. There is no one constructivist theory but most constructivists share two ideas:

- Learners actively construct their own knowledge.
- Social interaction is vital to knowledge construction.

### Gestalt psychology

'The whole is greater than the sum of its parts.' This frequently made observation captures the essence of gestalt psychology. Gestaltists believe that psychologists should be concerned with the total structured forms of people's mental experiences rather than individual elements:

'[Gestalt] ... refers to people's tendency to organise sensory information into figures and whole forms. Instead of perceiving bits and pieces of unrelated information, we usually try to make sense of events or objects by seeing them as a whole.

(Woolfolk et al. 2008: 298)

Gestalt psychologists refer to the notion of 'insight' when a learner suddenly becomes aware of the significance or relevance of something, rather like when the last piece of a jigsaw goes into place. These moments of illumination might be when a mental framework becomes complete or when a major connection is made. Such insight, however, is not just a matter of luck; it depends on teachers and learners building frameworks for learning.

Applied to learning this means, simply, that learners need the 'big picture'. This idea is at the heart of gestalt and of constructivism. In the same way as it is difficult to do a jigsaw without the picture on the box, it is difficult for learners to start with details and elements without a structure in which to locate them. Film studies students will benefit from a textual analysis of a film's camera work, sound, lighting and script, but a film is more than just the total of its elements – it is a complete work.

## Jean Piaget

The formalisation of constructivist learning theory is generally attributed to Jean Piaget (1896–1980). The key ideas from Piaget's work are that people construct knowledge from their active engagement with the world and through the processes of assimilation and accommodation.

Our mental schemas are not fixed; they are incomplete and always evolving. Constructivism is concerned with how they grow, develop and adapt. Piaget used the terms assimilation and accommodation. *Assimilation* is the process in which new information and ideas are added to existing schema leading to an increase in knowledge. The schemas do not change but they grow to include the new information. We can understand an increasing amount of information, but there will be times when new knowledge conflicts with existing. Piaget uses the term *accommodation* to describe the process by which schema change to make sense of new knowledge and ideas. Assimilation adds to existing schema; accommodation changes schema. These additions and changes happen throughout our lives.

## Jerome Bruner

Bruner (1915–) believed that learning is a social process in which learners construct their understanding of the world through communicative interaction. In addition, he regarded learning as a continuous, active process involving intellectual development and problem solving, not the production of a body of knowledge. From Bruner we get two important connected educational theories: a theory of learning and a theory of instruction (teaching). Bruner's *theory of learning* has three elements.

1   *Acquisition.* The acquisition of new knowledge which (in Piaget's) terms may be assimilated or accommodated.

2   *Transformation.* Basically, learners do something with this new knowledge. They manipulate it and apply it to work out problems. It might be used in a new situation (transference).

3   *Evaluation.* The learner assesses and evaluates the utility of the new knowledge in relation to the problem or task.

Bruner's theory of instruction has four elements:

1   *Readiness.* Learners should have a predisposition to learning. He believed the most effective motivation was for learners to be confronted with problems to be solved. The problem/s should arouse curiosity and uncertainty.

2   *Structure.* The content must be structured so that the learner can understand it. He suggested, perhaps controversially, that 'any idea or problem or body of knowledge can be presented in a form simple enough so that any learner can understand it in a recognisable form' (Bruner 1996). The content can, according to Bruner, be represented in three main ways:

   • by a set of actions or *enactive representation* – for example, a lecture in plumbing could provide a demonstration

   • using images or *iconic representation* – the plumbing lecturer can provide the information using pictures or a Powerpoint presentation

   • *symbolic representation* – the lecturer may present the information in the form of a diagram using symbols specific to plumbing and heating. The learners interpret this information using their prior experiences.

3   *Sequence.* Material must be presented in the most effective sequence to allow learners to acquire, transform and transfer learning. Bruner uses the term *spiral curriculum* to denote the method by which students revisit ideas and concepts over a period of time but at increasingly complex levels. In history, the very difficult question of the origins of World War I could be encapsulated in a visual chart showing the main combatants, alliances, etc., and revisited to develop an increasingly sophisticated understanding.

4   *Motivation.* The final element is concerned with the nature of pacing and rewards. Initially, learners may be motivated by positive feedback from teachers (extrinsic motivation), but ideally will move towards intrinsic motivation which comes from the satisfaction of solving problems and developing new ones to be solved. This intrinsic motivation can make the process cyclical, in that the learner will become ready to start a new, related stage of learning.

Bruner advocated the use of *discovery learning* as the most effective method to encourage the kinds of active, problem-solving learning implicit in his theories of learning and instruction. Problem-based learning is a very similar method, frequently used in health education and training in which learners start from a problem to be solved. They then draw on their learning and develop the new learning and research required to solve the problem. An excellent overview can be found in Harkin et al. (2001). Project-based learning, in which learning is based round an integrated theme, can include a discovery element.

Discovery learning is, essentially, an active student-centred approach in which the teacher's role is to provide opportunities for learners to work out problems and evaluate and transfer their learning. As Geoff Petty points out, it is 'teaching by asking' rather than 'teaching by telling' (Petty 2009). Petty goes on to stress that in many cases teachers will need to provide initial information and examples to kick-start active learning and, to ensure differentiation and motivation, some learners will need more support than others – this he describes as 'guided discovery'.

---

**Activity**

Consider an element from a course or module you teach. Briefly outline a task/s which would encourage discovery learning with your students.

For example – Motor Vehicle students could be confronted with a car which fails to start and asked to find out why and what can be done to rectify it.

---

## Lev Vygotsky

Vygotsky (1896–1934) developed his ideas during the Stalinist period in Russia. It was forbidden to discuss, disseminate or reprint his work until 20 years after his death. He believed education should liberate children (and people) by developing their thinking and learning skills and particularly the development of language. Vygotsky is most closely associated with *social constructivism* which sees learning not as an individual process but as a social and cultural process which happens through social interaction and dialogue.

Vygotsky maintained that education is an active process. However, people need help to learn and for Vygotsky the teacher is a more knowledgeable person who challenges the learner to achieve more by providing *scaffolding* to help them climb to higher levels. He refers to the difference between what the learner can do alone and what they can do with help as the *zone of proximal development (ZPD)*. Alan Pritchard (2009: 25) explains the ZPD as 'a theoretical space of understanding which is just above the level of understanding of the given individual. It is the area of understanding into which a learner will move next'. This move will be facilitated and aided by the teacher. Although the most effective learning will aim for the higher levels of the ZPD, the zone will be different for each learner and, consequently, we must know our learners as individuals in order to assess how high we can ask them to aim and to provide the right amount of scaffolding – too high, unsupported will feel threatening for some learners; a small rise with too much support will not represent a challenge, possibly leading to a decrease in motivation. As with scaffolding in construction, the framework is temporary. Once the higher levels have been attained and made safe for the learner to access alone, the scaffolding is removed.

Scaffolding activities might include discussion to guide and support learners as they learn new concepts, or practical tasks in vocational education may be supported by demonstration and observed practice. Scaffolding is not just provided by the teacher; learners can also support each other in their learning through groupwork problem-based learning.

## Active learning

Constructivism is essentially a theory of learning in which learners construct understanding from their experiences; it doesn't prescribe what those experiences should be. Constructivism, however, is generally associated with approaches based on *active learning*. Active learning doesn't mean learners are busily involved in physical activity, although they might be. Active in this sense means being actively involved in making meaning rather than just being given information. Passive learners are reactive rather than proactive and, typically, are involved in taking notes, listening, copying – just being 'filled up' with information. In passive learning the content is structured and organised by the teacher. Active learning is more likely to result from active teaching; surface learning is likely to be the result of passive teaching.

## Deep and surface learning

The notions of deep and surface learning developed from Marton and Saljo's (1979) work on the five conceptions of learning. *Surface learning* is characterised by rote learning, memory and low-level cognitive activities rather than on understanding. It can only usually be reapplied in the same situation in which it was learned. While memorisation is not in itself undesirable – learners may be required to memorise the periodic table or the lines of a play – deep learning only occurs when the information is connected to previous learning.

*Deep learning* is about really understanding a subject, making connections and recognising underlying principles. It is learning which is based on student-centred activities such as problem-based learning; reflection; case studies; application; evaluation and analysis. Deep learning is long lasting. It is associated with constructivism in that it requires the development of schema and the making of connections. Deep learning is best achieved when learners have their curiosity aroused and are set challenging problems.

According to Entwistle (2000), surface learning is characterised by students:

- intending to cope with course requirements
- drawing on lower level cognitive skills
- treating the course as unrelated bits of knowledge
- memorising facts and procedures routinely
- studying without reflecting on purpose or strategy
- finding difficulty in making sense of new ideas presented.

Deep learning is characterised by students:

- intending to understand ideas for themselves
- relating ideas to previous knowledge and experience

* looking for patterns and underlying principles
* checking evidence and relating it to conclusions
* examining logic and argument cautiously and critically
* becoming actively interested in the course content.

Deep and surface learning are best understood as metaphors for learning rather than theories of learning and we need to be wary of labelling individual learners as deep learners or surface learners. Learners can also take a 'strategic approach' in which they actively choose a more surface approach to parts of a course or a module that they have to pass but perceive as having little relevance. The adoption of a strategic approach could, in some cases, be evidence of rational choices and students being responsible for organising and structuring their own learning.

## Humanism

In essence, humanism in education could be summed up as the removal of barriers to learning and creating an emotionally safe and secure learning environment. It also revolves around the simple notion that we all need to feel good about ourselves.

You might have memories of your own or of friends' school experiences. Most of us can provide examples of teaching that has been threatening, humiliating and occasionally frightening. My own memories of maths in school are associated with fear – of failure, punishment or humiliation. Consequently, my number skills did not develop until I got my first job in a shop – a good example of 'situated learning'. These kinds of barriers are not confined to schoolchildren; 14–19 year olds and adult learners may well have similar psychological baggage which affects their learning and their feelings about learning. For adults returning to learning, the creation of a non-threatening environment is one of the keys to success. This, it could be argued, is an instance where humanism links to behaviourism.

---

**Activity**

Consider your own or another person's experience of education (in school, college or university).

* Identify an experience which was negative or something which was a barrier to learning.
* In what ways did it impede learning?
* How did it make you feel about that subject, about the school or college, about education?
* How did it make you feel about yourself?

The activity above may have illustrated the notion of the *self-fulfilling prophecy*, whereby an individual's self-perception is moulded by what others say about them and how they act towards them. Thus, a person who is frequently told they are a failure will come to believe they are a failure, with negative consequences for their future learning. Often in lifelong learning we are faced with the task of helping to repair those who have been damaged by early educational experiences. Humanist theorists regard every human as unique. Their aim is the education of the whole person and the development of individuals with positive self-esteem. Positive self-esteem is both a goal of education and a basis for lifelong learning.

## Carl Rogers

Rogers (1902–1987) is generally associated with the fields of counselling and psychotherapy, but he provides much useful advice for learning and teaching. As a therapist he believed that most people had the solutions to their problems within them and that the role of the therapist is to provide a safe environment in which they can express themselves openly and reach their own conclusions for the best way to deal with their problems. In this way the clients will develop confidence and self-esteem. Similarly, in education, Rogers argues that the most effective learning is student-centred learning in which the teacher acts a facilitator who creates a safe and secure learning environment and provides the necessary opportunities and resources for learning.

For Rogers one of the keys to learning, as well as psychological well-being, is the development of a positive self-concept. *Self-concept* is the view you have of yourself as an individual – this may be positive or negative – and it arises from your communication with others since childhood. As Legge and Harari point out:

> We all have a self-concept, but are we conscious of what that self-concept is and how it affects our lives? For example, individuals may feel they are too unlovable to form successful interpersonal relationships, but once they become aware of, and acknowledge this feeling, they can begin to understand why their relationships fail.
>
> (Legge and Harari 2000: 11)

*Self-concept* and *self-esteem* are closely linked but easily confused. Briefly, the former is how we view ourselves; the latter is how we feel about ourselves. Both are dependent on our communication with others, not least with our teachers. In the same way that teachers can contribute towards negative self-esteem by the self-fulfilling prophecy, they can positively affect learners by what some psychologists refer to as the 'Pygmalion effect' in which people can be encouraged by positive, friendly attentions. If they feel that they are valued by others, they may begin to value themselves. The 'Pygmalion effect' links to Rogers' notion of *unconditional positive regard* in which teachers have respect for learners and value them whatever they do. This might seem a very tall order when faced with a particularly difficult or demanding learner, but a refusal to be aggravated and the use of continued politeness may eventually be 'modelled' by the learner.

Carl Rogers' ideas on learning are expressed in his *Freedom to Learn* (1969). He sees the teacher's role as facilitating learning and creating the right climate for learning to take place. Some of his key principles of learning are as follows:

- People have a natural potential for learning.
- Learning is more likely to occur when it is perceived as relevant to learners' needs.
- Learning is more likely to occur when learners do not feel threatened.
- Much significant learning is acquired through doing.
- Self-initiated learning is the most lasting.

## Abraham Maslow

Abraham Maslow (1908–1970) provided a hierarchy of needs that he developed from his experience as a psychologist and psychotherapist. In his hierarchy Maslow suggests there is a range of human needs from basic to higher levels. The lower levels, particularly physiological, safety and belonging needs, are deficiency needs which must be satisfied before others can be addressed. Obviously, if we are homeless, cold, hungry and/or unloved we will not be especially concerned about our intellectual development. The higher levels, relating to our learning and cognitive needs and our need for self-fulfilment cannot be attained until the basic needs have been met (see Figure 5.3).

For teachers in lifelong learning, Maslow's hierarchy makes us think about the total experience of our learners. From physiological factors (is the room too hot or too

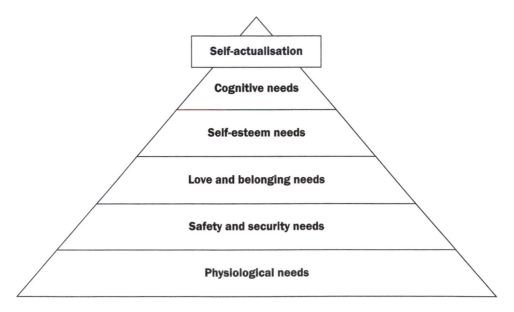

**Figure 5.3** Maslow's hierarchy of needs.

cold?) to relationships (do we give positive regard and developmental feedback?) to self-esteem needs ('I'm no good at English'), his hierarchy provides a useful device to help us understand learning and motivation.

## Learning styles

Learning styles of various kinds have been prevalent in the lifelong learning sector for nearly 20 years. The most widely used are VAKT (visual, auditory, kinaesthetic, tactile), Kolb's learning cycle and Honey and Mumford's variant of Kolb. One of the main attractions of learning styles is that they seem to offer a 'magic key' to unlock the mysteries of each individual's learning style, thus allowing teachers to use the matching teaching style so that everybody in the class would learn.

Coffield et al. (2004) carried out a comprehensive review of learning styles in which they identified 71 different models of learning style and evaluated their effectiveness. They concluded that in nearly all cases learning style methodologies had limited or no effect and, further, there was very little evidence to support their effectiveness. In addition, they point out that most learning style methods are tied to expensive training and resource packages and that there is, in effect, a 'learning styles industry' which is more concerned with selling products than enhancing learning. Coffield particularly singles out VAKT for criticism and he is worth quoting at length, if only to get a feel of the passion with which he expresses his views:

> There is **no** scientific justification for teaching and learning strategies based on VAKT and tutors should **stop** using learning style instruments based on them. There is **no** theory of VAKT from which to draw **any** implications for practice. It should be a dead parrot. It should have ceased to function.
>
> (Coffield 2008: 32, original emphasis)

Teachers are busy enough without being asked to administer and analyse learning styles questionnaires. It might be more appropriate to rely on the professional expertise of teachers at a local level to understand their learners and discover the best ways to help them learn rather than buy in expensive 'solutions' which have the appearance of scientific rigour but are of dubious value.

## Evidence from educational neuroscience

Initially, learning styles were seen a part of the 'brain-based' learning movement along with other activities such as 'brain gyms'. The claims for the success of these methods were frequently based on evidence from neuroscience. The rapid recent growth and development of neuroscience based on functional magnetic resource imaging (fMRI) has, however, provided evidence to undermine learning styles theories.

John Geake (2009) is critical of the claims of learning styles theorists' that the way in which we receive information through a particular 'sensory modality' is the same as the way in which we store it. So, for example, the belief that things learned kinaesthetically are stored in a 'kinaesthetic' part of the brain and that things learned visually are stored in a 'visual' part of brain is false. Geake (2009: 2) states:

> No improvements in learning outcomes have been found from teaching approaches which focus on differences in pupils' learning styles, save for an initial positive rise due to teachers' enthusiasm for a new approach. Importantly, there is no neuroscientific evidence for the existence of learning styles.

A major international research project carried out by the Centre for Educational Research and Innovation (CERI) centred on the development of educational neuroscience. This report also questions the uncritical use of learning styles, in particular the tendency to label learners according to their supposed style of learning: 'Labelling people as particular types of learners or as having particular learning styles is likely to limit rather enhance learning'. (CERI 2007: 201).

## Do we still need learning styles?

Should we abandon learning styles? The balance of evidence suggests that we should. Learning styles might be useful as tools for learner self-development, rather than as a means of categorising learners as particular 'types'. Coffield et al. state:

> A reliable and valid instrument which measures learning styles and approaches could be used as a tool to encourage self-development, not only by diagnosing how people learn, but by showing them how to *enhance* their learning.
> (Coffield et al. 2004: 51, original emphasis)

The most valuable message teachers in the lifelong learning sector get from learning styles is that people learn in many different ways. Consequently, teachers should have a wide, and continually developing range of techniques to draw on for long-and short-term planning.

## Educational neuroscience

Increasingly, educators are looking to neuroscience for the latest developments in understanding learning. Blakemore and Frith (2005) present an overview of recent research on the brain's development at various stages of life.

## Brain 'plasticity'

One of the key points which emerged from recent research concerns the brain's 'plasticity', which refers to the brain's physical changes and adaptations to new circumstances and new learning. This brain plasticity is a factor right through our lives, an idea which has clear implications for lifelong learning in that everyone can learn at any stage of their lives. It used to be thought that brain development was rapid during childhood and adolescence but before the age of 30 the architecture of the brain was fixed for life. It now seems clear that the brain is constantly changing and everything we do changes it:

> The brain's continuing plasticity suggests that it is well designed for lifelong learning and adaptation to new situations and experiences, and such adaptation can even bring about significant changes in its structure.
>
> (Howard-Jones 2007: 9)

A recurring question in human learning and development concerns the extent to which we are affected by our environment and how much is genetically or biologically determined – the so-called 'nature–nurture' argument. This is perhaps becoming a redundant argument, mainly because it is not possible for an organism to exist outside of an environment, so how could we ever tell which has the greater effect? More importantly, do we really need to know? As much as neuroscience can provide certainty, it now seems the case that the brain, to use an eloquent metaphor, 'is a sculpture carved by experience' (CERI 2007: 191). Learning is part of how this sculpting occurs and, as a recent report by The Royal Society suggests: 'Education is a powerful form of cognitive enhancement' (2011: 4).

## A note of caution

Neuroscience has helped us to debunk several myths about the brain and learning. As we have seen above, learning styles theories have come in for serious criticism, some of it from neuroscience. These theories are not dead yet but they are looking distinctly unwell. CERI (2007) provides a detailed unpicking of a number of other 'neuro-myths', including the following:

- left brain/right brain dominance
- the belief that we only use 10–20 per cent of our brains – the whole of the brain is active
- 'brain gyms'
- male and female brains are different.

We must, however, be wary of replacing one set of myths with another. Teachers, their managers, politicians and commercial educational organisations are very keen to find the latest 'answer' to a problem, often a non-existent one, and to use the latest body of research and theory uncritically. It is tempting to believe that because neuroscience is 'scientific' and undertaken by 'scientists', then the results will be infallible. Howard-Jones warns against expecting a 'new' science of learning:

> There has been much enthusiasm amongst policymakers for the creation of a 'new' science of learning . . . This may be because neuroscience seems a more secure basis for learning theory, with its images of blood flow appearing more concrete than abstract psychological concepts . . . A science of teaching and

learning which is chiefly based upon the brain is unlikely to develop in the foreseeable future.

(Howard-Jones 2008: 15)

Most serious neuroscientists and commentators provide caveats to the effect that this is still a young science and practical applications are a long way off. Some even suggest that we never will, and cannot, know all the 'answers'.

## Motivation

Learning is natural; education, unfortunately, is not. This is why we need to emphasise learning more than teaching. Compared to the span of human life on earth, formal education and its methods and purposes are relatively new. As Ian Gilbert says: 'The culmination of six million years' worth of neurological evolution is not the GCSE' (Gilbert 2002: 5). Everyone wants to learn. Unfortunately they might not want to learn what you want them to learn; at the time and place you want them to learn, or in the ways in which you want them to do it.

### Intrinsic motivation

Do you have a personal interest or hobby – perhaps stamp collecting, family history, Renaissance sculpture, the films of Alfred Hitchcock or ecclesiastical architecture? You might care to reflect on the genesis of this interest. Did anyone tell you to do it? I mention ecclesiastical architecture because many years ago I wandered into Lincoln Cathedral and pondered the construction of such a vast edifice. The purchase of a little book on church architecture from the cathedral shop fired a lasting interest. Intrinsic motivation comes from within the individual. It is generally driven by curiosity and the desire to learn and find out; it is learning for its own sake.

### Extrinsic motivation

This kind of motivation comes from outside of the learner. Many young people are extrinsically motivated by the promise of bikes or computers if they are successful in exams or SATs. Examples of extrinsic motivation include:

- To achieve an end or goal.
- A means to an end, for example, taking a course or qualification which is a requirement of your work. Learners who have been told to do something provide considerable motivational problems for teachers.
- Externally offered rewards – these include promotion or status-related rewards.
- Avoiding negative sanctions or unpleasant consequences; avoiding 'failure'. Many people studied extremely hard and practised IQ tests in the 1950s and 1960s in order to pass the 11-plus examination because their life chances could be significantly affected by success or failure.

## Adult learners' motivation

It is frequently assumed that adults return to learning because they choose to and because they are intrinsically motivated. The picture is much more complicated, however, and adult motivation comes from many different sources – educational, social and economic. Some will return to learning for something new and different to do; to develop an interest or learn a new skill. Others will return because they want to make real changes to their lives. People whose circumstances have changed, perhaps through redundancy or bereavement, may have a much more fundamental need to return to learning.

Some adults will return to learning brimming with confidence, even to the point of arrogance; others are likely to have real problems with confidence and self-esteem. This variety provides challenges and opportunities for teachers in adult education that require skilful handling and sensitivity. Unfortunately, there are instances I am aware of where adult learners have complained of teachers who treat them like children or lack respect for their age and experience. There are those who will be returning to learning very tentatively because of previous negative experiences of learning in school, and as a result will have self-esteem problems and lack self-belief. This can be particularly true of those coming to improve their literacy and numeracy skills. As Lawrence (2000, xvii–xviii) points out:

> What began a long time ago in school as an educational problem gradually becomes a social and emotional problem. With regular failure in a skill that society values, people eventually lose confidence in themselves generally. It should come as no surprise to discover there is an association between literacy skills and self-esteem. People who have low attainments in literacy have lower self-esteem than the rest of us.

## Motivation and 14–19 year olds

The old sector boundaries of education are changing. The 14–19 agenda was developed, in the main, to combat the very low staying-on rates in education post-16. The Increased Flexibility Programme provided opportunities for young people to spend time in FE colleges studying vocational courses. Recent government plans to make attendance at school, college or workplace training compulsory until 18 offers a whole new range of challenges for those working in the lifelong learning sector.

The opportunities for vocational education and skill development are undoubtedly a motivating factor for some young people who find the school curriculum doesn't suit all their needs and abilities. Courses, for example, in construction, engineering, hairdressing and business administration are increasingly popular. There is evidence to suggest that those who undertake such courses during the last two years of compulsory schooling are more likely to stay in education and training post-16. Others, however, may feel that they have been 'dumped' by their schools because their behaviour is perceived to be too difficult to manage. More serious is the suggestion that those likely to 'underperform' on the more academic courses will adversely affect the school's position in the league tables and therefore are best served by vocational courses elsewhere.

There is research evidence to support the view that many 14-16 year olds prefer their college experience to school and from these we can draw some conclusions about motivation for this age group. A key factor in the college provision was the attitude of the teaching staff, who were reported by many learners to be more patient with them and respectful to them. Harkin's (2006) research observes that:

> The characteristics of 'best' teachers, according to 14–16 year-old pupils attending college, are that they:
>
> • Are friendly, can share a joke, and show respect for students;
> • Know their subject and can make it interesting; and
> • Can keep order but without undue authoritarianism.
>
> (Harkin 2006: 328

In addition:

> This sense of a more 'adult' environment in college is also, more importantly, about the way the students perceive that they are treated and spoken to by teachers:
>
> *School teachers tell you off for nothing and just tell you to do something . . . they should be more like college teachers: let you do things in your own way; give you choice of what you want to do.*
>
> (Harkin 2006: 325)

The research also points to the motivational value of young learners being in real working environments and their learning being relevant to these environments. Several young people referred to working in garage or hair salon environments where they had opportunities to make independent choices about how things were done, for example, in dealing with customers and booking appointments.

## Attribution theory

Key to understanding learners' self-esteem is the idea of attribution – do they attribute their success or a failure to something they have control over and can change and improve or, conversely, do they believe that some people are just naturally bright and intelligent while others aren't. Carol Dweck (2000) suggests that learners have two different goal orientations. These are:

• *learning goals* – in which individuals strive to increase their competence, to understand and master something new;
• *performance goals* – in which individuals strive either to document, or gain favourable judgements of, their competence or to avoid negative judgements of their competence.

Dweck suggests that those with learning goals have a belief in themselves and their ability to learn. They view challenges positively, tend to be less put off by failure, persist in efforts to improve and tend to have an incremental rather than a fixed theory of intelligence. Conversely, those with performance goals tend to see ability as a fixed entity and attribute failure to low ability. They tend to give up or become upset in the face of difficulty. They tend to concentrate their efforts on getting favourable results and praise.

Much of the above discussion reflects our beliefs about ability and intelligence and the extent to which we believe these are innate and fixed or acquired and therefore susceptible to improvement. Claxton (1999) contrasts Chinese and Asian cultural attitudes towards learning in which, with effort and persistence, anyone can learn and achieve, with western cultures which hold 'ability' to be the major determinant of success in learning. Such is the pervasiveness of these notions of fixed ability that they disproportionately influence learners' self-esteem and confidence. As Claxton (1999: 27) suggests: 'On this Western view, it is one's own personal identity that is at stake. To be lacking in ability is to be wanting as a person.'

## A brief note on intelligence

Beliefs in innate ability match the belief in the importance and the measurability of something called IQ. Both in educational reality and public perception, IQ continues to be perceived as an innate and fixed quality which means that some people are 'bright', 'academic' or 'gifted' while others are not. You can read criticisms of IQ elsewhere, but suffice to say that many educationalists have criticised IQ tests as being a measure of a limited set of skills and abilities – particularly mathematical and logical – if indeed they are a measure of anything at all.

Recent conceptions of intelligence suggest that it is not fixed and people can become more intelligent, particularly if they believe they can. Lucas and Claxton (2010) consider the most recent developments in our understanding of intelligence and argue persuasively that intelligence is 'learnable' rather than fixed. They identify eight myths about intelligence which constrain teachers' and learners' perceptions of their possibilities and potential:

*Myth 1* Intelligence is essentially a one-dimensional commodity largely to be found in the kinds of thinking required by IQ tests.

*Myth 2* Intelligence is relatively fixed: educators make use of it, but do not really alter it.

*Myth 3* Mind and body are separate and truly intelligent activity is located in the mind.

*Myth 4* Intelligence is rational and conscious.

*Myth 5* Intelligence is a personal 'possession', and using tools which make you smarter is a kind of cheating

*Myth 6* Intelligence is an individual not a social concept.

*Myth 7* The concept of intelligence is universally valid, and not closely tied to the details and demands of one's particular 'habitat'.

*Myth 8* Intelligence is an intellectual function, separate from emotional and moral functions.

(Lucas and Claxton 2010: 9)

These new understandings of intelligence, they argue, can change our ways of thinking about learning and open up new possibilities for education. This message is reinforced by Frank Coffield in his essay for students when he states:

> Everyone can improve, and even the brightest of the bright can be shown how to become better at learning. In other words, you can learn to become more intelligent; your abilities are not fixed or set in stone at birth, or at the age of 17 or 14 or 21. Whatever your age, you can transform your own future and prospects by changing how you think about your abilities.

(Coffield 2009: 5)

## Multiple Intelligences

Howard Gardner's multiple intelligences theory (1993) was developed out of a concern that standard measures of intelligence have been based on linguistic and mathematical/logical abilities. This narrow definition of intelligence, he argues, does not allow everyone to demonstrate what they are good at or use different types of intelligence in their learning. Gardner originally proposed seven types of intelligence; an eighth, naturalistic intelligence, was added later. We should not make the mistake of assuming that an individual learner is a 'linguistic' learner or an 'interpersonal' learner, in much the same way that learners have been simplistically categorised as 'visual' or 'kinaesthetic'. Multiple intelligences are not learning styles; they indicate preferences and preferences are not fixed:

- *Linguistic* – these learners like language and words, reading and writing, speaking and listening.
- *Logical/mathematical* – learners with this preference like number activities, patterns, deduction, solving problems. They like scientific learning and making connections between pieces of information
- *Visual/spatial* – these learners are good at visualising, creating and using mental images; they like graphic organisers and reading images.
- *Interpersonal* – these learners like working with others. They are good communicators and empathic.
- *Intrapersonal* – these people are good at understanding themselves and their motivations and feelings. They tend to be reflective and use *metacognition* (thinking about thinking).
- *Bodily/kinaesthetic* – these learners tend to be 'sporty' types and have physical skill. They are good at coordinated body movement.
- *Musical* – are good at composing, appreciating and performing musical patterns. They are not necessarily musicians but they do enjoy rhythm; pitch; tone and beat, as in poetry or rapping.

- *Naturalistic* – learners with this preference have knowledge and understanding of nature and the environment. They are good at working outside and observing nature.

## Role of emotions in learning and motivation

Learning is always the interaction of cognitive and emotional processes, and learning always occurs in social contexts through interaction between learners and their environments.

(CERI 2007: 197)

Some educationalists argue that there is little place for the emotions in education. I wish to suggest that the emotions play an important role in motivation and successful learning and that part of a teacher's role is to create the conditions conducive to learning. Following from humanist ideas, the best conditions for learning are those in which learners feel emotionally secure and are unthreatening.

A certain level of stress is important for learning. It is a truism that tasks which are too far above a student's current level will produce anxiety while those which are not sufficiently challenging will result in boredom. Too much stress (bullying, harassment, humiliation) will negatively affect learning. Many of you will have experienced the feeling of 'not being able to think straight' when you feel anxious. This is because that part of the brain, the limbic system, which deals with emotions is active during times of stress and this blocks thinking and learning which happens in the neocortex.

## Adult learning

Adult learners tend to have different motivations and learning preferences from those in compulsory education. Basically, this is the assumption on which Malcolm Knowles' theory of *androgogy* is based. According to Knowles, education in schools is based on *pedagogy* and tends to be teacher dominated, with learners assigned a passive role having minimal control over their learning. The most obvious difference is that school education is compulsory whereas adult learning is, to a great extent, voluntary. Androgogy suggests a different model of learning in which adults are more self-directed and active. They see education as empowering and have high expectations of it and those who provide it. According to this theory adult learners are distinguished from younger learners in the following ways:

- Adult learners need to know why they are learning particular things.
- Adult self-concept – they need to perceive themselves as self-directed and responsible for their own decisions.
- Adult learners have a wide variety of experience which represents a rich resource for learners and teachers. They do, however, need to recognise bias and subjectivity in their opinions and experiences.
- Adults have readiness to learn those things which will help them to deal with real-life situations.

- Adults are motivated to learn things which are of interest or important to them. This, and their readiness to learn, implies that adults have intrinsic motivations for learning.

Knowles' ideas have been widely criticised, frequently because the distinction between adult and compulsory education seems too rigid. We probably know from our experience of adults who are not willing or motivated learners. In many schools the experiences of children are respected and included as part of the learning. Perhaps the best use we can make of Knowles and androgogy is that it gives us more ideas about how we should treat our learners and facilitate their learning. Clearly, adults wish to be respected as individuals, but this is equally true of 14–19 learners.

## Situated learning

Lave and Wenger (1990) and Wenger (1998) contend that it is at least as important to consider learning as something which results largely from our experience of participating in daily life. Our workplaces are 'communities of practice', which are strange and unusual when we first enter them but learning involves moving from the periphery to the centre and becoming a 'professional'. Learning which is meaningful and authentic, preferably in a work situation, is likely to be deeper and more effective.

Without too much thought we should all be able to identify communities of practice we are part of – work, hobbies or interests, voluntary work. The learning which takes place in these communities is so integrated and natural that the participants probably don't even realise they are learning at all. My sister started a history group in her village and in no time there was a community of practice in which the members, without a curriculum or plan, learned about and acquired skills in research, teamworking, using IT, fundraising, organising exhibitions and many more. Clearly, learning in post-compulsory settings cannot be quite so informal but situated learning theory makes us think about creating learning which is contextualised, authentic, meaningful and relevant.

## What can we learn from theories of learning?

This chapter does not aim, and would not be able, to cover the full range and complexity of learning theories. Rather, it provides an overview of the main theories relevant to lifelong learning. If you wish to follow up these ideas and others in more depth, suggestions for further reading are provided at the end of the chapter.

Theory is of little use unless we apply it to practice. The following points summarise the practical relevance of the learning theories when planning, preparing and facilitating teaching and learning:

- Positive rewards and encouragement are more effective than negative responses.
- Active learning should be preferred to passive.
- Active learning must connect to and extend previous learning.
- We should aim to develop 'deep' learning in preference to 'surface' learning.
- Learners need time to reflect on and practise learning.

- Learning is easier and more effective when a framework, or 'big picture', is provided. Advance organisers can help to do this.
- Learners need to construct their own learning. They need to construct mental maps.
- Learners need to 'play around' with ideas and concepts. They need to use learning and transfer it to other situations.
- Learning is a social process; we benefit from interaction with others.
- Learning is more effective when it is 'situated'; when it is relevant to the learners and authentic.
- Learners are motivated by challenges and problems to be solved.
- Teaching 'by asking' is as important as 'teaching by telling'.
- Scaffolding will help learners to reach the next level.
- Teachers should provide emotionally (and physically) safe and secure learning environments.
- Learners need to feel good about themselves and develop a positive self-concept. No one ever learned from feeling threatened, humiliated or anxious.
- Teachers need a comprehensive toolkit of teaching and learning techniques.
- People learn by experience and by 'doing'. We need time to reflect on and learn from our experiences.
- All learners benefit from being respected and treated as adults.
- We should have high expectations of all our learners.
- Intelligence is not fixed.
- Everyone can learn.
- Everyone can learn how to learn.

**For your journal**

Consider the extent to which you have consciously considered theories of teaching and learning in planning, preparing and delivering teaching and learning. For example, have you used a humanist approach to create a supportive learning environment? Have there been any examples of behaviourism in your sessions, particularly in relation to learner behaviour and motivation? To what extent has constructivism influenced the planning of learning methods and activities?

**Activity**

Read the following journal extract.

- Can you identify any elements of learning theory in this account?
- What conclusions can you draw about how people learn best?
- Describe the role of the teacher in this situation.
- What principles can you apply to your own teaching?

**Journal extract: Russell, trained as a teacher of construction**

I was feeling very confident this week. I experimented with a plastering session with _____ using my theory that 'you learn more by making mistakes than doing it right first time'. They were to skim and finish the low wall that they undercoated last week. This was their first time and the conditions cramped and the light poor. I had taught them to work in a confined space last week so now we could concentrate on the mixing. I allowed them to do it as they wished the first time. The mix was horrible, dry and lumpy and would not stay on. We reviewed the situation and all agreed it was too dry. I then let them mix it too wet and wet the walls as it is much easier to work but far too messy. The students were covered with plaster and one of the senior lecturers was raising his eyebrows at the mess. Once the students had experienced using wet plaster and seen the finish they could achieve their confidence grew. We reviewed the 'too wet' method again and cleared up. I asked them to mix it 'just right' this time and showed them a wall that had been finished by an experienced plasterer. The students without hesitation made a good mix and got to work. Before long they were handling the skim like professionals and took pride in making very good job of it.

## Further reading

Jordan, A., Carlile, O. and Stack, S. (2008) *Approaches to Learning: A Guide for Teachers*. Maidenhead: Open University Press.

Lucas, B. and Claxton, G. (2010) *New Kinds of Smart. How the Science of Learnable Intelligence is Changing Education*. Maidenhead: Open University Press.

Rogers, A. and Horrocks, N. (2010) *Adults Learning* (4th edn). Maidenhead: Open University Press.

Woolfolk, A., Hughes, M. and Walkup, V. (2008) *Psychology in Education*. Harlow: Pearson.

## Websites

Doceo. This comprehensive and generous site is a 'must see' for all teachers. www.doceo.co.uk.

# 6

# Teaching and learning methods

**What this chapter is about**

- Key elements of a range of teaching and learning methods
- Guidelines for using these methods in the lifelong learning sector

**LLUK standards**

This chapter covers the following standards:
BK 2.1; BP 2.1; BK 2.2; BP 2.2; BK 2.3; BP 2.3; BK 2.5; BP 2.5; BK 2.7; BP 2.7
CK 3.1; CP 3.1; CK 3.2; CP 3.2; CK 3.5; CP 3.5
DK 1.2; DP 1.2

To be an effective teacher in the lifelong learning sector (LLS) you will need to have a repertoire of teaching and learning methods to meet the demands of a wide range of learners. As you develop, you will probably prefer a regular suite of methods, but remember it's not just about what suits you but what suits your learners. You should always be prepared to try something new and to expand your repertoire. You will become able to merge several different methods into one session and even develop hybrids of methods which are unique to you. This is the kind of 'theory in practice' you can record and reflect on in your journal and also use as evidence of your CPD.

Teaching and learning methods are often categorised according to whether they are teacher dominated or student centred or tend to be active or passive, surface or deep. I'm not going to classify but will provide guidance and comments in each case. The best thing is to try out various techniques and see if they work. If they don't work, reflect and try to work out why. Do you need to modify or adapt the technique? Do you need to keep practising it? Or is it just not right for these learners for this purpose? Once again reflection is the key.

As you consider the range of techniques I have suggested, some of them might seem similar. Case studies, projects, discovery learning and problem-based learning all overlap to some extent. This doesn't matter. Categorisation is not really important and you will be able to draw certain aspects from each to develop your own methods. We will consider the following methods in this book, but there are many others which you can follow up elsewhere:

- lecture
- case study
- discussion
- student presentations
- demonstration
- brainstorming
- buzz groups

- projects
- role play
- concept mapping
- games and quizzes
- discovery
- problem-based learning
- coaching

## Lecture

Formal lectures, in which teachers address groups of students who listen and take notes, are rarely used in post-compulsory education. Traditionalists might deplore the demise of the lecture and consider it symptomatic of 'dumbing-down' and minuscule attention spans, but we have to do what works and use whatever gets results in terms of learning. Even in the best universities, students will frequently preface the word 'lecture' with the word 'boring', and the old maxim that 'a lecture involves the transference of the notes of the lecturer to the notes of the student without passing through the minds of either' still applies in a few cases. However, given the expansion of students in universities, lecturers are developing a wider range of strategies, particularly those which encourage active learning and deep learning (see Biggs 2003).

However, let's not reject the lecture completely. There may be times when it is appropriate for you to use one, especially as an introduction to a new course or module for degree students studying their first year in a FE college.

## Guidelines for preparing and delivering lectures

- A lecture should be enjoyable, stimulating and thought provoking. Think of it as a 'scene setter' in which you set out the big picture and outline the main issues. Students should leave it wanting to find out more.
- Students need a clear structure to help them navigate their way through the lecture and to identify the key elements.
- A clear structure begins with an introduction which states the purpose and key objectives and provides an organising framework for the students, for example: 'It is generally agreed that there are three main industries on which the Industrial Revolution was based – coal, cotton and iron. We will examine each in turn.'

- As the lecture develops, the main headings – in this case, coal, cotton and iron – form the basic skeleton of the lecture. Each of these will have subsidiary elements to guide the students.
- You can support the students by supplying printed diagrams showing the structure, possibly linked to a visual presentation.
- Use visual presentations, especially PowerPoint, sparingly.
- Be aware of your voice; an extended presentation requires the careful employment of pace, pause, volume and variety. Use some humour. We learn more effectively when we laugh.

However, it's fair to say that most teachers in PCET have never used, and probably never will use, a formal lecture.

## Case study

Case studies can vary to such a great extent that it's difficult to offer one simple definition. Case studies are generally student-centred learning activities based on real-life scenarios, events or problems with contextual information which provide learners with an opportunity to apply learning, develop higher order skills and diagnose and solve problems.

Case studies are frequently used in business courses to study particular businesses or business sectors and to analyse and evaluate their success or failure. Learners could, for example, study and analyse a real or fictional failing business and develop ideas for organisation, products and marketing to revitalise it. In engineering learners could examine specific engineering problems and develop innovative ideas and solutions. Case studies have a number of educational benefits including the following:

- They are invaluable in developing higher order skills (see Bloom's taxonomy) and thinking skills such as analysis, evaluation, synthesis, decision making and problem solving.
- They can be integrating activities in that they bring together a number of skills and learning around a theme. For example, in a business case study learners can use knowledge of economics, marketing, human resources and finance in the analysis of a business.
- Groupworking and team-building skills – case studies, particularly extended ones, encourage the development of cooperation, teamworking and role specialisation.
- Research and information gathering – larger case studies might require learners to use a range of resources and information sources to support their work.
- Time management – to be realistic, learners could be required to work within deadlines to produce response to the case study. The conclusion to the case study could be a presentation.

- Presentation skills – case studies provide ideal opportunities to prepare and give presentations which will help them develop skills they are likely to need in employment.
- Assessment – case studies can be both formative and summative methods of assessment.

There are many websites and textbooks that provide case studies you can use with your learners, but it's much more rewarding and relevant to develop you own. They can be detailed long-term activities that require the production of reports and presentations, or shorter ones based around specific issues with some specific questions to be answered or tasks undertaken.

**Activity**

*A learning group case study*
Choose a group of learners you work with on a regular basis and use them as a case study. You can use the group as a 'laboratory' for trying out new ideas and analyse and evaluate them.

This is an opportunity for you to integrate a range of knowledge and skills and to try out theory in practice. Here you can explore, for example, learning theories, communication, learning and teaching methods. You can study group dynamics and observe the effects of different subgroups and experiment with room settings.

If you are training to teach you might already be doing this as part of your PDJ, but you could choose one class for a more in-depth study. You will find it useful to present your ongoing study to trainee colleagues and discuss and develop ideas with them. As your career develops, this kind of activity can form the basis of an action research project.

An example of a brief, focused case study used to introduce the use of discussion in teaching and learning can be found in the following section.

## Discussion

In order to demonstrate the use of case study, this section on using discussion starts with a case study of a sociology teacher attempting to use discussion in his class. You should use this scenario to analyse and evaluate the teacher's use of discussion and to recommend guidelines for him to improve his technique. You will also find it useful to apply your guidelines to your own teaching practice.

**Activity**

*An introductory case study*

Ron is a very keen 28-year-old teacher recently appointed as a part-time sociology lecturer in a further education college in an inner city. The college has a wide ethnic and cultural mix. He has been asked to deliver a sociology input on a BTEC Health and Social Care course. The subject he is dealing with is the family. He has provided some inputs on types of family and the functions of the family. Ron has been told that discussion is a valuable teaching method and is keen to have a go.

There are 11 people in the class. Their motivations vary from very keen to a couple who are on the course because they couldn't really think of anything else to do. There are three mature students (30+) and one male student. It is September and only their third week in college.

The class runs from 11.00–12.30 on a Friday morning. At 12.10 the eager Ron says, 'Right. Let's have a discussion. What do you think about the family?' No response. Several students look at their notes or gaze out of the window. Some look at Ron as if wanting to help him out. Ron aims a question at an individual, 'Chantelle, what are your views on the family?'

Chantelle blushes and mumbles, 'Well. . . it's OK for some people.' An enigmatic response.

Dawn, a mature student, previously a shop steward in a garment factory, says, 'The nuclear family is another example of western cultural imperialism, isn't it?' Ron looks pleased. This is exactly his opinion.

'Any responses to Dawn's point?' There are none.

Darren says, 'It's like on *EastEnders*, isn't it?'

'Eh?' replies the temporarily baffled Ron. 'What do you mean?' His tone is not hostile but Darren declines further comment.

'Don't matter,' he mutters.

In a last act of desperation, Ron aims a question at Zeinab, who is normally keen to speak. 'What do you think, Zeinab? Do you agree with the functionalist view?'

'No,' says Zeinab.

After a period of silence Ron says, 'Well, you don't seem to have any opinions, do you?'

The class is set out like this:

```
    X    X              X              X    X

  [     ]            [     ]            [     ]
    X                  X                  X

  [     ]            [     ]            [     ]
                   X    X                  X

  [     ]            [     ]            [     ]

  [     ]
   Ron
```

1   Analyse Ron's use of discussion and his use of questions.
2   What should he do to have a better chance of success with discussion as a learning and teaching technique?
3   Produce a set of guidelines for effective use of discussion.

Discussion is something we take for granted, often regarding it as just 'having a chat' with learners or, worse still, it is derided as not 'proper teaching'. Discussion deserves serious consideration as a learning and teaching method, particularly in the development of active constructivist learning and thinking skills.

The essence of discussion is dialogue and the exchange and expression of ideas, opinions and knowledge. Discussions might range from a structured and planned learning experience to the unplanned but welcome opportunity to air some ideas. Inspectors are keen to see that sessions are not so rigidly planned that opportunities for discussion are missed. Discussion is an excellent method for developing thinking skills and higher order learning. Discussions are important when exploring opinions, beliefs and attitudes and encouraging learners to appreciate other points of view, but be careful because people can have strong views and may find it difficult to be objective (this includes teachers!).

Discussion is often considered to be a method more suited to the arts, humanities and social sciences which are mistakenly assumed to have more 'issues' to discuss, rather than science or mathematics which might be considered more in the realm of facts. Science is based on theories and debates, many of them controversial, and they need to be discussed. One of my trainee teachers described a session in which she introduced students to genetics through a discussion of ethical issues based around transgenic animals. This seems to me to be an excellent way to introduce a topic by making it relevant to real life and reminding learners that science is not neutral but has social, moral, religious and ethical implications.

Mathematics might seem to many teachers and learners not the place for discussion – what is there to discuss, they might ask? Research by Malcolm Swan, based on GCSE maths retake students in FE colleges, suggests there is considerable benefit to be gained from using discussion in maths sessions. Students retaking maths tend to improve by one grade on average, if at all, and much of the teaching is teacher centred and 'transmission based'. These methods have already failed the learners and merely repeating them does little to boost their confidence and motivation. But, as Swan says of the discussion-based resources which were developed:

> There is evidence here to suggest that learning is enhanced, particularly when they are used in student-centred ways. In particular, this means students' existing knowledge and misunderstandings are brought to the surface and discussed in the lessons. The greatest gains (approximately one standard deviation) were made in the group that used many lessons in student-centred ways. The more student-centred approaches seem to have prevented a general decline in confidence and motivation that may occur when traditional didactic approaches are used in FE classrooms.
>
> (Swan 2006: 240)

## Guidelines for using discussion

In the case study above, Ron did very little to plan for the use of discussion as part of learning about the family. If you are going to plan discussion into a session, here are few things to consider:

- Do you need some stimulus material or something to start the discussion? Ron could have provided an article about families, perhaps something which related family to adolescent behaviour. He could have used some statistics about the family or even an extract from a soap opera.

- Encourage learners and give them opportunities to explore ideas. Darren, in the case study, with support from Ron might have developed his thoughts about *EastEnders* into a useful vehicle for exploring issues about the family.

- Teachers shouldn't dominate discussion or force their ideas and opinions on the group; like good chat-show hosts their role is to encourage and facilitate inputs from others.

- As a teacher you will sometimes need to take the role of chair and to keep things under control and the discussion focused on the main point. Occasionally, you will need to thank contributors for their inputs but ask them to hold back a bit so that others can join in.

- It's a good idea to establish some rules: – only one person can speak at a time; no interrupting; no offensive or inappropriate statements or actions; listening to each other.

- The important thing is to make sure that everyone is involved, and willing to be involved, in the conversation. I've observed a number of sessions in which teachers are really enjoying an in-depth discussion with a few like-minded learners about an item of mutual interest while the majority of the group are showing clear signs of boredom.

- Don't let a discussion ramble on. When it's reached the end of its useful life, bring it to an end but don't forget to summarise the key points and relate them to the learning topic – better still, get the learners to summarise.

- Consider the room layout. Everyone needs to be able to see each other, so old school-style rows with people looking at the backs of heads is not appropriate.

## Student presentations

Student presentations are valuable learning experiences which develop a wide range of generic skills as well furthering subject knowledge. Unfortunately, many students dread them. However, this is no reason to avoid them. If we create the right atmosphere and provide support and guidelines for learners they can gain considerable benefit in terms of planning, organisation and confidence. A group presentation with the necessary research and preparation accompanied by a PowerPoint presentation, handouts and followed by discussion and questions can be very effective for developing communication skills and employability.

Presentations could be based around the use of seminars in which individuals or small groups of learners research a specified topic, or part of a topic, and present their findings to their colleagues. Presentations may also be the final part of a case study or a report on projects which students are currently working on.

A disadvantage of presentations is that they are time consuming in both their preparation and delivery. A class of 15–20 learners working towards an AS level might find the benefits are outweighed by the disadvantages resulting from time 'lost'.

## Guidelines for using presentations

- Ensure that learners know what they are doing, why and how. You will find it useful to prepare an assignment brief stating exactly what is expected and how long the presentation should last.

- If the presentation is part of an assessment, make clear to the learners what they are being assessed on: is it the development of subject-specific knowledge and skills; or their presentation skills; or both?

- If possible provide guidelines to the learners about preparing and delivering a presentation. In colleges, there may be study skills workshops or resources to help them. There is wealth of support in books and on websites about how to overcome nerves and anxiety related to presentations.

- In particular, stress that structure is important and that they should consider tried and tested methods such as cue cards; PowerPoint slides can provide a similar structure. Remind them not to write out a script and give a reading.
- Allow time for practice, or recommend they practise at home.
- Make learners aware of the importance of being a good audience as well as being good presenters. Presenters need to know that their audience is interested in them and going to support them. Create a classroom climate of low threat but high challenge.

## Demonstration

At its simplest, a demonstration involves showing other people how to do something; it is the display and explanation of a skill. The demonstration may be of practical/physical skills or of cognitive/intellectual skills. Examples in post-compulsory education might include the following:

*Practical/physical*

- hairdressing techniques
- first aid demonstrations
- science experiment
- computer file management
- sport routine/exercise
- bricklaying

*Cognitive/intellectual*

- mathematical calculation
- poetry analysis
- writing a business letter
- analysing a media text
- using apostrophes

Some teaching, particularly of practical skills, is not possible without using demonstrations – it would be difficult, for example, to teach bricklaying without demonstrating. Demonstrations allow the linking of theory to practice. Continuing the bricklaying example, learners will have been given information about the components of a mortar mix, the proportions in which they are combined and some general points regarding how the procedure is carried out. However, the teaching is only effectively done by demonstration, with the teacher explaining each step of the process. A good demonstration, especially if the end product is impressive, will leave the learners keen to have a go to see how well they can carry out the skill.

Practical demonstrations are nearly always followed by sessions in which the learners practise the skill observed by the teacher who encourages and motivates them by recognising correct practice but also patiently pointing out incorrect practice and reinforcing that particular element of the demonstration.

Teaching intellectual and cognitive skills is, like practical skill teaching, based on modelling a skill or procedure to learners followed by observed and corrected practice. An English teacher demonstrating the use of apostrophes explains the theory and the use of this punctuation mark, states the general categories of their use, and then demonstrates some worked examples using the board or a clearly visible medium.

The same English teacher carrying out an analysis of a magazine advertisement in relation to audience and purpose uses a worked example, then sets individuals or groups the task of applying the analytical process to another example.

## Guidelines for using demonstration

- Preparation – ensure that all materials are available and ready for use. It's embarrassing for you and unimpressive to students if you have to nip out and collect something you have forgotten.

- Preparation will involve breaking down the procedure into a series of connected key points. These will provide a framework for the learners.

- Practice – a good demonstration is like putting on a show. The first time you do it should not be in the class or the workshop. Try it out beforehand. You could even video yourself and analyse the result. If you are demonstrating a mathematical calculation, make sure you've checked it and can do it with confidence.

- Ensure that all health and safety requirements are in place. If it's a science experiment, does everyone need lab coats and eye protection?

- Arrange the room and ask learners to move so that they can all see clearly. You might need to find ways of making things more visible. In a demonstration of computer file management it's difficult to get everyone round one computer so you will need to consider using a data projector.

- Does the demonstration link to previous learning and knowledge? Have you prepared the ground so that learners can see the demonstration as part of a continuum of learning?

- Consider the pace of the demonstration. Don't rush it. You can even slow it down to an unnaturally slow pace and observe learners' reactions to see if you need to speed up.

- Allow time for questions, particularly if they are for clarification or repetition of something missed, but also be prepared to deal with some questions later if they interfere with the flow of the demonstration.

- Avoid unnecessary jargon or terms which learners haven't previously encountered. The use of acronyms and abbreviations can be particularly annoying when people aren't familiar with them.

- To check learning, try a second demonstration in which the learners tell you what to do. After demonstrating the application of a sling, a first aid trainer could repeat the demonstration and ask the learners to tell her what to do at each stage.

- Don't make the demonstration too long otherwise you'll start to lose your audience. Can it be broken down into two or more demonstrations with student practice in between each? You will want to consider the level and previous experience of your learners when making these decisions.

**Activity**

Identify links and explain the connections between:

- demonstrations
- Kolb's learning cycle (see Chapters 2 and 5)
- communication
- active learning

## Brainstorming (thought showers or word showers)

This is a technique that can be used to generate quickly a large number of ideas or possible solutions to a problem. It can also be used to introduce a topic and get people thinking. When I taught communication studies I began the course by asking learners to brainstorm as many different methods of communication as they could think of.

A brainstorming session should ideally last between 5 and 15 minutes. You will need to set clear rules and guidelines – no shouting all at once, no obviously silly or offensive ideas – and keep a brisk pace going. You, the teacher, will write the ideas onto the board or flipchart or you could ask a member of the group to do it. Sometimes you might want to use the brainstorming session as a warm-up exercise where the topic and the solutions are less important than getting the group active and participating. Try, for example, brainstorming the possible uses of a brick. It's a good idea to use brainstorming with a concept map or spider diagram to organise key ideas round a central theme. Figure 6.1 shows an example.

### Buzz groups

The 'buzz' is the noise that results from this activity. This method entails breaking a large group of learners into several smaller groups (ideally 3 or 4) and giving them a

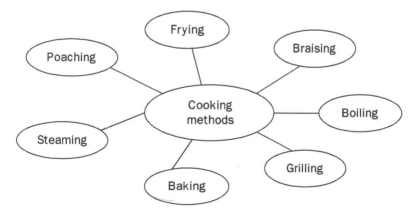

**Figure 6.1** Concept map as part of brainstorming activity.

question to answer or a problem to work on for about 5–10 minutes. For example, I recently set a large group of trainee teachers into buzz groups to consider some of the causes of behavioural problems in classes of young learners. The time limitation is important because it increases the urgency to get the job done and heightens the 'buzz'. When the time is up, it's usual to ask each buzz group to feed back their ideas to the whole group. It's a good idea to ask for one or two ideas from each group in rotation. If you go round the groups asking each one to report all their ideas the final group might find all their suggestions have already been covered.

When you set up this activity be clear about what the task or question is and state specifically how much time is available. You might find it useful to appoint a leader or spokesperson for each group. Tell the groups how you want the feedback – just an oral response or do you want them to produce flipchart diagrams or come up and use the board?

Buzz groups are ideally for adding variety to learning sessions and getting the learners involved and thinking. A wise teacher will know from observing her learners when she has been talking for too long and needs to have a change. Buzz groups are an easy activity to introduce unplanned when you feel a change of pace or activity is required.

## Projects

What is a project? You will probably have memories of doing project work at some stage in your educational career, at school, college or university. In the lifelong learning sector a project could include, for example: an art and design project; an engineering project; an extended essay or report in English or psychology; a magazine project; a research project; a family history research project; making and/or marketing a product. What, if anything, do all these different examples have in common? The term 'project' can be very vague and covers such a wide range of endeavour in so many curriculum areas. Jane Henry (1994) suggests six main points which define a project:

1   The topic is usually selected by the learner. There may be limitations on the choice introduced by the teacher or the examining or awarding body.
2   The learner finds their own source material and carries out their own research.
3   The learner presents an end product (a written report, a presentation, an artefact.)
4   The project is usually independent. Group projects may sometimes be appropriate.
5   The project covers an extended period.
6   The teacher acts as a facilitator/adviser/'critical friend'.

Using projects has many advantages for learners, the most obvious being that they are examples of independent learning which the learner has some control over in terms of content and activity. This can be highly motivating, especially if they can synthesise skills and knowledge across a curriculum area or areas. A magazine or web design project gives learners the opportunity to combine, for example: word-processing; digital photography; desk-top publishing or web design; not to mention, further links into market research and design. Projects clearly provide significant opportunities for the development of generic skills.

## Guidelines for developing and using student projects

- Projects need to have a proper focus and be clearly structured. Given that projects are essentially student-centred this may seem a contradiction. Students need a project or assignment sheet which tells them clearly what they are expected to achieve and the time in which they have to do it. Timing is very important. Too little time will be discouraging for learners and they will feel they can do nothing more than a cursory piece of work; too much time can lead to a leisurely approach, frequently followed by furious last-minute activity. As C. Northcote Parkinson suggested in his famous 'law': 'Work expands so as to fill the time available for its completion.'

- Ideally, the project or assignment brief should indicate the assessment criteria and state clearly what learners have to do and/or produce.

- The teacher is the facilitator. This means that they have an active involvement and should not use project work as an opportunity to let students get on alone while they nip back to the staffroom to do some marking. The first use of projects and the initial stages of any project require close observance and support from teachers.

- During the early stages of the project it is essential to get learners to develop a clear statement of intent or a learning contract. This might be adapted or modified according to suggestions from the teacher concerning feasibility and practicality. These learning contracts can become part of the regular review process.

- To facilitate and support project work it will be necessary to have regular meetings and tutorials with learners to help them assess their progress, review their work and consider the next stages. It is advisable to draw up a tutorial or meetings schedule and ensure that learners turn up for them and bring the necessary materials. Get the students to put these dates in their diaries; better still develop a project logbook. Long-term projects could include presentations of work in progress, with discussion and criticism sessions, to fellow learners.

- Extended practical projects may need to be supported by extra skill development workshops in, for example, desktop publishing or using digital cameras. This requires advance planning and liaison with colleagues.

- Resources will need to be booked according to need and availability. Schedules need to be negotiated and agreed with learners and resource providers.

- Some projects will require support for the development of study skills, such as using library, report writing, finding and interpreting information. Some projects require learners to undertake primary research for which they will need help with research methods, for example, questionnaire design.

- Group projects can be especially difficult to manage, especially when members of the group are assigned to particular roles. As a media studies teacher I well recall group video projects, involving scriptwriting, filming, sound and editing, sometimes lasting a term or more. It is vital that students know their role and are committed to fulfilling it. In group projects individual logbooks are necessary to record the activities and progress of each learner, together with their own evaluations.

In short, project work is a valuable learning experience which at its best encourages the development of independent and motivated learners, but without firm management and clear guidelines learners can lose focus and interest.

## Role play

Role play is a popular technique with many teachers. In some curriculum areas, particularly health, nursing and counselling, it is a staple of the teaching and learning process. Used well it can be a fruitful and illuminating activity, particularly in the development of emotional intelligence; rapport and empathy. Used less well it has little value and can even be upsetting for learners.

In essence, a role play involves the creation of a situation in which learners act out particular roles, followed by discussion and analysis. A simple example is the use of role play in retail to explore dealing with difficult customers. Participants in counselling courses frequently use role play to develop their listening skills. In human resources and trades union training role play can be used to simulate negotiations on pay and conditions or the resolution of disputes.

Role play has the advantage that it can simulate 'real world' situations for learners to explore without the threats of a real situation. It provides opportunities for learners to 'get into role' and experience how it feels and the emotions involved. Used well it is a valuable way of developing confidence and reflective skills. However, role plays can feel very uncomfortable for many learners and some will even refuse to take part; no one should ever be pressured to take part in role play if they don't wish to. At the other extreme will be those who relish being in the limelight and will use the role play as an excuse to perform to an audience, especially if it gets laughs. The danger here is that the participants and the audience miss the whole point of the exercise and learn little or nothing from it. We should remember humanist principles of learning which suggest that learners thrive in an emotionally safe environment; for many, role play is not an emotionally safe activity.

### Guidelines for using role play

- You should first consider why, indeed whether, you need to use role play. Retail students acting out the awkward customer and sales assistant scenario could probably learn as much from a training video made by professional actors.
- If role play is right for the learners and the learning need you should set it up and prepare it carefully. There's nothing to be gained from suddenly springing a role play on to an unsuspecting group.
- This preparation could involve the writing of 'role cards' or information sheets giving the players all the information they need about the situation and their roles.

- It will be necessary to simulate the physical elements of the situation in some way, even if it's simply moving the furniture to represent a shop or a hospital ward. More advanced role plays can include props, for example, phones, computers, office equipment.

- Teachers must monitor role plays carefully and be prepared to step in or to intervene if students get so deeply into their role that they act out inappropriate behaviour. It will be necessary to tell some groups that however authentic the role play is aiming to be some kinds of behaviour and language are not acceptable.

- Following the role play, it is essential to debrief the participants and the audience to get them out of role and all the emotional elements should be defused and discussed.

- The discussion will include the analysis and evaluation of the role play, summarising key learning points and relating practice to theory; this part is the real value of role play.

## Concept mapping

Concept mapping is the most widely used term to describe this kind of activity; other terms include 'mind mapping', 'spider diagrams', 'tree diagrams' or simply 'mapping'. Concept mapping was developed by Joseph Novak of Cornell University in 1972 from the work of the educational psychologist David Ausubel. Concept maps combine several key ideas in teaching and learning – active learning; constructivism; advance organisers; and visual learning.

Concept maps are attempts to represent schemas. Schemas are mental models which each of us build to represent, organise and understand our world. You will be developing your own schema relating to teaching and learning which will be adapted and modified as you assimilate new information and ideas. Concept maps are constructivist in that they help learners to organise, process and represent schema, make connections and fit new information into their existing knowledge. Concept maps are particularly useful for people who have a visual learning preference and for dyslexic learners. They allow fleeting ideas represented by spoken or written words to be held static so that connections can be seen and new information assimilated. Information presented visually in this way can lead to improved retention and creativity. Concept maps have a wide range of uses in teaching and learning, as well as business and many other areas of work. They can be used for:

- creativity
- brainstorming
- memory
- revision
- critical thinking
- problem solving
- summarising (e.g. an article)

- planning a report, essay, project or assignment
- assessment
- communicating complex ideas.

## Guidelines for concept mapping

1   Start with a central idea, such as cooking methods, as shown in Figure 6.1, p. 119). Write the idea or key concept in a box or oval.

2   Start putting in secondary ideas which spring from the central idea. Connect them to the main idea with lines.

3   Each secondary idea can lead to several further (tertiary) ideas.

4   Do it as quickly as you can. You can refine it later.

5   Introduce your own symbols and ways of representing ideas using, for example, different colours or shapes.

6   You can start to link some of the primary and secondary ideas on the map where you see connections.

For an example, see the concept map of the Industrial Revolution in Chapter 5 (Figure 5.1, p. 86). English teachers often find it useful to get students to produce concept maps of, for example, plays. They can introduce pictures of the main players and start to connect them; to show relationships and work out causes and consequences. I have also seen a concept map that provides an overview of the origins of World War I – it's a very crowded map!

There are several concept mapping computer packages which you can use. If you work in a large college or other institution ask your IT people what's available. These packages are particularly effective when used with an interactive whiteboard so that you can expand and collapse the diagram as part of an explanation. Tony Buzan has developed a related technique known as mind mapping which uses visual and graphical elements and colour in their production. He has produced several books that you might find useful to refer to (see Bibliography).

### Activity

Concept maps are useful tools when you are planning courses or teaching sessions. They can help you to discover relationships between different areas of your teaching. In addition, these maps can be used to give students a visual overview (advance organiser of the course)

Take a course you currently teach and work out key topic areas, or use the ones provided in the specifications to make a concept map. Extend the map as much as you like as long as it remains helpful to do so.

Mapping and using visual or graphic organisers is an extremely fruitful area to consider for your teaching and for your students' learning. You can follow this up by searching the internet for 'graphic organisers'. You will find a bewildering array of ideas including tree diagrams, hierarchies, organisation charts, cause and effect diagrams, maps and many others. For concept mapping software see: MindGenius (www.mindgenius.com/); Free Mind (freemind.en.softonic.com).

## Games and quizzes

It's OK to have some fun and have a laugh once in a while. Indeed, many education-alists believe that laughing is positively beneficial to learning. Using games and quizzes not only provides opportunities for enjoyment but also for active and experiential learning. There is such a wide variety of educational games in textbooks, on the internet and commercially available that this section is only intended to alert you to the possibilities of using games and to find and develop your own.

Educational games usually involve competition and or cooperation and can be based on individuals competing or teams competing. Games will help to develop a range of skills in learners, including team building and cooperation; problem solving and communication skills. They can be used as icebreakers to help groups relax and get to know each other. Games need to be chosen and deployed carefully to match the needs and level of the learners. A game that seems too simple or childish might offend or patronise some; a game that is too competitive will not suit those who don't like competition – or are poor losers!

## Some examples of educational games

### Broken information exercises

These involve a situation or a problem being broken down into a series of printed cards so that each learner has some information but nobody has all of it. The group has to cooperate to piece together the information. 'Murder Hunt' (Ginnis 2002) provides clues that learners have to put together to solve a murder case and explain the circumstances of it.

### Decision-making games

These involve learners having to work together to make and justify decisions which the whole group agrees on. Classic examples are the Desert Survival exercise in which learners imagine their plane has crash-landed in the desert. They have to rank in order of importance to their survival a number of items saved from the wreckage. A further example is the Lifeboat Game in which learners have to make decisions about which people to throw overboard because there is insufficient food and water. This game is good for examining attitudes, emotions and prejudices, but needs to be handled carefully.

### Bingo

This can be played straight for developing numeracy skills or adapted to revise and practise words and concepts (Ginnis 2002).

## Quizzes

Learners at most levels generally enjoy a quiz now and then. They provide an element of competition which is a motivating factor for most of them. Quizzes are also a useful method of assessment, particularly of more fact-based, rote learning, for example: history dates and events; the periodic table; characters in literature.

You can be as inventive as you like with games, provided your students enjoy them. There is some educational benefit and there are no health and safety issues. Think of family games you play at Christmas and use and adapt them as appropriate. Many numeracy teachers use cards and dice to develop number skills; some even use darts!

## Discovery learning

Discovery learning, at least in schools, has had a very bad press. Many educationalists, politicians and journalists decry discovery as just another example of 'trendy teaching', or worse still not teaching at all. Such thinking is often founded on a belief in education as a form of social control, with the emphasis on discipline and rote learning. This is a shame because discovery is how most of us have been learning for most of our lives. Lefrancois (2000: 209) defines discovery learning as: 'the learning that takes place when students are not presented with subject matter in its final form but rather are required to organise it themselves. This requires learners to discover for themselves relationships among items of information.'

Discovery learning is not about telling learners to go away and find out. It requires guidance and support from teachers. Discovery learning is developed from the work of Bruner (1960) who emphasised the importance of understanding what is being studied by working out the key principles of an area of knowledge and discovering interrelationships between things. The essence of discovery learning is finding out, working things out and making connections. Discovery links to several other key themes and methods in this book: active learning; deep learning; thinking skills; and using questions as part of teaching by asking. It also links to concept maps and advance organisers in that it requires the understanding of structures and the 'big picture' as a precursor to learning the details.

Working with trainee teachers I have used an example of discovery learning based on Greek and Latin word roots. Students are provided with word roots, prefixes and suffixes and invited to make and explain the meaning of as many words as they can make. This method also works well to develop specific vocabularies; some of my trainee teachers in the ambulance service used it to help trainees learn medical terms and vocabulary.

Briefly, here, in no particular order, are a few examples. See what you can make with them. (Some classical scholars will criticise my definitions!)

- geo = earth
- morph = shape
- ology = study of
- a, -ab, abs = away from
- bio = life

– graph(y) = writing/writing about
– auto = self
– poly = many
– psyche = the mind
– tele = from afar
– skopos (scope) = to see

You've probably come up with words such as *geology, telescope, autobiography*. The trick, of course, is that once you have learned the meanings of the parts you can work out the meaning of previously unencountered words.

Woolfolk et al. emphasise the importance of intuitive thinking in discovery learning and encouraging learners to make imaginative leaps, even if they sometimes make mistakes. They provide an example of learners making guesses based on incomplete evidence in order to discover some general principles: 'After learning about ocean currents and the shipping industry, for example, pupils might be shown old maps of three harbours and asked to guess which one became a major port. Then they can check their guesses through systematic research' (Woolfolk et al. 2008: 344).

Most things – language; art, music, engineering, numbers, film, fashion – are made up of a range of basic elements which are combined together in a variety of different ways. Whatever you're teaching, try to identify some of the basic elements and let people play with them – rather like children playing with bricks – and see what they can discover or create.

## Problem-based learning (PBL)

Most learning begins with learning something particular (knowledge and skills) and then, hopefully, using it to solve problems. PBL works the other way round. It begins with the problem and asks learners to identify what knowledge and skills they already have but also what additional learning they need in order to solve the problem. John Biggs believes that:

> PBL reflects the way people learn in real life; they simply get on with solving the problems life puts before them with whatever resources are to hand. They do not stop to wonder the relevance of what they are doing or at their motivation for doing it.

(Biggs 2003: 232)

This sounds remarkably similar to discovery learning but while discovery learning involves finding things out around a theme or topic, PBL is more focused around finding the solution to a specific problem.

Problem-based learning began in medical and health education as a response to the situation in which some health professionals had a wealth of knowledge but fewer problem-solving skills. If you think about it, turning up at the doctor's or at the hospital with a complaint is about asking a health professional to make a diagnosis and solve your medical problem. Similarly, turning up at a garage with a spluttering, underperforming car is about asking a motor vehicle technician to solve your car's problem.

Much of our working lives is concerned with solving problems. It doesn't take too much thought to extend the above examples to include business, engineering, science, design, construction, health and social care, and social work training.

PBL, as far as I am aware, has not been widely used in post-compulsory education and lifelong learning. In FE colleges, in particular, teachers feel that they do not have sufficient course time to indulge in PBL and similar strategies. This is a real concern, but sometimes it's necessary to take risks. John Biggs states that PBL 'is not so much a method as a total approach to teaching, which could embody several possible TLAs [teaching/learning activities] and assessment methods' (Biggs 2003). In this respect, PBL provides an ideal integrating focus on BTEC, diploma courses and similar vocational courses, but might be less viable for A-level students.

PBL has a number of advantages. First, it recognises that learning is a process of construction by the learners, not just reception of information. Because PBL is constructivist it develops greater knowledge retention and recall skills, as well as higher order skills. It provides an integrating focus for learning which can bring together skills and knowledge from within a particular subject or across the curriculum. PBL also develops subject-specific skills; for example, in business studies learners might draw on but also develop accounting, budgeting and marketing. A case study of a failing business could easily be the basis for a problem-based learning activity. In addition to subject-specific skills PBL develops general, or transferable skills such as teamwork, time management, decision taking and communication.

The kind of PBL practised in universities might be too large-scale for use in lifelong learning, but we can use the principle and adapt to some smaller scale activities. Let's consider a few possible problems:

- problems with a car
- problems with behavioural difficulties in children
- problems in IT or electrical equipment
- problems of accessibility and mobility in a building
- problems with the profitably of a company (this might have begun life as a case study).

## Guidelines for using problem-based learning

- The most obvious first step is to state clearly what the problem is.
- As a teacher, you need to decide on the time frame for completion and the time available within the course as a whole.
- You might also want to decide what degree of autonomy you will give to your learners in organising the work and providing a solution.
- Connected to the above point, you might suggest that learners work as a formal group with meetings, agendas and minutes.
- The group will probably want to break into subgroups working on specific smaller tasks and report back to the whole group.

- You might want to build in some taught sessions as part of the programme which will act as a stimulus for further learning and application of learning.
- On completion of the exercise, it's important to have debriefing sessions and ask learners not only how they have solved the problem but also evaluate their acquisition of subject-specific and transferable skills and knowledge.

## Coaching

Coaching is frequently associated with sport, in particular the development of particular skills such as serving in tennis. Increasingly, coaching is used in the lifelong learning sector as well as in training for business and human resources.

- Coaching is a one-to-one technique.
- It usually lasts for short periods.
- It focuses on improving performance and the development of specific goals and skills.
- It helps people to evaluate how well they are doing and what they need to learn.
- It is essentially non-directive – it doesn't tell people what to do but supports them in their own improvement and development.
- The basis of coaching is giving and receiving feedback.

Coaching can be difficult to distinguish from mentoring. A mentor is generally considered to be a person who has more experience, skills and knowledge than the learner or trainee; people learn *from* mentors. A coach doesn't necessarily have to be higher status or more experienced person. MacLennan (1995) makes the distinction between a mentor as someone we learn *from* and a coach as someone we learn *with*. He defines a coach as follows:

> Someone for the performer to work WITH. Coaching is the process whereby one individual helps another; to unlock their natural ability; to perform, to learn, and achieve; to increase awareness of the factors that determine performance; to increase their sense of self-responsibility and ownership of their performance; to self-coach to identify and remove barriers to achievement.
>
> (MacLennan 1995: 4)

Coaching is based on a dialogue between learner and teacher. It requires the teachers to use their skills of non-directive support and questioning techniques to help learners assess, evaluate and develop their work. So rather than saying 'I can see what your problem is' or 'What you should have done is. . .', the teacher uses questions such as 'Tell me what you think is going on?' or 'What do you think went wrong and how could you improve it?' 'What do you think you need to do next?'

The GROW model of coaching is used in training and development as a means of developing coaching skills. It is based on a cycle of four elements:

- Setting **G**oals
- Assessing current **R**eality
- Generating **O**ptions
- Setting a **W**ay forward.

The model is shown in Figure 6.2.

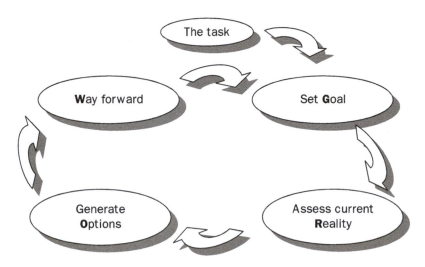

**Figure 6.2** The GROW model of coaching.

1   The **G**oal – *what do you want to do or achieve?*
   - What is your goal? What do you want to achieve?
   - How will you know when you have achieved it?
   - What is the aim of today's discussion?
2   Current **R**eality – *what is happening now?*
   - What is happening? What are you doing at present?
   - What difficulties are you encountering?
   - What's holding you back?
   - What have you achieved so far?
   - What have you done so far?
   - What results have your actions produced?
3   **O**ptions – *what could you do?*
   - What options or courses of action do you have?
   - What else could you do? What alternatives are there?
   - What if. . .?
   - What would be the benefits/advantages of these options?

4   **W**ay forward – *what will you do?*
  - What options or strategies have you chosen?
  - Will they meet your objectives?
  - What do you need to make this happen? What steps will you take?
  - Can you foresee any difficulties?
  - What resources do you need?
  - Do you need to develop new skills/knowledge to achieve this?
  - Do you need any support?

## The self-coach

You may have noticed similarities between the GROW model of coaching and the experiential learning cycle. All of these models are based on a cycle of improvement that is not only essential for effective learning but also for reflection and continuing professional development. The GROW model can be used by more experienced learners as a form of self-coaching in which they ask themselves the questions and explore the options. Clearly, self-coaching is another from of reflective practice and, as such, can form part of your PDJ.

---

**Activity**

*A coaching role play*
Working in groups of three, assign the roles of coach, coachee and observer.

Decide a topic from your teaching area which involves a task or a project to be completed.

Using the techniques and skills mentioned above, the coach should focus on the coachee and help them to develop their goals.

The observer can use the examples of questions shown above to analyse and evaluate the coaching process.

Coach and coachee can discuss their experiences of the roles.

---

In summary, the range of techniques discussed above is only intended to be a representative sample. You should research and develop others, particularly those which are suited to your subject specialism.

## Further reading

Eastwood, L., Coates, J., Dixon, L., Harvey, J., Ormondroyd, C and Williamson, S. (2009) *A Toolkit for Creative Teaching in Post-Compulsory Education*. Maidenhead: Open University Press. A very useful book which provides 50 learning activities for developing creativity.
Ginnis, P. (2002) *The Teacher's Toolkit*. Camarthen: Crown House.

## Websites

The Excellence Gateway subject resources page contains a lot of useful links to a wide range of teaching resources and methods, especially subject specific. www.excellencegateway.org.uk/tlp/subject-resources.html.

# 7

# Resources for teaching and learning

**What this chapter is about**

- Critically examining a range of resources including: printed, projected, non-projected, digital
- Selecting appropriate resources
- Designing, making or adapting resources as appropriate
- Design principles for printed and projected resources
- Advantages and disadvantages of different resources
- Evaluating and improving teaching and learning resources

**LLUK standards**

This chapter covers the following standards:
BK 1.3; BK 2.1; BP 2.1; BK 2.2; BP 2.2; BK 2.3; BP 2.3; BK 3.1; BP 3.1
BK 5.1; BP 5.1 BK 5.2; BP 5.2
CK 3.5; CP 3.5
DK 1.2; DP 1.2

## What is a resource?

The precise definitions of and differences between methods, strategies, techniques and resources occupies considerable space in some texts. I don't intend to add much to that debate here. Methods and strategies are generally concerned with the selection, combination and use of various teaching and learning activities, such as discussion, role play or demonstration. Resources are the things which teachers and learners use to support that learning. They are sometimes referred to as 'learning aids'. Thus a demonstration of using a microphone in music technology might be supported by real microphones and/or a PowerPoint presentation.

## Why use resources?

This is probably a more important question than what a resource is because if we consider *why* we use resources, we are on the way to using them appropriately to suit the learners and the learning outcomes. It will help us to become more reflective in the selection, use and evaluation of a range of resources. These are some of the reasons why we use a range of resources:

- *Add variety* – effective learning requires a range of inputs and stimuli to engage and maintain the interest of learners.
- *Appeal to different senses* – spoken input from a teacher loses its effect quite quickly. The introduction of a visual or moving image, sound, objects or a combination of these will arouse other senses and can help to re-engage your learners.
- *Reinforce learning* – multisensory inputs such as a spoken description of photosynthesis accompanied by an animated projected diagram can help to reinforce learning.
- *Help understanding* – the use of visual images, particularly, can help learners to see 'the big picture' and connect ideas more effectively.
- *Aid retention* – if learning resources help learners to visualise and connect learning they will also aid retention of learning.
- *Develop thinking skills* – using a range of resources can help learners not only to retain information but also to use it more effectively for analysis, synthesis and evaluation.
- *Support explanations and demonstrations* – effective use of resources makes it easier for teachers to explain concepts and facilitate demonstrations.

**Activity**

Think about the range of resources you use.

Why do you use them?

Are they the best resources for the job?

Have you evaluated their effectiveness?

To what extent are they planned into your sessions to support and develop learning?

Do your resources tend to make learners active or passive?

## Being visual

Very young children look at pictures and then start to associate words with them. Thus, a picture of an apple is accompanied by the word 'apple'. As the child becomes older the picture is removed and only the word (spoken or written) remains. Hearing or seeing the word 'apple' will produce a mental referent or image in the child's mind. This transition from recognising pictures to recognising words is the transition from *iconic* to *symbolic representation*. Icons are representations – photographs, pictures or drawings – which actually look like the real thing, as in the picture of the apple. Words are symbols which don't physically resemble the real thing; they've just become associated with it. Pictures of apples are the same in English or French; the words 'apple' and 'pomme' are not the same.

There is a temptation to assume that maturity means we should be able to understand most things by words rather than by visual images. The phrase 'Do you want me to draw you a picture?' is generally intended as an insult to people unable to understand something represented in written or spoken words. However, when we encounter a new concept or idea it can be difficult to visualise it and to connect it to previous learning; a visual image often helps understanding. Obviously, a physics teacher will show a visual image of various atoms when explaining them, or art students will need pictures by Van Gogh before they can discuss his work, but perhaps we can consider using visuals in less obvious cases. As a social sciences student, initially I struggled to grasp Marxist theory but it became clearer when I drew a big box labelled 'Proletariat' with a much smaller box labelled 'Bourgeoisie' above it. Having started with a simple static framework I could add an increasing number of complicating factors. It's easier to start simple and add complexity. The level of simplicity you start at is negotiated with your learners.

## Choosing, using and evaluating resources – the ASSURE model

Heinich et al. (1999) recommend a six-stage model for the use of resources. The model fits in with reflective practice and can also be used as a method of reviewing and evaluating resources in your PDJ and session evaluations. The stages are as follows:

**A**nalyse learners

**S**tate objectives

**S**elect resources

**U**se resources

**R**equire learner participation

**E**valuate and revise

### Analyse learners

Knowing your learners is the key to planning and preparing effective teaching and learning, especially the selection and use of resources. Factors that will influence your choice of resources include level, age, motivation and previous learning and experience.

### Level

Resource choices will vary according to the level of your learners. Those working at Entry level will require different content and style of resources on punctuation and grammar from students on an AS English language course. The style is also important. Many pre-prepared worksheets for Skills for Life have rather childish drawings and presentation which are inappropriate for adults with reading and writing difficulties.

### Age

Materials designed for 16–19-year-old learners may prove unsuitable for adults. Design features and references in the text to popular culture probably won't work for adult learners. It's also important to bear in mind that younger learners may have become habituated to fast-moving, short attention span activities such as they might experience through digital technology at home.

### Motivation

It's often assumed that those in further and adult education are there because they have chosen to be. Unfortunately, this isn't always true. Less willing learners will appreciate resources and teaching methods which involve and interest them in the topic.

### Previous learning and experience

You will need to choose and plan your resources with consideration of prior learning and experience. Learners encountering difficult concepts for the first time need to have them clearly introduced and explained.

## State objectives

When choosing teaching and learning resources you need to be clear about why you are using them and what it is that you want your learners to know or be able to do – what is the learning outcome? The objectives could be those, or one of those, you have written for your lesson plan. In a numeracy session, for example, the objective 'learners will add and subtract numbers' could involve physical resources (counters, sweets, blocks) rather than paper-based sums.

Using objectives based on Bloom's taxonomy (knowledge, comprehension, application, analysis, synthesis and evaluation) will help you to define the learning experiences and appropriate resources.

## Select resources

Having analysed your learners and identified the objectives, you will need to select resources which are most appropriate for learners and purpose. The bulk of this chapter is concerned with the discussion of a range of resources for teaching and learning. One of your first tasks as a beginning teacher is to familiarise yourself with the range of resources available to you where you work but also from other sources. In larger organisations there are likely to be media technicians and IT technicians who can advise you on resource provision. The most frequently used resources, which we will examine in more detail later, include:

- whiteboards
- PowerPoint presentations
- flipcharts
- DVD/video/Youtube
- printed resources (handouts, worksheets, readings, gapped handouts)
- models and 'realia'
- libraries and learning centres
- visits and trips
- IT/internet/digital technology
- interactive whiteboards
- overhead projectors (OHP).

In many cases, you will be producing your own resources. These might vary from the relatively straightforward design and production of printed resources, PowerPoints, or card sort activities to more complex pieces of equipment. I have seen trainee teachers produce quite sophisticated resources: for example, a 'lightbox' to demonstrate the colour spectrum or a PowerPoint projection including film clips for textual analysis.

## Use resources

This step is the whole point of the exercise – actually using the resources. However, be wary of diving straight in and using your resources without adequate trial and preparation. There is a series of five simple steps, recommended by Heinich et al., which will guide you through preparation and use of resources. These are the '5 Ps'.

1   Preview the materials. Don't use anything you haven't previewed first to check for suitability and appropriateness for learners. The first time you see a DVD shouldn't be when you use it in the session. It might be too long, contain inappropriate content, or simply just not work. You might find that you need to edit a DVD or just show part of it.

2   Prepare the materials. The resources need to be built into the structure of your session plan and the order of their use determined. It's a good idea to have a column on your session plan for resources and to summarise them on the front sheet. If the resources include equipment for learners to use, be sure you have enough of them readily available and try to anticipate any other equipment they might need.

3    Prepare the environment. Check equipment is available and working. Some projected resources require a darkened room so you need to check that blinds are working and effective and also adjust seating arrangements so learners can see and hear properly

4    Prepare the learners. The content and objectives of all learning sessions should be made clear to learners from the start. You must prepare your learners for the resource you are about to use. If it's a video or DVD, explain why you are showing it and what you want the group to get from it. A video might be supported by a question sheet or prompt sheet of things to look for.

5    Provide the learning experience. In other words, use the resource. If you have gone through the previous steps carefully, you will lessen the chances of things going wrong.

## Require learner participation

Learners should not just be passive viewers or consumers of resources. This book is based on the belief that learning should be active and based on constructivist principles of learning. A video should stimulate discussion, analysis and evaluation of its content and its application to the topic. PowerPoint presentations shouldn't merely present; they should leave spaces where learners can offer responses and ideas. Printed resources become more meaningful to learners if they can personalise and interact them with them in some way.

## Evaluate and revise

All resources can and should be refined and improved with subsequent use. In some cases they might be rejected as unsuitable for purpose. Evaluation and revision is part of being a reflective teacher committed to continuing improvement. Part of your resource evaluation might be done by 'reflection in action', by watching your learners and their reactions to the resource. You can easily detect 'death by PowerPoint' by observing your learners' body language. You can also seek specific feedback on it and ask learners if it helped their understanding of the topic. Course or module evaluation questionnaires usually include feedback on resource provision and use.

Obviously, the ultimate test of a resource is whether it achieved the required purpose. One test of this is the learners' performance: can they do what you wanted them to do or do they know what you wanted? You should also ask yourself, and your learners, if the resource can be used differently or adapted in some way; whether it represented an effective use of time. Did the resource arouse learners' interest and attention? Did it stimulate discussion or encourage learners to engage with the task? All of these questions should stimulate analysis and evaluation of the resource and any necessary modifications and improvements for future use.

## Resources for teaching and learning

This section is an introductory survey of a range of resources; it is not an exhaustive list. You will find others or observe colleagues using others. You will also start to develop your own which will be hybrids of these, or something completely new. The use of PowerPoint is discussed in the section on technology.

## Whiteboards

Whiteboards have almost completely replaced chalkboards in educational establishments. Rather than discuss the merits and demerits of whiteboards, I offer some bullet point guidance to their use:

- Avoid 'absent-minded professor' style rambling, scrawling coverage of the board. Keep the content well organised and to a minimum.

- Use the right pens. Ensure that the pen you are using says 'dry-wipe' or 'whiteboard marker'. Permanent markers are not suitable and require special solvents to remove them. Never keep permanent and dry-wipe markers in the same place.

- An interactive board is *not* a whiteboard. You cannot write on an interactive whiteboard with any can kind of marker other than the stylus provided with it. If you're planning to use an interactive board, it's best not to bring any markers into the room.

- Keep the writing legible, clear and a size that can be read by all. If in doubt walk to the back of the room and see if you can read it.

- Use capitals and lower case printed letters. Don't use capitals only, they are more difficult to read.

- Organise your board use with headings, subheadings, boxes and bullet points.

- Use diagrams and concept maps.

- Keep board writing to a minimum. As far as possible use it to provide advance organisers and to summarise key points. You might find it useful to write your objectives on the board before the start of the session. If you have extensive written input, plan it into your session and prepare an overhead transparency (OHT) or PowerPoint.

- Try to avoid lengthy periods with your back to the audience as you write and don't speak to the board.

## Overhead projector

Data projectors and PowerPoint have not taken over completely. It's probably still true to say that the most widely used method of displaying information to groups, especially large groups, is by using overhead projection. Lifelong learning takes place in a variety of situations, many of which will not have enough funds to install expensive data projectors and interactive boards.

First, let's get the terminology right. An OHT is an overhead transparency, the acetate on which you write or print what you want to project. An OHP, an overhead projector, is the device you put the OHT on to project it. The chief advantage of an OHP is that you don't have to have your back to the audience as you do when using a whiteboard. The key to using an OHP effectively is to practise and experiment. If you're a trainee teacher you should get the opportunity to use one – if not ask for it.

Guidelines for using overhead projectors:

- Experiment and practise so that you can be confident in classes. Practise placing and moving the OHP, adjusting the focus, moving the projector nearer or further away to alter the size of the image. Practise pointing things out by pointing at the transparency, not the screen.
- Design – the best OHTs are used as frameworks for learning. Keep the number of words to a minimum. Try to limit the number of lines to 8–10, double spaced and use bullet points to increase emphasis and focus.
- Design – use 20 point minimum font size to ensure that the OHT is visible by all. Go to the back of the room and check visibility; you shouldn't have to ask people if they can see.
- Use capitals and lower case, not all capitals. Use landscape rather than portrait layout.
- OHT pens come in a variety of colours in both permanent and non-permanent forms. However, it's probably best to design your OHT on a computer and then use inkjet or laser printer transparencies to print directly on to. Alternatively, you can photocopy directly on to transparencies but be sure to use ones which are specifically designed for this purpose; using write-on acetates in a photocopier will cause serious damage – not to mention embarrassment!
- You can amend and annotate your OHTs in use with non-permanent marker pens.
- Do not copy a page from a book directly on to a transparency. People will not be able to read it and you will rarely need everything that's on the page. Isolate key points or quotes and prepare them using the guidelines above.
- Don't have a series of transparencies of things for learners to copy down. There's little point in copying things. If you have designed your OHTs well, you can give learners copies which they can amend and personalise.
- Don't leave the projector running longer than necessary; the noise is annoying and the continued projection will be distracting if you've moved on to the next point.

## Flipcharts

Flipcharts are large pads of paper, usually supported on a stand, which can be used in a similar way to a whiteboard when there isn't one available. Flipcharts can be used in more informal, student-centred sessions where you want to record and refer back to the narrative of the session and identify the key points. Individual sheets can be torn off and given to learners to use in group activities, which are then stuck on the walls for student presentations and reference purposes. Some teachers use prepared flipchart sequences which they can take to learning sessions at a variety of venues. However, the production of these is time consuming and is not really necessary where OHPs or data projectors are available.

## DVD, video and audio

I have to admit that in my early days of teaching liberal studies to day-release, vocational students in a further education college, I frequently found myself with little time to prepare and only a vague idea of what to teach. Like many of my colleagues, I found the answer in an extensive collection of videos kept in a cupboard. 'Show 'em a video' was the maxim of the hard-pressed liberal studies lecturer. This is very bad advice and under no circumstances should it be followed. Being a reflective teacher, however, I learned a lot from this experience; mainly, not to use too much video.

Audio recordings are still used but generally in specific subjects or topic areas. Studying poetry is enhanced by hearing the poems recited and it's easy to locate recordings, often by the poet, from various websites. Music obviously needs to be heard. Audio allows learners to concentrate on the sound and structure of musical pieces, without the competing stimulus of the visual element. Digital technology is making it much easier to find and select music; you can even incorporate sound clips into PowerPoint presentations. Video recordings, and increasingly DVD, provide valuable learning experiences provided that their use is properly planned and prepared.

### Guidelines for using video and DVD

- In the session planning and resource selection stages, it is important to be sure if and why you need to use video recordings. In some instances it is the only alternative: if hairdressing students want to observe a particular technique by a famous stylist, a video or DVD might be the only way. Video and DVD offer the possibility for learners to see experts operating in a particular field. Your reason for using video could be to provide variety in teaching techniques. There's nothing wrong with this provided the piece is relevant and brief.

- You can use video to provide an introduction or an overview to a topic, to provide 'the big picture'. A video can be used to stimulate discussion and explore issues, particularly in science, social science or humanities. Some training videos, in sport for example, can be used to demonstrate and exemplify good practice or technique.

- Having prepared the session you need to prepare the learners. State clearly what the video extract is, why you are using it, and how it relates to the topic. It can be useful to point out what learners should look for or particular questions they might consider. A question sheet or key points sheet can be distributed prior to viewing, although there is a danger that learners will concentrate on the printed sheet and only look for those suggested.

- If you are using a video recording, have it set at the right starting point to avoid embarrassing searching while the group grows restless. Be sure that you know the controls of that particular machine and that the conditions – lighting, seating, visibility – are appropriate. Ensure the quality of sound and vision.

- Break up the viewing of a long extract to allow for checking of learning and discussion. Remember that people watching TV and videos at home have made a choice; in teaching you have imposed your choice. Learners will have varying attention spans and you should monitor the learners for signs of boredom or distraction.

- DVD and digital technology is more manipulable and this makes selection and editing easier. You can record your own DVD of particular extracts so that you don't have to sit or fast forward through irrelevant material. Video clips can be inserted into PowerPoint presentations and thus be more integrated into the session.

- There must be a proper follow-up to the use of video. This is more likely to happen if you have prepared learners beforehand. Remember, a video is not an end in itself, it has a purpose. That purpose may be: to stimulate discussion; to identify key points; analysis; recognition of good practice; or criticism and evaluation.

- Whatever happens, don't let the end of the video coincide with the end of the session. If it does, there will be no time for discussion or feedback and learners will not easily recall in the next session.

Video sites such as YouTube carry a bewildering variety of short films and video clips, some of which will be very useful in your teaching though most won't be. However, with careful selection and previewing it might be more convenient for you to use this than go to the trouble of setting up the equipment. Another site for useful video clips and films is BBC Learning Zone Broadband Class Clips www.bbc.co.uk/learningzone/clips/.

## Printed resources

### Handbooks

Course handbooks are vital if learners are to have 'the big picture', even if it's a short course. Learners feel ill at ease when they can't see the framework of what, why, when and how they are doing things. A course handbook provides this information and forms an intrinsic part of the course induction. It's worth spending time on the original version of the course handbook; subsequent versions will only need additions and improvements. Make it look professional and well presented by taking time and seeking advice on the design and content. It's one of the first things learners will see and helps to form an impression of the organisation and its staff. Remember, the more informed and supported learners feel, the more likely they are to achieve. The exact contents of a course handbook will vary from course to course, but the following provides some suggestions:

- Details course, title, level, relevant extracts from the specifications.
- Details of staff, locations, where resources can be found.
- Course map showing the sequence and timings of the units or modules. Try to provide visual map of the course structure.
- Schedule or scheme of work. You don't need to give learners the same scheme of work document as you use but a schedule of dates with key topic areas shown is useful for them.

- Key dates, for example a calendar showing dates of assessments, visits, tutorials and support sessions.

- Resources – give your learners a reading list and details of relevant websites and journals.

- Assessments – indicate the range, frequency and type of assessment during the course.

Design the handbook so learners can add to it and personalise it and make sure it's a working document that is regularly referred to by learners and teachers. You can make them available electronically via an intranet or virtual learning environment (VLE) for students who prefer to work this way and access things from home.

Module handbooks provide specific details of each element of the course and serve as an introduction to new modules or units. They can also give specific details of the assessments and include overviews of any relevant theories or key ideas. A good module handbook will serve as an advance organiser for a module and will aid learners in making sense of and organising their work.

## Handouts

What is a handout? The easy answer is that it is a paper-based resource that you hand out to learners. But do we think enough about why and how we use them? Do our learners know clearly what they are for and what to do with them? Student feedback often criticises the use of too many handouts. Conversely, handouts can encourage laziness and poor attendance. If students think that the handouts equal the lesson, all they need to do is collect them at a later date. Let's identify the range of handouts and why they are used.

### Information sheets

A handout giving background, facts, information or statistics can be a useful accompaniment to input from the teacher. The content should be kept to a minimum and not contain information irrelevant to the topic. The handout should support the input, not distract from it. You should, wherever possible, make it interactive in some way so that learners can add to it and personalise it. This helps to make the learning meaningful.

### Worksheets

These give learners something to do; they have to answer questions, add information, or complete it in some way. An obvious example would be an English grammar worksheet on using apostrophes. You can obtain or produce a range of worksheets at different levels so that you can differentiate the learning within a group. They can also be used independently by learners in their own time.

### Activity sheets

These are similar to worksheets, but are generally used to support a student (often group) activity. Examples would be: a problem that learners have to solve; a mini-case study; a discussion point. An activity sheet can provide guidance and instructions for a particular exercise or group activity.

### Notes

These might be more appropriate for a lecture where you provide copies of your notes or PowerPoint presentation to your learners. Again, the question is why? You might feel it is wasted effort for learners to write as much as they can of what you say or to copy every slide you project so you provide them with copies of the notes. It's important to ensure that learners do something with them to make them personal and to incorporate the learning.

### Readings

It is sometimes appropriate to give learners a reading – perhaps an extract from a book, journal, newspaper or magazine article. Be prepared to edit and keep it to the minimum required. Avoid photocopying a page from a book because it can look scruffy and unprofessional. Scanners are easy to use and a scanned copy can be stored electronically, retrieved and modified as required. Newspaper articles can generally be downloaded from the site and adapted to purpose. You might want to provide some questions and activities at the end of the article.

### Gapped handouts

Gapped handouts are a useful learning and assessment device. The text of the handout leaves gaps for learners to fill or to answer questions. A particular form is the cloze exercise in which learners have to supply specific words to fit in the gaps, either from a list provided or from memory. An example of a cloze exercise in literacy on the use of 'their' 'there' and 'they're' could include the following examples:

'_____ coming for dinner'

'I left my bike over _____'

'Have you seen _____ photographs?'

## A house style for printed resources

This is not just a case of style over content. Using a document template for your printed resources not only looks professional but can also help your learners to organise their files and resources more easily (see Figure 7.1). Use the organisation logo and perhaps a course logo you have designed. Include the course and unit or module title and a space for the learners to write the date. Dating printed resources is one of the most useful things you can do to help students organise the work in their files. If the budget will run to it, you could print different modules on different coloured paper, but check with your learners to see if it suits them – some dyslexic learners prefer everything on yellow paper.

FAB
College
*Further and
Better*

AS Media Studies

Module 2:     Analysing Media Texts

Date_____

**Figure 7.1** Example of handout template.


## Design guidelines for printed resources

It's worth spending some time considering the design and presentation of your printed resources to make them more attractive and easier to use. The Basic Skills Agency guide to readability can now be downloaded from the NIACE website (www.shop. niace.org.uk/media/catalog/product/R/e/Readability.pdf). This guide provides valuable design advice for materials for all learners, not just those with reading problems. Its suggestions include the following.

### White space
Avoid handouts that are too crowded. Leave space between paragraphs and wide margins to allow for easier reading and to give room for learners' annotations. Acres of densely packed text are offputting for anyone. Avoid using newspaper-style columns.

### Line spacing
Lines too close together can be difficult to read. Consider using 1.5 line spacing. In some cases double line spacing might be necessary.

### Font choice and size
Modern computers provide a huge variety of fonts, many of which just look silly. You can use a fancy font or WordArt design for a logo or heading, but for text the best choices are shown in Figure 7.2.

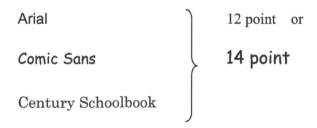

Arial

Comic Sans

Century Schoolbook

12 point   or

**14 point**

**Figure 7.2** Recommended fonts and sizes for printed resources.

**Headings**
Use headings and subheadings to organise the text. The heading can be in a larger or emboldened typeface to provide emphasis. Don't use capital letters for headings. In general, it's best to avoid overuse of capitals.

**Illustrations and clipart**
These can help to break up text and make it more interesting and readable. You should choose the amount and style of illustrations to suit your learners. Some might feel patronised by excessive and or irrelevant clipart.

## Learning centres and libraries

If you teach in college, school or university you will almost certainly have access to a learning centre. Most people working in information services prefer the term 'learning centre' because they don't just provide books. A well-equipped learning centre is likely to provide at least the following:

- books
- academic journals
- newspapers and magazines
- video/DVD and audio recordings
- CD-Rom
- internet access
- inter-library loans and electronic access to materials in other places
- study skills materials
- photocopying/laminating/binding facilities.

In addition, your learning centre should provide access to vast stores of research and knowledge through information systems such as the Educational Resource Information Centre (ERIC) which is the world's largest educational database. Similar services are provided by EBSCO that specialises in electronic journals; InfoTrac for online newspaper archives, and several publishers who provide e-books. There are many reference services, such as the Oxford Reference Online, that provide dictionaries, thesauruses and a wide range of specialist dictionaries.

**Get to know your learning centre colleagues**
People who work in learning centres are proud of what they do and want to use their skills and knowledge to help you. In many organisations they are encouraged to provide sessions for learners on, for example, finding books or finding electronic resources. If you're planning a new course or preparing for a new year, you might find it useful to include learning centre staff at your planning meetings. Learning centre staff can advise you on finding information, developing the stock of books and materials for you and your learners, and even helping you to devise assignments.

Digital technology is bringing a convergence of the activities of learning and teaching, learning and information services and information and learning technology (ILT). To provide the best for your learners you should develop good working relationships with these colleagues. Your induction into the organisation should include these elements; if it doesn't you should seek it out.

If you don't work for a large organisation, or at an outreach centre, you may not have such easy access to facilities. If you have computers and internet access you will be able access almost as much information as anyone else, although some subscriber services will be beyond the reach of your budget. If you have space you can start your own mini-library of books and other printed materials relevant to your teaching area. Your learners can be co-opted into this enterprise by locating and providing resources which the whole group can share.

## Models and 'realia'

'Realia' is a horrible word; it simply means real things. In junior school we had a nature table to which I, being a country kid, contributed armfuls of sticky buds and the occasional tadpole. Sometimes we need not only to see things but also to touch, move and manipulate them. At the first FE college I worked in the motor vehicle department had an excellent cutaway engine which could be turned by means of a handle to show the movement of pistons, valves and other elements. Such sophisticated working models are rare now because of expense, but it's worth approaching manufacturers and employers for help or for old things you can modify or adapt.

Models can be used to support demonstrations. I recently observed a trainer in the ambulance service explaining anatomy using a full-scale, accurate skeleton which could be disassembled and assembled. It was particularly useful in asking the learners to identify bones, groups of bones and the relationships between them.

In the skeleton example, scale and accuracy are important, but models don't always have to be so accurate. In science teaching models of atoms enlarge the structure and allow learners to disassemble and manipulate the electrons and protons. Many objects can be pressed into service to demonstrate and explain, for example, marshmallows and spaghetti or straws can make quite intricate models. I recall my brother using a football, marbles, apples and oranges to explain the solar system to me. The exact proportions and distances could not be accurately scaled down but the demonstration really captured my imagination.

## Visits and trips

Sometimes you just have to go and see things. Anyone studying the Industrial Revolution in England will find the learning significantly enhanced by a visit to Ironbridge and Coalbrookdale to see where it all began. Museums and art galleries are the obvious choices for visits and the educational facilities are becoming increasingly sophisticated and interactive. Most museums and art galleries have websites which show some of their major exhibits. A virtual visit is not as good as the real thing but it can help you to plan and prepare for the actual visit and decide what you most need to see and do.

Visits can be arranged to give learners insights into particular areas of work, for example; business and retail, childcare, health care, construction and engineering. Before taking learners on visits you must check the policy and guidelines relating to visits and seek permissions from parents if necessary. You must also ensure that appropriate insurance and health and safety regulations are arranged.

## Using technology

It isn't compulsory to use ILT in your teaching. There is still a lot to be said for the possibilities of simply a room, some learners, a teacher and a whiteboard. Increasingly, teachers and students use several different kinds of technologies every day of their lives as naturally as they might use books and pens. People of all ages use social media, 4G phones, iPads, electronic readers and probably several devices which will come into existence between the writing of this book and its publication.

Using technology will not make a bad teacher good; an ineffective teacher with a PowerPoint and a data projector will probably remain ineffective but in new and surprising ways. An effective and reflective teacher will use technology to enhance and develop their *teaching*, not just their use of technology. We are frequently told that work in the future will be interconnected and rapidly changing; this includes the work of teachers. Confronted by the full panoply of technological devices and possibilities, many teachers may feel overwhelmed. You can't and shouldn't be expected to use everything; just concentrate on what is most immediately useful for you and your learners' needs. Clarke (2011: 3) suggests:

> New technological and e-learning approaches are continually being developed. You do not have to jump on every bandwagon but it is important to include technology in your CPD activities so that you are aware of the possibilities and are able to judge if a new development would be appropriate.

The importance of CPD in technology applies to learning providers at least as much as it does to individual teachers. The British Educational Communications and Technology Association (Becta) no longer exists but undertook considerable work in supporting the development of ICT in education. One of its later documents (Becta 2009: 4) outlines some of the ways in which technology is changing colleges but suggests that 'if technology is changing the way colleges operate, it is having too little impact on the role of the teacher'. According to Becta, colleges are currently spending up to 80 per cent of their IT budgets just on keeping their systems running, leaving little for innovation. This problem is exacerbated by young people coming into learning whose personal IT equipment is more advanced than that of learning providers. To support colleges in their ICT development Becta provided a range of services, some of which should still be available in archive, including the 'Generator Technology Improvement Tool'. Becta suggest that teachers need ongoing support and training 'without fear of judgement. Training and development should be about raising confidence and enabling staff' (Becta 2009: 8).

### 'Digital natives' and 'digital immigrants' – do they really exist?

The answer is probably that we don't know, but it might be useful to consider this widely used phrase to see if it has any useful meaning. The concept of 'digital immigrants' and 'digital natives' was developed by Marc Prensky (2001), partly to highlight the rapid growth of digital technology and the assumed gap between old and young. 'Digital immigrants' are people above the age of about 25 who, though they try to learn and catch up with the latest digital technology, have not grown up with it. 'Digital natives' have never known life without digital technology and its concomitant devices. Prensky suggests, somewhat controversially, that their brains may have developed differently.

Recently the divide between 'natives' and 'immigrants' has been criticised as overly simplistic and, more importantly, not accurate. It may well be the case that children and young people have been accustomed to digital technology for as long as they can remember. However, this doesn't mean that they are all equal in their abilities and their interests, just as all young guitar players don't have equal facility or motivation. There is also the question of access in that children from poorer families may not have such a 'technology-rich' environment. Neither does age necessarily mean there is a 'digital divide', as evidenced by many 'tech-savvy' senior citizens. Steve Jobs was not born in a digital age, but he developed many of the devices which 'digital natives' use so naturally and easily. We should not necessarily assume that technology has widened access and reduced inclusion. Research evidence suggests that information technologies in education have, to some extent, tended to reinforce existing inequalities in access and achievement:

> The evidence is strong that, despite many efforts to use technology to overcome social exclusion, it has tended to reinforce social divisions, with people who use the internet for learning, or for gathering information, tending to be those with the highest levels of previous education, and the best access to traditional learning.
>
> (McNair and Quintero-Re 2008: 82)

In summary, the notion of digital native and digital immigrants might have been useful in reminding us of the rapid development of technologies, but such a simplistic divide does not help us to understand and plan for the complex nature of our learners' needs in the lifelong learning sector.

### Technology and motivation

One of the key questions in all sectors of education is how to motivate learners. Technology can do much to interest and motivate learners but we shouldn't assume that just because young people enjoy engaging with technology at home and with their friends that any use of technology in learning will automatically motivate them. Clarke (2011: 40) outlines a number of motivational benefits from using technology, including:

- flexibility – freedom to access learning when and where they prefer
- communication – opportunities for information exchange and mutual support
- independent learning
- improved access for disabled students
- encouraging learners to create and publish resources
- developing self-reflection through e-portfolios and blogs.

## Terminology – what do we call all this stuff?

Powell et al. (2003) developed Figure 7.3 based on the original by Markos Tikris of the Learning and Skills Development Agency to explain the relationship between the key terms.

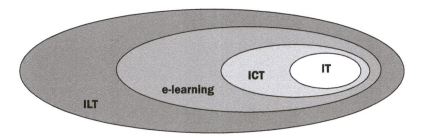

**Figure 7.3** The relationship between the key elements of ILT.

- *information technology (IT)* simply refers to the equipment such as computers, printers and scanners. The computer is the hub around which all the various technologies converge and interact.
- *information and communication technology (ICT)* is what you get when you connect computers within an institution via a local area network (LAN) or an intranet, or beyond it via the internet.
- *e-learning* is the use of IT/ICT to support teaching and learning specifically not including the management of the business. E-learning ranges from the provision of, for example, computers and CD-Roms in a teaching room through to the provision of wholly online learning which can be accessed at any place and time. The mixing of traditional teaching and learning with e-learning in various proportions is often referred to as *blended learning*.
- *information and learning technology (ILT)* refers to the application of IT/ICT to the main business of the organisation, learning and teaching, but also the management and business systems.

The picture has been further confused by arrival of terms such as *m-learning* (mobile learning), *blended learning, online learning* and *technology-enhanced learning*. One of the most frequently used terms is *e-learning*, which is the one I prefer. Some people just talk about 'technology'.

## Using ILT to enhance and develop teaching and learning

You might not consider yourself a champion of e-learning but it's almost certain that you will have been involved in some way, even if only limited. If you have used word-processing and clipart to produce handouts; accessed the internet, or used a PowerPoint then you're already on the way. You will want to follow up this introductory survey with more specific and detailed reading.

### Data projectors

Data projectors are the starting point for projecting anything from an electronic source to whole groups of learners. The most common uses are projecting PowerPoint presentations, projecting the teacher's computer display so that it can be seen from a distance and showing video film or clips.

At present it's probably still true that most rooms used across the lifelong learning sector – FE colleges, work-based learning, adult and community learning – will not have data projectors. Some rooms will have fixed projectors, in other cases you will need a portable one. If they are available to you, make sure you get the proper training in their use and know where you can find technical support in case of problems. Unless you're an expert, it's not a good idea to stand on a table and start fiddling hopefully with the equipment. You will also need to know how to connect your laptop to the system and connect to a network if available. Learn and practise the use of the technology before you meet the learners.

### Interactive whiteboards

The interactive whiteboard looks like an ordinary whiteboard but with a computer image projected on to it. The teacher or learners can touch the board to control the computer or write on the board electronically. The interactive whiteboard has many uses and here are a few:

- You can display any file from your computer or display internet pages.
- You can project PowerPoint displays. You can just tap or double-tap the board to progress the slides or bring in animated sections.
- Using the stylus markers provided, you can use it like a conventional whiteboard, with the added facility to turn your writing into text and save it. Never have a conventional whiteboard marker anywhere near an interactive board.
- You or the learners can annotate PowerPoint slides using the stylus pens.
- You can save your 'board work' and convert it to handouts for your learners or store it on an intranet.
- You can use drag and drop and reveal techniques, particularly in PowerPoint, and invite learners up to the board to operate these facilities.

- Drawing packages in Microsoft Word, Visio or other programs can be used to add visual elements.

- Interactive boards usually have object galleries of clipart and shapes. I've used these successfully with trainee teachers who have dragged and dropped tables and chairs around on the board to explore different room layouts.

- A whole range of programs can be used with interactive boards. Concept-mapping programs are excellent; they can be prepared beforehand and expanded and collapsed to explore connections.

- Learners and teachers can control the board and edit displays using a wireless keyboard and mouse or a tablet PC.

## PowerPoint

When we prepare a PowerPoint presentation for the learning session, we forget that it might easily be the second, third or even fourth time that day that learners have been exposed to this resource. 'Death by PowerPoint' is a result of this program being used in dull, didactic sessions where teachers bring up a succession of slides and talk learners through them. Trainee teachers are warned of the dangers of 'chalk and talk'; the new hazard is 'click and talk'. While there are no recorded cases of 'death by PowerPoint' there are certainly instances in which learners have been bored into a state resembling death quite closely. PowerPoint used in this way is nothing more than a 'posh' use of OHTs, especially if learners are required to copy the content of each slide. Excessive reliance on this program, like excessive use of OHTs, can have a 'distancing' effect in that it separates teachers from learners and comes between them. In the worst instances, teachers stop being teachers and just operators of technology and readers of slides.

### A critique of PowerPoint

PowerPoint is a useful tool, but don't let it become the only tool in your box. Like other resources, it's there to support teaching and learning, not to dictate the form and structure of it. So what's wrong with this technology? Basically, nothing; it's how is used that's the problem. In one of the first critiques of PowerPoint, Edward Tufte claims:

> The core ideas of teaching – *explanation, reasoning, finding things out, questioning, content, evidence, credible authority not patronizing authoritarianism* – are contrary to the cognitive style of PowerPoint.

Tufte goes as far as to assert that 'bullet outlines can make us stupid' (Tufte 2006: 13, original emphasis). The main criticism is that PowerPoint encourages, almost compels, teachers to adopt a linear structure. Such linear structures, organised around bulleted lists and stock PowerPoint templates with frequently annoying or irrelevant clipart, can all too easily reinforce teacher-dominated sessions with learners as mere 'viewers', probably not even bothering to take notes because they know they will be given a printout of the slides.

Teachers in the lifelong learning sector are becoming more familiar with constructivist learning theory and the importance of finding ways to help learners construct and critique their own learning. A useful method to support this kind of activity is a concept map, a device which doesn't feature on PowerPoint templates. Constructivist learning and teaching and concept maps show learners that knowledge and ideas exist in complex and changing networks, not in the simple linear steps which form the basis of a PowerPoint presentation.

### Towards a more creative use of PowerPoint

Having apparently demolished the potential of this resource, we can now consider how it can be used effectively in teaching and learning. The best use of PowerPoint involves applying it in a way that provides a framework for the session. If there are things that you would regularly write on a whiteboard in more or less the same way, you could put them on to a PowerPoint slide; the slides then become a backdrop to the session rather than the main focus of it.

The judicious use of bullet points can be a useful device for summarising the key points of a topic or of a learning session and it's a good technique to use custom animation to introduce them one by one. You should remember to include learners' summary points, otherwise it just gives the appearance that the teacher knows all the answers. PowerPoint can be used successfully with an interactive whiteboard to add learners' points and convert them to text.

---

**Activity**

*PowerPoint*
Analyse and evaluate one of your own PowerPoint presentations. Consider, for example:

- How many slides are there? Do you need that many?
- Is it a 'framework' for the session or does it include most of the content?
- How 'crowded' are the slides? (See the design hints for using PowerPoint.)
- Are the learners passive or does the presentation encourage activity and involvement?
- Ask your learners what they think about the use of PowerPoint.

---

## Design hints for powerpoint slides

- Font size should be 24pt minimum. Design templates are often set with 40pt for titles and 28pt for body text; this can be too much, so feel free to adjust it
- Line spacing should ideally be 1.5 or even double. As with OHTs, avoid too many lines per slide, perhaps 6 maximum.

- Avoid too much content. Slides which are crowded with text and/or graphics can be too 'noisy' and make it difficult for learners to see the main points. Remember – less is more!

- PowerPoint provides some nice design packages which automatically adjust and coordinate design, colour and font. However, you should consider designing your own, especially if you want a 'corporate image'.

- White backgrounds can be too dazzling so use a gentler pastel shade. Some font colours, particularly bright and light ones, are difficult to read. It's generally best to stick to dark colours for fonts. If you have learners with dyslexia or sight difficulties, ask them what they prefer so that you can design slides to suit them.

Be creative with PowerPoint. It can do a lot of things that many teachers don't even know about, let alone use. Features include: action buttons; animation; incorporation of video and sound; hyperlinks to other presentations, programs and websites. Try designing a PowerPoint package that is non-sequential and gives you the opportunity to go to different places in the presentation using action buttons. I've designed a package on using thinking skills where I can choose a topic area from the introductory page and go to it by action buttons. You can develop packages that use 'drag and drop' as matching exercises and invite people up to the board to use them. You can also use reveal techniques to uncover answers to a quiz or an assessment or to uncover concealed information. Using action buttons you can devise assessments or quizzes where people select an answer to a question and the button reveals the right or wrong answer with explanations and further information. You can download quiz timers and question ladders (see Further reading) to make them more fun. There are many gaming packages that you can download, sometimes for free.

### TurningPoint

Another way you can enhance your presentations is by using TurningPoint, an audience response system based on PowerPoint technology that gives learners the opportunity to participate and interact in learning sessions by voting and submitting responses to interactive questions using a keypad. The results of the interaction can be displayed in the form of graphs or charts. The technology and equipment will require some investment but it's worth investigating (see www.turningtechnologies.com).

### Digital cameras (still and video)

Using photography with students used to be so difficult that teachers rarely bothered. With digital cameras, some of which are very cheap, it's no longer a problem and even fairly basic phones have a camera included. Think of ways in which you can motivate and involve your learners by letting them use digital cameras to include images in their work and presentations, to include in blogs or on websites. Just experiment. If an image is no good, just delete it; all you are using is battery power. For example, a session on body language and facial expression could be enhanced by learners taking pictures of different expressions and using them to assess others' understanding of non-verbal communication. Clearly, the possibilities can be further extended by using video clips.

## The internet

The internet is so commonly used that I don't need to explain what it is. Its use is widespread in colleges and schools, not to mention controversial. Let me express my bias immediately. I feel uncomfortable when learners' first action in any research or problem solving is to look on the internet. However, whether or not I feel uncomfortable is largely irrelevant because it's what young learners do. My problem is the tendency to regard everything found on the internet as of equal value. A search for information on Mozart will bring thousands of hits, many of which will be reliable, trustworthy and accurate; others, however, will be the products of Mozart obsessives who have a less than impartial interpretation of him and his works. Quality control is a problem with the internet. On the other hand, the internet is a very democratic medium that allows people with no previous opportunities for publishing to share ideas. It can break down the notion of experts and amateurs.

Having offered some words of caution we must accept that the internet is a central part of life and therefore we need to embrace it as part of our work as teachers. It offers quick and easy access to a vast amount of information which can be accessed at any time in any place. Specialist websites exist for all areas of learning. Teachers in the lifelong learning sector are increasingly well catered for; check out the Gold Dust resources available through the LSIS Excellence Gateway.

### Evaluating websites

The internet provides huge amounts of very useful information; it also appears to provide an even larger quantity of rubbish. As teachers we need to be able to critically evaluate websites and to judge their authority, credibility and reliability – and to encourage our learners to do the same. You could use the 'Who? What? To whom? How? Why? formula set out in Chapter 3 'Communication and the Teacher'. Pritchard (2009: 16) offers some key website attributes against which we can make judgements:

- *Authority* – who has written the site? What are their credentials or qualifications to support their authority? Does it contain advertising, if so does it influence the content?

- *Purpose, audience and relevance* – what is it for? Who is the intended audience; is it generalist or specialist? Is it aimed at a particular age group?

- *Objectivity* – does it contain any bias? Does it confuse fact and opinion? Is it well referenced? Does it represent a range of views?

- *Accuracy and currency* – how accurate is it? Check it against something you know to be correct. Is it up to date? When was it last updated?

## Blogs

This is shorthand for 'weblogs'. These are online personal logs or diaries which groups or individuals develop to share ideas and points of view. Many of your learners will write their own weblogs and will want to use this format to record their learning journals and submit them for assessment. Some colleges actively encourage this and have developed systems to accommodate them. Personalised learning is likely to become electronic with the development of e-portfolios. Futurelab's report 'Personalisation and Digital Technologies', states that 'many learners today are already creating personalised environments for themselves outside school using digital resources' (Green et al. 2005). Blogs need motivated learners to keep up the regular inputs required.

## Wikis

Wikis provide a way in which learners and/or teachers can work collaboratively to build a joint document or create a shared body of knowledge and ideas. All of the group members edit the pages and add information. As Clarke (2011: 36) points out, wikis require a systematic approach and agreement to work together. Wikis also provide opportunities for self-assessment and peer assessment.

---

**For your journal**

Use the ASSURE model to develop use and evaluate a learning resource.

Consider your use of PowerPoint. Do you use it sparingly or does every lesson include a PowerPoint presentation? Why do you use it? In what ways does it enhance the learning experience?

For your ILP, as well as your journal, you should consider your ILT skills and knowledge and identify areas you need to develop or improve.

Review your printed resources and your use of them. Have any learners complained of an excess of handouts? Always ask yourself why you are using handouts and what learners do with them. Do they just file them or do they personalise and integrate into their own notes and resources?

---

**Journal extract: Martyn, training to teach popular music**

I've been developing the use of Facebook for the students. They'll able to showcase their music, have a forum for discussion/moans and (most importantly) have a less formal outlet for written work which can provide assessment criteria without the stress. I launched this project and EVERYONE is up for it.

## Further reading

Clarke, A. (2011) *How to Use Technology Effectively in Post-Compulsory Education.* London: Routledge. A very useful and concise introduction with lots of links in the Resources and Tools sections.

Whalley, J., Welch, T. and Williamson, L. (2006) *E-learning in FE*. London: Continuum.

## Websites

A6 training and consultancy company offers a range of timers for activities which can simply download and incorporate into PowerPoint presentations. Also offers useful advice about the use of wikis and concept mapping. www.A6training.co.uk

Generator Technology Improvement Tool. www.generatorfeandskills.com/

Joint Information Systems Committee for leadership in the innovative use of ICT in education and research. www.jisc.ac.uk

# 8

# Planning for teaching and learning

There is a strong relationship between thorough planning and effective teaching. Syllabuses and programme requirements should be translated into clear and comprehensive schemes of work that are understood by learners. Individual lessons should be well planned, but lesson plans should not be so inflexible that they cannot be adapted to reflect the progress of learners.

*(Handbook for Inspecting Colleges*, Ofsted 2006: para. 182)

## What this chapter is about

- Why is planning necessary?
- Planning a course
- What will I teach – where does the content come from?
- Planning a scheme of work
- Writing aims and objectives
- Producing session plans
- Using individual learning plans
- Differentiation and personalised learning

## LLUK standards

This chapter covers, at least, the following standards:
AS 1; AK 1.1; AP 1.1
CS 2; CK 2.1; CP 2.1
DS 1; DK 1.1; DP 1.1; DK 1.2; DP 1.2; DK 1.3: DP 1.3 DS 2; DK 2.1; DP 2.1; DK 2.2; DP 2.2 DS 3; DK 3.1; DP 3.1; DK 3.2; DP 3.2

## Why is planning necessary?

Consistently good teaching and learning don't just happen by accident; they are the result of thorough planning and preparation. Someone not involved in education might observe an impressive session where the teacher is performing at the top of her game: the learners are learning; the session flows effortlessly; it is clearly structured; there is a wide variety of active learning methods; there is an excellent working relationship between teacher and learners; in short, everyone is enjoying themselves. The observer might regard this is a matter of talent, natural teaching ability or luck, but appearances are deceptive. Much like the swan which appears to glide effortlessly on the water, there is considerable effort beneath the surface. Even the quality of the relationship between teacher and students is rarely a matter of good fortune, it has to be planned for and worked at.

Effective planning is a fundamental part of the process of being a reflective teacher; it is part of a cycle of PLAN–DO–REVIEW. In Chapter 2 on the reflective teacher we considered Donald Schon's concepts of reflection in action and reflection on action and suggested that continuing improvement comes from reflecting on and evaluating the effectiveness of teaching and learning sessions and drawing conclusions which will inform the planning of future sessions. In this sense, planning for teaching and learning is part of your continuing professional development and improvement.

Effective teaching and successful learning are not possible without proper planning. In short, you have to make a planning journey from the specifications or syllabus, or the competences, or the content you have negotiated with learners, to the detailed planning of individual sessions and the subsequent evaluation of those sessions. Figure 8.1 encapsulates this process.

There are three main elements to planning teaching and learning in post-compulsory education and training: long-term planning; session (or lesson) planning; individual learning plans (ILPs).

## Long-term planning

This could be for a term, a year, a module, or a sequence of sessions. A module or a sequence of sessions could be regarded as medium or short–term planning. This is generally done as a *scheme of work* document. The purpose of this long-term planning is to provide a big picture for the teaching team and the learners, showing when and in what order the content will be delivered. Schemes of work show less detail than session plans. Their main function is to ensure that the necessary content is delivered in the time available and that the teacher and learners don't get behind or ahead of schedule, to ensure a range of teaching, learning and assessment techniques, and to plan and provide resources.

## Session (or lesson) planning

This is the planning and preparation of individual teaching and learning sessions. These are usually paper documents which the teacher uses to guide him through

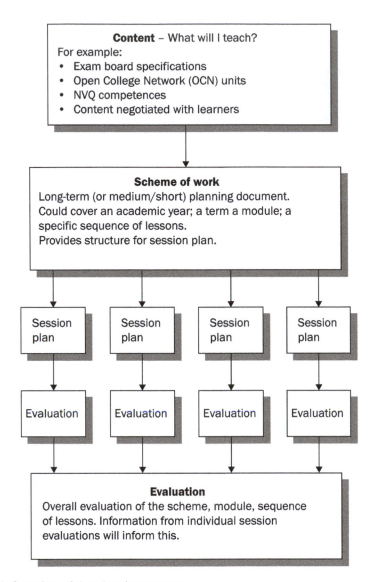

**Figure 8.1** Overview of the planning process.

the session to achieve the aims and objectives. Particularly as a trainee, you are likely to meet teachers who say they don't bother with lesson plans, generally claiming that they don't have time to do them. While it may be true that experienced teachers produce session plans which are fairly rudimentary, it is equally true that limited planning will result in limited and ineffective learning. Sessions can only be planned effectively one at a time using the session you have just delivered as a starting point.

## Individual learning plans (ILPs)

Increasingly learners and teachers will use ILPs – you will have produced one yourself if you are currently doing teacher training. ILPs are especially valuable in groups of learners who are working at different levels and progressing at different rates. ILPs, particularly in Skills for Life, are planned together with learners based on information gained from initial and diagnostic testing. They are regularly reviewed and amended by learners and teachers.

## Principles of planning

The first question a new teacher is likely to ask is 'What will I teach?' In most cases the content to be learned and assessed is provided by an examining authority (AQA, OCR, Edexcel) or by some other national or regional awarding body, in the form of specifications, or a syllabus. The form of external assessment is usually prescribed, frequently in the form of national examinations. The Open College Network (OCN) provides units with specific learning outcomes at a variety of levels. These are widely used in access and adult education courses. In NVQ-style courses, vocational competences are prescribed stating what learners should be able to do. Occasionally, teachers will be able to negotiate content to a greater or lesser extent with their learners.

Even though the content and forms of assessment are largely prescribed, the specifications do not stipulate the order of delivery, the amount of time allowed for teaching and learning, specific details of content, resources and formative assessment. The teacher, frequently as part of a team, will need to plan the course delivery and produce the scheme of work. This can be one of the most challenging, yet creative, tasks that teaching staff undertake. However, time spent thinking through and producing the scheme of work will make a significant difference to the success of the learning.

The scheme of work gives teachers the 'big picture' from which they can plan each of the sessions. A properly planned scheme of work is a working document – not a pristine document you keep in a file just in case of inspection. The scheme will probably be annotated and adjusted to some degree, although major changes to the structure and timings should be unnecessary and should be avoided. Its purpose is to keep you on track and ensure that you have covered the content, met the aims, carried out assessments and kept to the schedule. You can't afford to dwell on one particular topic because it's your 'favourite bit'. I've witnessed several occasions on which teachers have got halfway through but only covered 20 per cent of the scheme.

## What factors influence planning?

Before you begin planning your scheme there are many factors you need to consider. For the sake of consistency, I will use the same model I set out in Chapter 3, 'Communication and the Teacher', based on the five key questions:

- Who? – the teacher
- What? – the content

- Whom? – the learners
- How? – methods, strategies, resources
- Why? – the aims and purpose of the learning

Obviously, the five questions interlink and will have consequences one upon another. For example, a group of 14–16 year olds attending a college one day per week will probably need a different approach from adult learners at an outreach centre or a group of A2 students studying physics. If you want learners to develop autonomy and thinking skills, you will need to include teaching and learning methods that encourage active and deep learning. Teachers often feel that time is limited and they will have to use didactic, teacher-centred methods in order to cover all of the specification's content. This can be a mistake; limited time doesn't necessarily mean not using student-centred learning.

### Who? – the teacher

This is an unconventional starting point for planning but it is useful to consider yourself – the teacher – in relation to what you are planning to teach. We all have our specialist subjects, but the reality of life in post-compulsory education and training is that we are frequently called upon to stretch our expertise to areas we have not previously taught or even considered teaching. During my time teaching in colleges I moved from teaching general and communications to day-release students to delivering A-level communication studies and, subsequently, media studies, English language and teacher training.

You need first to consider how closely your knowledge and skills match those required in the specifications. This could be as basic as an English literature teacher reading and researching the set text or an IT lecturer familiarising herself with a new software package. You might need to develop your teaching and learning techniques to cope with new learners: for example, there has been a considerable growth recently in the number of 14–16 year olds taught by college lecturers. Teachers need support in providing for these new learners and developing new teaching and learning strategies as well as coping with some young people who may have challenging behaviour or a history of underachievement. You will have to study the specifications closely to assess your own development needs. Is your subject knowledge current? Are you up to date with the latest initiatives and research? If you're delivering as a member of a team you will need to assess the strengths of the team members and allocate teaching and learning accordingly.

### What? – are you going to teach?

If you are working from published specifications you must first make some decisions regarding the content. Are there any sections which you can edit or omit and still meet the aims and assessment objectives? You may not need to include everything in the specifications or it may be possible to condense or edit some elements. Some of the required skills and knowledge shown in the specifications can be taught as integrated units of work

The working arrangements of most teachers, particularly in FE colleges, are such that much planning has to be done before the first meeting with the learners, but for others, perhaps in adult and community education, there will be opportunities to negotiate the content and sequencing, possibly even the assessment of the course with your learners. Clearly, this is desirable since it gives learners more 'ownership' of the course and offers the possibility of integrating their own learning and experience. You need to consider the order in which you will teach the specifications. Is there a particular order suggested or implied in the specifications or can you be creative in the sequencing of learning?

Finally, what level is the course? All courses (including A-level, GCSE, NVQ. Diploma, Functional Skills) are expressed in terms of the National Qualifications Framework (NQF, see Appendix). The level indicates the level of assessment and attainment which are expected of learners at that particular stage and, as such, represents a key consideration in your planning and preparation.

## Whom? – the learners

To risk stating the obvious – learning is for learners. Consequently we need to know as much as possible about them. The following overview is not comprehensive but provides some examples of things you should consider.

First, we should consider the needs of the learners. As we shall see when we consider planning for differentiation, it is inappropriate to consider any group of learners as an undifferentiated group who have more or less the same needs and characteristics. At a fundamental level, you might have learners who have special or particular needs, such as those with hearing or sight difficulties, or wheelchair users. All learners are individuals and won't appreciate or respond to the same learning and teaching methods. Catering for these differences is difficult, especially if you are doing your planning before you meet your learners, but you can at least ensure that your planning includes a variety of teaching, learning and assessment strategies.

Second, your new students will arrive with many different experiences of learning, life and prior knowledge. You could possibly assume that learners starting an AS-level course will have similar experiences, skills and knowledge from GCSE, but even then they will have had varying success.

A group of adult learners, however, will be extremely diverse, many having had negative experiences of previous learning and with a bewildering array of existing skills and knowledge.

Other factors include motivation and commitment to learning, confidence, social and communication skills. The key to effective planning is to know as much as you can about your learners as soon as possible.

## How? – will learning happen?

The most important aspect of planning is to decide how learning will happen. Obviously, this is related to who the learners are and why they are there. If their need and your purpose is to get them passing examinations in a limited amount of time you will probably tend towards more didactic, teacher-centred learning. However, as we have seen earlier, such methods are not necessarily compatible with the development of confidence, deep learning and independent learning. You have to plan the optimum strategies to meet the needs of the institution for results but also the need to create a stimulating learning environment.

How much time is available for learning? The trend in FE colleges during the last 15 years has been towards fewer taught hours per course. How can you best accommodate the same or more content in less time? How many sessions per week will there be and how long is each one? When I taught media and film studies, learners were constantly frustrated by the need to watch films in two halves! Is it possible for some parts of the course to be given over to the students to learn for themselves? Geoff Petty (2009: 340) suggests that elements which involve straightforward, factual learning can be run as independent learning units. Clearly, there are risks in such an arrangement because it requires student commitment and organisation, but there is also a bonus in terms of development of learner autonomy and independent learning.

The range, suitability and availability of resources will affect your planning. Increasingly, teachers use ICT in their delivery extremely effectively, but learners often complain of, for example, 'death by PowerPoint'. Over-reliance on one particular resource will become tiresome for learners and teachers alike. I am always rather suspicious of trainee and experienced teachers who begin their planning by designing a PowerPoint presentation.

### Why? – the aims of the learning

There are many reasons why teachers provide courses and learners choose them – desire for success and achievement; to pass exams and gain qualifications; acquire knowledge and skills; or to develop confidence. An implicit, often explicit, aim of learning is to develop independence and responsibility in learners. All these factors will influence your planning and choice of methods.

Learners and teachers frequently have conflicting aims and purposes. While many begin their learning programmes with enthusiasm and commitment, others will be less willing, possibly even hostile. It is often assumed that all learners in post-compulsory education and training are there because they have made an individual choice to learn. Unfortunately this is not always the case. For example, a student in an FE college on a programme of 4 AS levels might have chosen yours as a last resort or because it's the only one that fits his timetable. It's part of your job to enthuse such learners and sell them your subject or area of expertise. There will be other elements which you will have to include in your planning and delivery, such as:

- inclusive learning and teaching
- functional skills
- technology
- differentiation
- employability
- developing independent learners
- developing thinking skills.

These will all be considered in detail in other chapters.

## Planning the scheme of work

**Preliminary tasks**

Find a copy of the specification/syllabus/competences for one of the courses you teach. If you haven't got one, ask a colleague or download one from the awarding body's website.

- What are the stated aims of this syllabus?
- What part/s of it are you teaching?
- What do you already know?
- What skills do you already have?
- What do you need to research?
- Take one section (a module, perhaps) and start to think about the order in which you would deliver it.

Because we can't teach everything at once, we need to break the specification content into *topics*, or 'chunks' of learning, each of which has a specific focus. These topics are assembled into an order that the teaching team thinks will provide the most effective learning experience. This ordering or sequencing of content can be difficult to decide and you will probably be familiar with colleagues in other establishments who deliver the same programmes as you do but in a very different way. For example, one team delivering an AVCE media communication and production course might develop a scheme for each of the units – some more theoretical, some more practical – while a different team might deliver holistically through a series of integrated projects.

## How is the scheme of work sequenced?

Your first task in planning a course or sequence of lessons is translate the key elements of the specifications into a broad list of topics and to consider how they should be sequenced and how much time should be allotted to each. For example, an AS English language course might include the following topics in two modules:

*Module 1 – Language framework*

- Grammar
- Punctuation
- Semantics
- Phonology
- Design/layout

*Module 2 –Writing for specific/purposes and audiences*

- Audience

- The writer
- Subject matter
- Purpose – to inform, to persuade, to instruct, to entertain
- Mode of writing

These are the topics prescribed by the examining body, but teachers can be creative in the ways in which they sequence and deliver them. One method would be to arrange them in more or less the way in which the specifications imply, one element following another. A more imaginative way might be to adopt a themed/problem-solving approach involving the examination and analysis of texts bringing the various elements of the topics as required. The approach could begin with some 'big' questions for example: 'Why and how is this article in *The Guardian* different from this article in *Hello* magazine?' 'In what ways are the audiences different?' 'What are these different texts aiming to do – amuse, inform, persuade?'

There a many different organising principles for producing a scheme of work. The following list is not exhaustive:

### Easiest first

This seems the most obvious method and will probably be true of all schemes. It would be difficult to plan for students to make complex joints in wood occupations if they hadn't previously been introduced to and practised using tools and basic techniques. Learners have to move from the 'known' to the 'unknown', from the simple to the complex. This echoes the idea of the *spiral curriculum* (see Bruner, Chapter 5, pp. 90–92) in which the same area of work can be revisited but at successively higher levels and learners can become more independent and use higher order thinking skills.

### Themed

As suggested above, it might be a more effective learning experience to integrate all the various topics into a project. This could even be developed as *problem-based learning*. For example, a childcare problem-solving approach could begin with a 'big' question such as 'Why do some children appear to be well behaved and others not?' There is much scope here for initial discussion to bring in learners' ideas and experiences and to introduce elements of theory to support or modify these inputs.

### Assessment requirements

Assessments, particularly external, are a fact of educational life and need to be planned into schemes. Some learners will be taking exams quite soon; in AS courses students starting in September might take their first exam in the following January. Remember, however, that not all assessment is so formal; there are many ways of checking and developing understanding. As far as possible, you should use assessment *for* learning, that is, formative assessment based on developmental feedback to help learners' progress (see Chapter 9, 'Assessment for Learning').

### Most interesting topics and activities first

This can apply to teachers and learners. As a teacher you might feel most confident delivering what you know or like best first. This can be a trap because it might not be the most appropriate sequencing for the learners. Doing interesting things first can be an important way of 'selling' your subject to the learners and getting them enthused and involved straightaway, especially if it involves questions or problems to be solved which, like soap opera cliff-hangers, keep them coming back for more.

## Writing the scheme of work

Having identified the main topics and considered the sequencing, your next step is to produce the actual document. Many larger learning organisations stipulate a particular format for the scheme, but if you need to design your own you should consider using the following columns on your grid:

- Date/session number
- Content/topics
- Learning and teaching activities
- Resources
- Assessment
- Key skill opportunities.

Although the scheme of work is a planning document produced by teachers for teachers and learners, you should remember that managers and inspectors will ask to see it and will often make judgements about your planning based on a fairly cursory examination. Clearly, a wide range of learning and teaching activities and assessments is important for successful learning, but you need to make it obvious on the scheme. Figure 8.2 shows an example of a scheme of work.

## Session planning

I have chosen to use the term 'session planning' rather than 'lesson planning' in this book mainly because 'lesson' planning has connotations of school-type learning in formal classroom settings. 'Session planning' seems more appropriate to the wide range of provision and learners in post-compulsory education and training.

Session planning is the most fundamental and important of all the tasks which teachers are required to do. Inspection reports from Ofsted all make the same point that: poor learning sessions are invariably badly planned sessions. Even given the wide range of learners and learning in post-compulsory education it is generally the case that all good sessions are good in similar ways and all ineffective sessions tend to have the same faults. Some of the most frequent criticisms of session planning are that the purpose, aims and objectives are not clear to learners; there is too much teacher talk and too little learner activity; learners are treated as an undifferentiated mass and there is little differentiation; there is lack of structure and poorly handled transitions; no clear conclusions and no 'rounding out' of sessions.

**FAB**
**FE College**

*Further and Better*

**Scheme of work**  Course:  AS Media Studies

Module: Key Concepts  Year: 2006-7

| Week | Topic / content | Learning / teaching activities | Assessment / checking learning | Resources | Key Skills |
|---|---|---|---|---|---|
| 1 | Representation<br>• Age<br>• Gender<br>• Race/ethnicity | Teacher input – introduction to representation<br>Groupwork – analysis of advertisements<br>Discussion<br>Poster activity | • Question and answer<br>• Poster display<br>• Discussion | Handout - definitions<br>Advertisements – Magazine and TV<br>Poster paper / scissors/ glue sticks | |
| 2 | FHM case study<br>• Introduce case study | Teacher input<br>PowerPoint presentation on representation<br>Reading<br>Discussion<br>Note taking | • Question and answer<br>• Discussion of examples<br>• Reading and discussion | Case study<br>Readings<br>PowerPoint presentation | |
| 3 | FHM case study<br>• Group workshops and preparing presentation | Small group activity preparing presentation<br>Learning centre research<br>Internet search<br>Prepare resources for presentation | • Teacher support<br>• Discussion | Learning centre<br>Internet access | WWO<br>3.1; 3.2; 3.3<br>Comm 3.2<br>ICT 3.1; 3.2<br>3.3 |
| 4 | FHM case study<br>• Student presentations | • Student presentations | • Student presentations | Data projector<br>OHP | Comm<br>3.1a; 3.1b |

**Figure 8.2** Scheme of work example.

## Why is session planning important?

### For effective teaching and learning

Basically, session planning is important because without it the learning and teaching are likely to be poor and ineffective. Poorly planned lessons will be characterised by their lack of structure, vague transitions between topics or sections, and teacher and learner uncertainty. Occasionally, teachers can take a session at short notice and 'fly by the seat of their pants', but generally it doesn't work

### So you and your learners know what you are doing

Clarity of purpose is vital to successful teaching. This begins with the teacher being clear about what they want learners to achieve, knowing the learners' starting point and previous learning, knowing how best to achieve their aims and objectives. If your students ask 'What are we doing?' and 'Why are we doing it?' there's probably something wrong with your planning. The purpose should be made clear from the start of the session.

### To provide structure

Poor sessions are generally poorly structured. In short, there should a clear beginning, middle and end with a variety of activities to mix teacher inputs and learner activities. One of the most difficult tasks for trainee teachers is judging how long each activity will last. This is why trainees spend so long on session planning, but without practice in planning they will not develop this vital skill. Each section should be introduced and explained to learners and learning summarised and checked before moving on.

### Learners' attention span is limited

In universities the traditional method of teaching has been, and in many cases continues to be, the formal lecture. The best examples of lectures are interesting, motivating and serve as a stimulus to further study. In post-compulsory education, however, the lecture is rarely used because even the most dedicated students can only listen attentively to a teacher for about 20 minutes. Excessive teacher talk nearly always produces feelings of frustration, boredom or annoyance – not the ideal conditions for learning. Unfortunately, some teachers still take the view that it is the learners' responsibility to be interested and maintain attention whatever inputs and teaching style they use. Thorough planning allows you to vary the teaching and learning activities to create and maintain learners' attention, interest and activity.

### So you don't get lost or miss vital elements

Without a written plan there is a greater chance that you will lose your way, miss vital elements, or introduce new learning for which your students are not prepared. More importantly, without a plan you are more likely to repeat things you've done previously – learners get particularly frustrated when this happens.

### To build up a bank of materials and resources

Developing a regular planning habit will help you to build up a bank of resources and materials for future use and development. Like many other teachers, I still keep a teaching file which contains the session plans and copies of printed resources I have used in each session. Rarely have I been able to take a previous session and use it unmodified for a subsequent one, but previous plans do provide starting points and the basis for continual improvement. These files are the most valuable resources you will create. I feel reassured by physical files full of paper, but increasingly teachers will store these electronically which further facilitates their modification and improvement. Electronic files can be kept as shared resources to be used by other teachers and by learners and shared through virtual learning environments (VLEs) such as Moodle.

## What is a session plan?

Many experienced and long-serving teachers will tell you that they don't have or do session plans, often claiming that there is no time to produce them. This is not good advice and there are several things wrong with such assertions. Generally these people mean that they don't produce a detailed written plan for every session. Further questioning would be likely to reveal that they do some form of planning, even if only of the most rudimentary kind. As you become more experienced your own lesson plans will probably become more concise but they will remain the key to your planning and to continuing improvement.

Session plans vary considerably in their format and style. Many teachers design their own formats, while others are obliged to use a standard format supplied at their workplace. Standard plans at least provide some consistency and are frequently well designed to encourage teachers to consider aspects of planning which they might otherwise overlook. However, it is questionable whether a standard lesson plan can be designed to cover all learning in a particular institution from tree surgery to A-level physics. One should be prepared to modify and adapt them according to need. If they are provided as word-processed templates it shouldn't be too difficult to adjust the layout and size of the boxes to suit individual needs. The Ofsted *Handbook for Inspecting Colleges* states that inspectors 'will not be prescriptive' . . . and that 'Colleges should not assume, for example, that lesson plans must be in a particular format' . . . (2006: para. 182).

In the prevailing atmosphere of increased accountability, session plans are key documents expected by managers, auditors and inspectors – this is an entirely reasonable and legitimate expectation. However, it is important to state that session plans are produced *by* teachers *for* teachers; they are not management tools to ensure compliance.

A session plan must be a written document that you can store in a file or electronically. However, the aim of session planning is not merely the production of this written document; it is the act of thinking and working out what you want to do and how you will achieve it. As Michael Marland says: 'The key to this planning, however, is not the writing down . . . [it] is the ability to think through a lesson in advance, as it were, to preview rapidly the entire stretch of time' (Marland 2002: 120).

So, what is a session plan? I would define it as follows:

*A session plan is a written guide which shows you the teaching and learning strategies, resources, assessment techniques and other key information you need to use with a particular learning group to achieve specified aims and objectives in an effective, struc-tured and enjoyable way.*

Minton (2005) refers to session plans as 'cue sheets'. This is a useful definition since it reminds us that a lesson plan is there to keep us on track and to remind us when and in what order we have planned to do things. An effective session plan means we don't have to keep all the details in our heads and allows us to concentrate on the imme-diate matters in hand. Bourdillon and Storey (2002) describe session plans as 'mental maps' because they are the physical result of imagining our way through the session.

Trainee teachers are frequently worried that they are expected to stick rigidly to their session plans and to achieve all the aims and objectives they have set. A session plan, however, is not a straitjacket; it is a guide which can be adapted and adjusted as the session develops. Inspectors will not be impressed by teachers who push their plans through relentlessly but ignore opportunities for discussion and interesting diversions which contribute to learning, especially if they relate to learners' experiences. If you regularly need to make changes and adaptations you should reconsider your planning in general. However, minor changes and adjustments should be immediately recorded on the session plan. This not only shows vital information for planning subsequent sessions, but also shows evidence of evaluation and reflection–in-action as you monitor the session's development. Clearly, lesson plans will vary in their format and style, but they should all have similar basic elements, including:

- Basic information – date, time, course, level, number of learners
- Aims and objectives
- Key topics/content
- Learner activities
- Teacher activities
- Timings and structure
- Assessment/checks on learning
- Resources
- Evidence of differentiation
- Space for comments, evaluation, notes and reminders for the next session.

## How do I plan sessions?

Essentially, planning can be reduced to three questions:

1   Who are the learners and what is their starting point?
2   What do you want to do/learn/achieve?
3   How will you facilitate and assess the learning?

Before we consider these questions it must be stressed that session planning is an activity which can only be done satisfactorily one session in advance. I have met a number of teachers who have written, or been instructed to write, batches of lesson plans in advance of delivery. One teacher proudly proclaimed that he had written a scheme of work and all the session plans for an entire year ahead. This is not session planning; it is merely the production of a very detailed scheme of work. Each learning session must be planned using the previous session as the starting point of the next. If this is not done teachers cannot truly claim to be meeting the needs of their learners or reflecting on and adapting learning as it progresses.

The starting point of planning is recalling and reviewing what was done in the previous session. Were all the objectives of that session met? Did the learners achieve? Were there any points which need to be reinforced or covered again? In addition, we need to consider the session in relation to the scheme of work and to confirm what has already been covered and what learners already know or can do. Once you've ascertained where you and the learners are now, the next part of the process is to plan what will happen this session and what you want the learners to achieve. This takes us to aims and objectives.

## Aims and objectives

There is considerable debate in more academic texts concerning the precise meaning and use of learning aims and objectives; the differences between them and other concepts such as learning outcomes or general and specific objectives. Some educationalists argue that teaching by aims and objectives is mechanistic and based on behaviourist theories of learning. As part of your continuing professional development you should engage with these debates and reach your own conclusions. Despite these debates, however, aims and objectives are still widely used to provide clarity and structure to learning sessions. The next section provides a simple introduction and guide to their use.

## Aims

Aims are general statements of what the teacher wants to achieve with the learners. They provide a 'big picture' which shows the destination of the course or of individual sessions. They are usually descriptive in that they state where learners are going, but don't describe how they will get there or what they will do on the journey. Aims can be expressed at two levels:

- course, module or unit aims
- session aims.

### Course aims
Course aims indicate a very general overall destination. They encapsulate the whole of what a student is intended to learn and are sometimes used in marketing and promoting courses. For example, the aims of a counselling skills programme could be stated as: 'To introduce participants to the principles and practice of counselling, active listening, reflection and empathy'. Course aims are frequently prescribed by examining and assessment boards.

### Session aims

Session aims are not used by all teachers, but they can be useful to put into a nutshell the purpose and direction of a session for teachers and learners. Examples of session aims could be:

- 'To understand and develop the use of the apostrophe and the comma'
- 'To be familiar with the main types of sports injuries'
- 'To introduce the concept of socialisation and identify the main agencies of socialisation'
- 'To examine strategies for motivation and control with 14–16-year-old learners in further education colleges'

In summary, course planning requires teachers to adopt prescribed aims or to create their own to describe the key purposes and destination of the course. At session level, the aims describe the purpose and destination of each particular session. Having established session aims, the next part of the process is to decide the learning objectives.

## Objectives

While aims tend to be descriptive, objectives are prescriptive, that is, they prescribe precisely what the learners will know or be able to do at the end of the session. Objectives should be measurable or observable so that the learning can be assessed. My trainee teachers, in their early planning attempts, tend to use the word 'understand' when writing objectives: for example, 'Learners will understand photosynthesis'. 'Understand' might be useful for a session's aims but it doesn't state what it is that learners will do or produce which demonstrates their understanding. To assist in writing precise objectives it can be useful to use the SMART acronym to check them. SMART encapsulates the key requirements of learning objectives – they are:

- **S**pecific – objectives relate to a specific learning activity and state clearly what learners will do
- **M**easurable – the objectives can be measured, observed or assessed in some way. Thus, *list, define, analyse, evaluate* are measurable but *understand* is not.
- **A**chievable – there's no point setting objectives that learners cannot achieve at their current level. Students need objectives that give them opportunities for achievement.
- **R**ealistic – objectives should be realistic in terms of students' level of development, the resources available and the aims.
- **T**ime-bound – objectives should be achievable within a specified time. Students are motivated by a series of relatively short-term objectives that give small, cumulative steps to achievement.

## Bloom's taxonomy

Learning objectives have to relate to levels of learning. There will be differences between what your students at Entry Level 3 will be able to do and to work towards as opposed to those at Level 3. A taxonomy is a system of classifying general principles. Benjamin Bloom developed his taxonomies of educational objectives using three domains of learning:

- the *cognitive* domain – concerned mainly with thought processes
- the *psychomotor* domain – concerned mainly with manual skills and practical skills
- the *affective* domain – concerned mainly with emotions, attitudes and feelings.

Using objectives based on Bloom's taxonomy will help you when writing schemes of work, producing lesson plans, writing assessments and giving feedback to learners. We will be concerned here mainly with the cognitive domain – defining and describing each level, providing a range of active verbs to use in writing objectives for each level, and examples of objectives at each level.

### The cognitive domain

In the cognitive domain, Bloom identified and described six levels of learning from the simple to complex.

1  Knowledge
2  Comprehension
3  Application
4  Analysis
5  Evaluation
6  Synthesis

*Note*: the verbs provided at each level are not necessarily restricted to that level alone. Neither are the lists complete, they are intended simply to illustrate examples at each level.

### Knowledge

This is the base level and refers, for example, to the observation and recall of information; knowledge of dates, places, names; knowledge of facts and ideas.

When writing learning objectives and/or assessment objectives at this level, the following verbs may be useful:

| | | |
|---|---|---|
| list | define | describe |
| identify | show | label |
| quote | name | repeat |
| reproduce | recognise | write |

collect                 measure                 match
select

Example: media studies – learners will define uses and gratifications theory.

## Comprehension

This level is to do with understanding information and ideas, comprehending meaning, interpreting, ordering and grouping. Examples of verbs for writing objectives and assessments at this level include:

| | | |
|---|---|---|
| summarise | interpret | explain |
| estimate | comprehend | clarify |
| give examples | report | rewrite |
| present | illustrate | restate |
| convert | classify | extend |

Example: media studies – learners will explain uses and gratifications theory.

## Application

At this level learning objectives are concerned with, for example, the use and application of learning; using theories, concepts and methods' solving problems. Verbs for writing objectives at this level include:

| | | |
|---|---|---|
| apply | demonstrate | calculate |
| solve | examine | modify |
| change | classify | discover |
| construct | operate | predict |
| produce | prepare | practise |
| adapt | derive | use |

Example: media studies – learners will apply uses and gratifications theory to the study of soap opera.

## Analysis

This refers to recognising and explaining relationships between components and elements; seeing patterns and organisation; recognising and understanding parts and wholes. Examples of useful verbs at this level include:

| | | |
|---|---|---|
| analyse | separate | order |
| connect | classify | deconstruct |
| arrange | divide | relate |
| infer | distinguish | contrast |
| categorise | diagnose | break down |

Example: textual analysis in media studies – learners will analyse a magazine cover in relation to audience, purpose and effect.

## Synthesis

This refers to the combination of knowledge, skills and ideas to create new understandings, to relate knowledge from several areas, to draw conclusions and develop new ideas, practices and artefacts. Examples of verbs for objectives and assessment at this level include:

| | | |
|---|---|---|
| combine | integrate | rearrange |
| create | invent | design |
| prepare | produce | propose |
| generate | organise | compose |
| adapt | synthesise | modify |
| plan | implement | reconstruct |

Examples: in media studies – learners will combine skills in video production with knowledge of film techniques to create a short pop video.

In IT – learners will combine knowledge of and skills in the use of word-processing, spreadsheets, scanners and digital cameras, and publishing packages to create a community magazine.

## Evaluation

This level is concerned, for example, with developing and using criteria to make critical and aesthetic judgements; comparing ideas and discriminating between them; evaluating effectiveness; assessing the value of different theories; the valuation of evidence; and the recognition of subjectivity. Examples of verbs used at this level include:

| | | |
|---|---|---|
| assess | decide | test |
| recommend | judge | discriminate |
| evaluate | determine | conclude |
| appraise | criticise | critique |
| value | question | discuss |

Examples: in media studies – learners will evaluate the validity and effectiveness of uses and gratifications theory in explaining media effects on audience

In IT – learners will assess and evaluate the suitability of the community magazine they have produced in relation to its audience and purpose.

## The psychomotor domain

This learning domain is concerned with manual tasks and physical movement. The taxonomy starts from copying from others to the learning becoming automatic. It is similar to the journey from unconscious incompetence to conscious competence (see Chapter 1). For example, in craft, engineering or construction it could be used when learners are acquiring skills in tools and processes. It could also be related to sports coaching and other physical activities.

### Imitation
The learner observes a skill demonstrated by another and tries to repeat or replicate it. The learners will be able to, for example – *copy, repeat, replicate.*

### Manipulation
The learner is able to perform the skill from instruction or memory. The learners will be able to, for example – *build, recreate, perform.*

### Precision
The learner can carry out or reproduce the skill reliably, usually independent of help. The learners will be able to, for example – *demonstrate, show, control.*

### Articulation
Learners can adapt, combine or integrate skills consistently and with expertise. The learners will be able to, for example – *construct, combine, coordinate.*

### Naturalisation
Learners demonstrate automatic, unconscious mastery of one or more skills at strategic level. The learners will be able to, for example – *design, manage, invent.*

## The affective domain

This domain is concerned with feelings, attitudes, emotions and behaviour. It could be used, for example, in the field of personal and social skills development. The development arises from becoming aware of attitudes, feelings and behaviour and moves towards increasing internalisation of them as core values. This domain might also be about encouraging learners to acquire and internalise safe working practices or health messages or, at a more fundamental level, challenging and modifying stereotypical attitudes towards, for example, gender, ethnicity, disability and culture.

### Receive
Learners become aware of, or are willing to hear, a particular message. The learners will be able to, for example – *listen, ask, read, acknowledge.*

### Respond
At this stage learners begin to react and participate to particular ideas or messages. The learners will be able to, for example – *respond, contribute, write.*

### Value
Learners start to adopt ideas and values voluntarily. The learners will be able to, for example – *argue, persuade, criticise.*

### Organise
At this stage learners are starting to organise ideas and beliefs and to develop a value system. The learners will be able to, for example – *defend, contrast, compare.*

### Characterise

Learners adopt and internalise values and ideas and behave consistently with them. The learners will be able to, for example – *display, influence, practise.*

## How to structure a learning session

People, learners in particular, like structure. Feedback from learners in schools, colleges and universities indicates that they do not like teachers who are unprepared and whose learning sessions are unstructured and vague. A clear structure helps learners to see where they are going; how they are going to get there; to reinforce their learning and connect it to existing knowledge and experience. This applies not only at course and module level where learners need handbooks and maps to provide them with the 'big picture', but also at session level.

Michael Marland (2002: 119) refers to the rhythm of a lesson. This is an apt metaphor which we can usefully extend. Like an enjoyable piece of music, a good session has rhythm and, to develop the musical theme further, structure, variations in pace, loudness and softness, periods of reflection and periods of activity. In your sessions, as in music, there should be smooth transition from and links between one passage and the next. There will be no 'silent' sections where nothing is happening. When you are producing a session plan, you are in a sense composing a piece to suit your learners and their needs. At session level, there are three basic elements: beginning, middle and end; or introduction, development and conclusion. We will examine the important elements at each stage.

## Introduction

Like a good salesperson, a good teacher hooks her audience immediately. First impressions count and a well-planned and well-delivered introduction will set the tone for the whole session. The opening of a session, particularly the first time you meet a group of learners, may be referred to as the 'establishment phase'. The following points are general guidelines but you should make a point of thinking them through and allowing time in your plan for them.

First, do not turn up late for the session; it makes you look unprofessional and your learners will feel that you don't respect them. Turning up late with disorganised materials and without prepared resources will not inspire your learners with confidence in your organisation and ability. Whenever possible, arrive before your learners. Get your resources sorted out – laptop set up, board pens ready, printed resources to hand – so that you can make an immediate start.

Begin the session promptly and don't wait for latecomers; other students will resent it when they've made the effort to be on time. Lateness should be challenged appropriately. Don't interrogate people in front of the whole group; they might have a genuine reason for the delay. In some learning situations, perhaps in adult and community learning, you will not need to be so disciplined regarding arrival times, especially if learners have personal or domestic constraints. Remember adults want to be treated as adults. Equally, however, they will expect a rigorous and structured approach to the organisation of learning.

Make a firm and decisive start to your session. Speak clearly and loudly to gain everyone's attention and explain what the aims and objectives of the session are. It might be appropriate to share your objectives, exactly as you have written them, with the group. This is acceptable provided the objectives have meaning for the learners, but it can look somewhat sterile and mechanistic. However you introduce the session, you must make clear what it is about, what people are going to do, why they are doing it and how it fits with previous learning. There should always be an introduction to the session. Even if it's a workshop or practical session, it's useful to 'touch base' with the whole group to review progress and see if there are any issues which concern all the learners. If you have regular practical sessions based on individual work, it's advisable to ensure that you schedule time on the lesson plan for learners to record what they've done and what they need to do next time. This makes a starting point for subsequent session.

Effective learning requires continuity between sessions. As a general rule, the introductory phase should include a review and recap of the previous session. This can be done in several different ways:

- Ask learners to tell you what you and they did.
- Use lower order questions to recall content and check learning.
- Use higher order questions to extend learning and thinking and, possibly, use this as a way into the current session.
- It might be appropriate to ask if anyone has been able to apply their learning since last time or if they have any examples or experiences which illustrate any of the things they covered.
- A brief activity such as a gapped handout or a wordsearch can be used for revision.
- Try to include a stimulating activity to enliven and enthuse your learners. Perhaps pose a question or a problem to be solved during the session.

## Development – main body of the session

This is where the content is delivered, the objectives met and, most importantly, the learners learn. Effective learning uses a variety of teaching and learning techniques which are clearly structured and timed with smooth and seamless transitions between them. It is important to estimate and plan the length of time needed for activities and inputs and share this with the group. They will lose focus and motivation if activities are not timed and just seem to drift to a vague conclusion. Estimating timings is a significant challenge for trainee teachers requiring some experimentation and risk taking.

In general for a whole group session there should be a change approximately every 20 minutes. This will vary according to the learners and isn't a formula which has to be rigidly adhered to – if all the learners seem to be involved and interested then it's acceptable to continue with that activity or input. Reflective teachers recognise the signs which indicate when it's time for something different. Careful planning helps you to manage transitions smoothly without any gaps or periods of inactivity. Research suggests that learners enjoy being kept busy and don't appreciate inactivity. Some learners who present with challenging behaviour and poor motivation might exploit any gaps in the session to behave inappropriately.

Your planning should ensure that the main body of the session allows for regular checks on learning and opportunities for people to show what they've learned. Remember, assessment doesn't necessarily mean a formal test; it can be a discussion, a series of questions or asking students for examples which demonstrate learning. A typical session could involve the following elements in the structure:

- Introduction and recap.
- Begin by asking rather than telling (asking retail students to tell you what they think are the key elements of good customer service is more effective than telling them).
- Teacher talk/input.
- Student activity.
- Feedback and discussion of activity and conclusions drawn.
- Another, different activity.
- Feedback.
- Students recording activity/completing journals.
- Conclusions.
- Summary of learning.

The session plan example later in this section will indicate a structure of activities in more detail.

## Ending

The ending should round off the whole session and bring it to a clear, crisp conclusion. Some sessions just fade away without any real review of the learning or indication of what will happen next; others just suddenly stop unannounced, rather like falling off a cliff. The elements of good ending include:

- a clear statement or signal that the session is moving into its final phase
- a review of the learning
- summary of the main learning points
- final checks on learning
- possibly a plenary activity
- asking if learners have any final questions
- link forward to next session with a brief statement of content and inform learners of anything they need to do in preparation
- prompt finish on time – you might wish to thank the learners for their attention and effort.

**Activity**

*Initial planning*
Your initial planning will probably involve several scraps of paper on which you start to list topics, their possible order and begin to estimate timings, for example:

9.00 Introduction

- Content overview/aims and objectives
- Recap previous session

9.40 Student input/activity – What is customer service?

9.50 Discussion and examples

10.05 Video

- Viewing (10 minutes)
- Discussion (10 minutes)

10.25 Consequences of behaviour (groupwork?)

10.50 Summarise main points

11.00 Conclusion

Do you use this method in your initial planning? If not, what, if any, methods do you use?

Figure 8.3 shows an example of a session plan. It indicates the main elements of style and layout, but is intended for guidance only. You will probably be asked to use a standard format.

## Individual learning plans (ILPs)

In the *Handbook for Inspecting Colleges*, Ofsted states that inspectors should take into account where relevant 'how well staff work with learners to develop ILPs that are informed by initial assessment, meet learners' identified learning goals and are reviewed and updated regularly' (2009: 53).

Colleges and other providers of post-compulsory education and training have been using ILPs with their learners for several years. ILPs were originally developed for use with learners on Skills for Life, ESOL and 14–19 programmes but they are increasingly seen as a useful tool in managing and improving learning for all students.

**FAB**
**FE College**
*Further and Better*

Session Plan  Course_____

Date_____  Time_____  Site/ room_____

AIM/S
- To introduce learners to the purpose and use of the phonetic alphabet in the study of language

OBJECTIVES: At the end of this session learners will be able to:
- Define phonemes
- State the need for the phonetic alphabet
- Recognise some of the main symbols in the phonetic alphabet
- Express simple words in written form using the phonetic alphabet

RESOURCES/ MATERIALS
- Introductory Handout
- Word list handouts
- Worksheets

| Time | Content | Teaching and learning activities | Assessment/checking learning | Resources |
|------|---------|----------------------------------|------------------------------|-----------|
| 9.00 | Introduction and aims of session | ▪ Teacher input | | |
| 9.05 | How do you pronounce these words? | ▪ Student activity<br>▪ Discussion of problems of writing the sound | Discussion<br>Questions | |
| 9.15 | Phonemes – definition | ▪ Teacher input<br>▪ Discussion<br>▪ Student notes | | Definition handout |
| 9.25 | Phonemes – relation to linguistics | ▪ Teacher input | Discussion<br>Questions | Module booklet |

| | | | | |
|---|---|---|---|---|
| 9.35 | Problems with standard alphabet | • Student activity<br>  Work out some problems of using standard alphabet to indicate pronunciation | Student activity<br>Feedback and discussion | Word list |
| 9.45 | Phonetic alphabet | • Teacher input – worked examples | Discussion<br>Questions | Explanatory handout |
| 10.00 | Student practice | • Groupwork<br>• Practice<br>• Feedback – response to activity | Student practice<br>Discussion and correction | Word list |
| 10.30 | Summary | • Teacher input<br>  - review objectives<br>  - summarise main points | | |
| 10.40 | Conclusion | • Set problem for next session<br>• Overview of next session | | Worksheet for next session |
| **Evaluation notes** | | | | |
| **Next session** | | | | |

**Figure 8.3** Sample session plan.

This trend is likely to continue as learning providers move towards systems of 'personalised learning' (see below). If you are training to teach in post-compulsory education and training you will have agreed an ILP with your course tutors. This ILP forms the basis of your continuing professional development (CPD) while working in the lifelong learning sector (LLS).

## What is an ILP?

An ILP is a plan which is drawn up as a result of initial and diagnostic assessment of learners and negotiation between them and teachers to set goals and objectives for individual achievement and progression. They are regularly reviewed and discussed between teacher and learner and feedback provided to aid learning and development. ILPs are an integral part of what has become known as the 'learning journey'; that is, the recognition by an individual of the need or desire to learn; the identification of long-term goals and the development of targets to reach those goals. The steps in the planning and management of an ILP might look like something as follows:

### Life or career goals

This might be that a learner wants to work in construction, more specifically in bricklaying. Other goals might be, for example, to achieve independent living. Support for learners begins at this stage with initial advice and guidance.

### Long-term goal

These goals are what the learner wants to achieve by the completion of his time in college or in training. This goal could be stated as a specific qualification such as 'Achieve Level 3 in bricklaying'. Other goals might include learning to drive and some basic elements of running a business. For some learners these goals include working towards target grades based on analysis of their entry profile. This can be a useful motivational device, but many learners will be demotivated by them because they have negative experiences of being graded and expectations placed on them.

### Short-term goals (or targets)

These are the small achievable steps, agreed with teachers and trainers, which learners take to achieve their goals. They could include qualification-specific targets such as completing a specific building project or acquiring a particular skill. Others might include working on literacy, numeracy or IT targets or personal skills like time management or budgeting skills. These targets are reviewed at each meeting with the teacher.

### Learners' use of ILPs

The ILP should be something that learners feel that they have ownership of and that its main purpose is to support their learning and progress. Used properly they are valuable tools for students to reflect on and for developing their independence and autonomy. These are some of the ways in which learners might use them in practice:

- recording what they want to achieve
- identifying goals and progression routes and options
- negotiating learning and development targets
- recording details of resources, support and guidance they will use
- recording and reflecting on assessment feedback for formative development
- making links between formal and work-based learning
- reflecting on:
  - what they have learned
  - what went well
  - what went less well and how they can improve.

Increasingly, there are opportunities for learners to use technology to record their progress and achievements and to develop their ILPs. Technologies such as PebblePad provide a vehicle in which learners can reflect and record and also include scanned documents, photographic and video material and a range of links.

### Teachers' use of ILPs

ILPs give teachers real opportunities to listen to learner voices and to plan learning which suits their needs, their circumstances and their aspirations. They will more easily be able to integrate the processes around initial and diagnostic testing, planning, tutorial support, performance, achievement and progression. In addition, they can plan, with learners, opportunities to extend learning into the workplace and the community.

### ILPs – benefits and disadvantages

There is little doubt that ILPs contribute to effective and successful learning and to the planning and provision of teaching. The advantages of their use include:

- encouraging learners to take responsibility for learning and helping them become more effective learners
- recognising the importance of prior learning
- motivating learners by agreeing achievable steps related to their individual context and progress so far – developmental feedback is an essential part of this process
- recognising and overcoming barriers to learning
- as a means of differentiation and formally recognising that all learners are individuals
- provide structure for reviews and tutorials
- helping colleges and providers to plan their provision.

However, it is important to remember that we are primarily concerned with the process and development of learning rather than the production, monitoring and auditing of paper and electronic documents. The ILP documentation is there to support learning. As John Callaghan (2004: 8) says, writing in the context of using ILPs in ESOL: 'Formal procedures for identifying learners' needs – including ILPs – are consuming amounts of time disproportionate to their value, as well as distorting the process of goal-setting and reducing possibilities for other kinds of activity.' The challenge, therefore, is to create ILP systems that are meaningful and useful to learners while being efficient and avoiding unnecessary bureaucracy.

The Ofsted Good Practice Database, which you can access through the Excellence Gateway, provides advice and examples to support you in developing ILPs (www. excellencegateway.org.uk/page.aspx?o=108288).

## Planning for differentiation

Differentiation worries some teachers. Frequently, this is because they are exhorted to do it but without support and training in the best ways of achieving it. However, in many ways the concept of differentiation reminds me of something which really is obvious and doesn't need research to prove. We know that people of all ages outside of educational institutions do things differently and learn at different rates and in different ways. However, when people are put into learning groups, in schools, colleges or any other setting, there seems to be an expectation that they will progress at roughly the same rate while covering the same content and using a fairly limited range of teaching, learning and assessment methods.

### What is differentiation?

> When we plan for differentiation in the classroom we are attempting to meet the individual needs of each student while providing a challenging learning experience for all students in the class.
>
> (Le Versha and Nicholls 2003: 96)

Differentiation means enabling and ensuring that learners from a wide range of backgrounds and varying experiences of education and with different abilities and different experiences can achieve. Differentiation aims to reduce the frustration and lack of self-esteem which many learners experience when the teaching and learning doesn't suit them. Differentiation is closely allied to motivation and behaviour. Two motivational states which affect learning are anxiety and boredom. Anxiety occurs when teachers expect too much of their students, boredom when they expect too little.

### How do teachers differentiate learning?

In common with all aspects of effective teaching, the key to differentiation is knowing your students and being alert to feedback on their progress and recognising problems or different levels of progress. At first you will know them through initial testing and assessment, but increasingly you will build a more comprehensive picture of each learner's style, preferences and abilities as you work with them. Some lesson plan formats require teachers to indicate differentiation by showing;

- what *all* learners must do/achieve
- what *most* learners should do/achieve
- what *some* learners could achieve.

This system could be amended by reference to:

- core activities
- support (similar to the notion of 'scaffolding')
- extension – having extra materials available at a higher level, often as independent activities.

Stradling and Saunders (1993) suggest there are five types of differentiation:

1  *Differentiation by task.* Learners cover the same content but are set different tasks at different levels of difficulty.
2  *Differentiation by outcome.* Learners are given the same tasks but different outcomes and a range of responses are anticipated from learners at different levels.
3  *Differentiation by learning activity.* Resources and materials cover the same content but are differentiated according to learners' needs. For learners with communication difficulties, resources can be provided in a different form – for example, large print for those with sight difficulties. Extension activities could be available for learners who complete tasks early or are working at a higher level. This links to the next point.
4  *Differentiation by pace.* Learners cover the same content at the same level but take more or less time to achieve.
5  *Differentiation by dialogue.* This refers to the interaction and discussions between learners and teachers in which their progress is monitored and varying levels of support provided. A useful method here is to consider the use of 'peer teaching' in which learners developing at a faster rate can help and support others; an added consequence being that one of the most effective methods of learning is to teach someone else.

**Activity**

List as many ways as you can think of in which learners are different. For example, age, previous achievement.

For each of these, consider what strategies and methods you would use to meet their differing needs and abilities.

## Personalised learning

Personalised learning means tailoring the curriculum and the teaching methods to meet the needs of all students. There are clear links here to differentiation and the use of ILPs. It could be argued that the lifelong learning sector has been more receptive to individual and personalised learning than schools have been. The Department for Education and Skills (DfES) issued a consultation document in 2006, '*Personalising Further Education: Developing a Vision*', which sets out its plans to introduce 'a range of changes to strengthen personalisation in FE and make a reality of the 14–19 Skills Strategies'. In summary, personalisation is defined as:

> In an educational setting, personalisation means working in partnership with the learner and employer – to tailor their learning experience and pathways, according to their needs and personal objectives – in a way which delivers success.
>
> (DfES 2006: 7)

The development and use of initial and diagnostic testing and ILPs provides a firm foundation for the introduction of personalised learning, but as in so many educational developments, the key beneficiary of all this activity should be the learners. It is important to remember that personalised learning, like all effective learning, involves the learners; it is something that is done *with* them, not *to* them. The role of technology in supporting personalised learning is considered in detail with cases from a range of colleges and learning providers through the Excellence Gateway (www.excellencegateway.org.uk/page.aspx?o=275606).

---

**For your journal**

- Provide examples of how you have planned for differentiation.
- State differentiation strategies you have used.
- Evaluate the effectiveness of these strategies.
- Follow up and research further on differentiation; note and consider for use any strategies which are new to you.

---

**Journal extract: Lisa, training to teach music and drama**

I feel that the students benefited from having a structure of the aims and objectives in front of them on the board. The discussion at the beginning and the end of the session showed that the students were able to write their own targets for the session ahead, and during the end of the session they could evaluate and assess each other's learning. The discussion allowed the students to be interactive with each other, and it also brought them together as a community. The students were able to experiment with learner autonomy, by allowing themselves to be more independent.

**Jasvir, training to teach IT**

There was a time when I never followed my session plans; I just thought they were there for managers or observers to look at. I used to be a little disorganised with my paper-work for the course and the resources, I did not know whether I was coming or going. I now realise the importance of having a session plan and how it helps the structure of my lesson, assessment and meet the criteria for the course within the timescale. I now always make sure I follow the session plan and that learners have met the aims and objectives of the session.

# 9

# Assessment for learning

---

**What this chapter is about**

- What is assessment?
- Why and how do we assess?
- Types of assessment: initial, diagnostic, formative, summative, ipsative
- Norm referencing and criterion referencing
- Principles of assessment
- Competence-based assessment and assessing NVQs
- Assessment methods
- Giving feedback
- The emotional impact of assessment

---

**LLUK standards**

This chapter covers the following standards:
BS 1; BK 1.1; BP 1.1; BK 1.3; BP 1.3; BK 2.1; BP 2.1; BK 2.2; BP 2.2; BK 2.5; BP 2.5
DK 1.1; DP 1.1; DK 2.2; DP 2.2
ES 1; EK 1.1; EP 1.1; EK 1.2; EP 1.2; EK 1.3; EP 1.3; EK 2.1; EP 2.1; EK 2.2; EP 2.2;
EK 2.3; EP 2.3; EK 3.1; EP 3.1; EK 3.2; EP 3.2 EK 4.1; EP 4.1

---

As an experiment I'm going to start this chapter with some 'teaching by asking' rather than 'teaching by telling'. This is a challenge in a textbook because, to be effective, this technique requires a two-way dialogue using open questions. However, let's give it a go. Consider each of the questions as fully as you can – it's probably best done as a group activity – and see what conclusions you can draw and what connections you can make about assessment. Other questions of your own might arise; include them in your discussions.

**Activity**

Consider the entirety of your learning experiences in a variety of settings –
school, college, university, training at work – and discuss the following:

- What kinds of assessment did you experience – tests, examinations,
  coursework assignments, others?
- How did you feel and what was your emotional state during and after the
  assessment
  ○ if you were successful?
  ○ if you were unsuccessful?
- If you were successful, did you feel you had learned something or just
  passed a test?
- What, if any, were the consequences of the assessment
  ○ if you were successful?
  ○ if you were unsuccessful?
- Did assessment help you to learn? If so, what forms of assessment worked
  best for you?
- Did you understand why and how you were being assessed?
- Describe the quantity, quality and usefulness of the feedback you received.
- Did you find assessment motivating? Did you look forward to it or dread it?
- Did you at any time, as a result of assessment, feel like a failure?
- If you felt like a failure, what were the effects on your subsequent
  learning?

As a result of your thinking and discussion you will inevitably have brought up
some of the key issues relating to assessment, for example, its uses and purposes, or
its emotional impact. These issues will most likely reflect the main questions of this
chapter, which are:

1  What is assessment?
2  Why do we assess?
3  How do we assess?
4  How does it affect learners?

From the outset, I want to express a fundamental belief about assessment. The prin-
cipal purpose of assessment is to help people to learn; it should not be about testing
people to see at what point they will fail. We must remember, however, that although
assessment is primarily *for* learning we also live in the real world and learners will, in
most instances, want assessment *of* their learning and certification and accreditation

of their learning. Assessment information and data will also be required by you, your managers, learning providers, governors, funding bodies, LSC, Ofsted, potential learners, employers, marketing and publicity teams. The trick is to get the balance right and to use assessment primarily *for* learners and learning.

## Why do we assess learners?

There are many reasons why we assess learners and their learning. These reasons could be grouped under the following headings.

### Because we are required to

Much of the teaching and learning in the lifelong learning sector (LLS) is assessed by external agencies, such as examination boards and awarding bodies, and the assessment information and data are made publicly available. Generally, our learners come to us to undertake courses that lead to formal, summative assessment by external bodies and the attainment of a grade or statement of achievement.

As indicated above, we are required to measure our learners' and our own performance and if it is unsatisfactory we may lose funding and, in the worst-case scenario, be closed down. We are in receipt of public money and it seems reasonable that we should be asked to provide evidence that this money is well spent. This evidence comes, in part, in the form of assessment results and grades. An over-reliance on summative assessment and grading, however, can be counter-productive and lead to an 'examination culture' in which results become an end in themselves and the wider aspects of learning are neglected. In schools and colleges teachers may feel under pressure to 'teach to the test'.

### For grading, selection and progression

In a pub quiz we compete against others by trying to answer more questions correctly than they do; we are then ranked in winning order and receive prizes and congratulations, or commiserations, accordingly. In short we are graded. We do this for fun and the consequences are of little importance. We might not like the idea of grading in educational settings but it is a fact of life and its consequences are considerable. Success in gaining employment or entry to university is based on being assessed and graded. Some of you may be teaching on courses where you are regularly required to grade your learners as they go through the course and to report estimated grades to examination boards.

Adult learners over a certain age will have memories of a significant grading and selection exercise – the 11-plus examination. Many of these people will still feel that they are 'failures', not just in their education but as people.

### To find out if learning has taken place

We use assessment to find out if and to what extent our students have learned and how they have developed. Without some form of assessment it would be impossible to ascertain whether progress has been made by all or just some of our learners. This can be done by informal methods, such as questioning and discussion, or by more formal methods such as essays or phase tests. Much of this assessment is used to check learning and understanding regularly prior to moving on to the next sections. Reflective teachers use checks on learning and understanding to adjust and adapt teaching as necessary. Without some form of assessment we can't give feedback to learners. We now know that positive and structured feedback is the most effective form of teaching and assessment. Effective feedback is motivating, which leads us to the next point.

## To motivate and encourage learners

Learners and teachers tend not to consider assessment motivating, but for some students it is. Many learners will like to be tested and will find assessment, particularly tests and examinations, both stimulating and rewarding. Unfortunately, there are at least as many who find such assessments to be fear inducing. Learners who are usually confident and able can be stricken by 'performance anxiety' when it comes to testing. Unfortunately, most 'high-stakes' assessments are, to a greater or lesser extent, based on tests and examinations. So, if only in the interest of equality and inclusivity, there should be a range of assessment techniques in your teaching and learning toolkit.

Assessment can discourage learners by giving them the impression that they have not performed well enough or are simply not clever enough. Effective assessment is an aid to learning and helps learners and teachers not only to recognise achievement but also to identify areas for improving or extending learning. We should use assessment to motivate learners, not demotivate them.

## Diagnosing learners' needs

If learners are to be successful there needs to be an assessment of their starting points. We need to know what learning, skills and experience they arrive with when they come to us. Initial and diagnostic testing helps us to plan the learning for groups and individuals and to provide support and meet individual needs. The information from these tests can form the basis of ILPs which are regularly reviewed in consultation with the learners.

## Evaluating and developing learning programmes

To use a shopping analogy, learning providers must offer courses that meet learners' needs, are useful and enjoyable, help them to progress and provide good value. We need to be accountable to our learners. When we buy unsatisfactory goods we should complain and ask for our money back. There is no reason for us to expect that learners will accept unsatisfactory learning 'products'. There are many ways in which learning is evaluated; one of them is assessment of learning which feeds into a continuing drive for improvement.

**Activity**

Consider two or three different kinds of assessment you have recently carried out with your learners.

- Why did you use them?
- Did your learners know why they were being assessed?
- To what extent do you think they valued the assessment?
- Could you have assessed them differently?
- How did the assessment contribute to their learning?

## Main purposes of assessment

Having considered the general reasons for and aims of assessment, we can now examine the main purposes of assessment which are:

- initial assessment
- diagnostic assessment/testing
- formative assessment
- summative assessment
- ipsative assessment.

### Initial assessment

As the name suggests, this type of assessment happens at the beginning of a course of learning, or even before the learning starts if we include activities such as pre-entry advice and guidance, application and enrolment. Initial assessment will be a key part of the induction process for new learners and, as such, should be handled sensitively to welcome learners in rather than scare them with formal testing and assessment procedures. Initial assessment has developed mainly in the realms of functional skills, work-based and vocational learning, but increasingly it is valued as part of the learning journey for all students.

Initial assessment may include diagnostic assessment (see below) but it comprises a much wider range of assessment and information gathering, including, for example: career intentions and suitability; qualifications and achievements; prior learning and experience; key skills; functional skills. Learning style inventories are often used at this initial stage, but all too often learners and teachers do not know why they do them or what they are used for. Frequently they are filed away and not referred to unless, perhaps, an inspector is visiting. Initial assessment is also used to identify any particular requirements learners might have. Wheelchair users will expect access to buildings and facilities; people who have hearing difficulties may require rooms with induction loops or perhaps a communicator. We have legal obligations to anticipate and meet the needs of all learners.

Muriel Green, writing about initial assessment in work-based post-16 provision, states that initial assessment is:

> . . . . a staged process that helps the learner cross the threshold to the most appropriate post-16 provision. . . . It is really important to 'get it right', so that the learning and support opportunities offered are the best possible match with the interests, abilities, aptitudes, aspirations and needs of the individual.
>
> (Green 2003: 5)

Given the emphasis on retention and achievement of learners, it will be apparent that initial assessment is designed to benefit not only the learners but also the learning provider. The formula is quite simple: get the right learners on the right courses; help them to stay on programme and to achieve; help them progress to the next stage. Initial assessment is crucial to the first stage in this formula.

## Diagnostic assessment

Diagnostic assessments or tests are used to discover how current performance or abilities differ from the expected or required level of performance. It can be used to identify specific problems that a learner may be experiencing and to provide appropriate learning support. As part of the initial assessment process diagnostic testing can be used to assess learners' abilities in functional skills. As we noted earlier, the temptation to sit new students in front of a literacy or numeracy test on their first day should be avoided. Tummons (2010: 13) points out that diagnostic assessment can be a continuing process rather than just a tool used prior to the start of a course. He distinguishes between:

*Diagnostic assessment before a course*

- provides initial guidance and advice
- identifies entry criteria for the programme together with any possible claim for the accreditation of prior learning.

*Diagnostic assessment before and during a course*

- reviews learner progress through progress review and tutorial meetings
- identifies learners' strengths and development needs
- identifies learning strategies and activities that the learner uses or may need to develop.

## Formative assessment

The main developments and debates in assessment practice revolve around the issues of formative assessment and summative assessment. *Formative assessment* is an integral part of the teaching and learning process and its aim is to promote learning and to motivate learners; it is assessment *for* learning. *Summative assessment* is the summing up or checking of learning at particular stages by, for example, testing or some kind of formal assessment. Such testing may involve making judgements about learners against national standards as, for example, in a GCSE or A-level examination: it is assessment *of* learning.

Formative assessment, used properly, is such an integral part of the teaching and learning process that one could argue that it shouldn't even be called assessment. When we consider teaching and learning methods, many of them questioning, case studies, projects – are also assessment methods.

Some of the most significant work on formative assessment has been carried out by Black and William (1998). The influence of their work is evident in the Qualifications and Curriculum Authority's guidelines on assessment for learning (QCA 2001). Black and William provide some basic premises to support the use of formative assessment which are worth quoting in full. Their work is the result of research in schools but the conclusions are equally valid for learners of all ages, particularly adult returners who have basic skills needs. Consequently, I have substituted the word 'learner' for 'pupil' in the following:

> The research indicates that improving learning through assessment depends on five, deceptively simple, key factors:
>
> • the provision of effective feedback to learners;
> • the active involvement of learners in their own learning;
> • adjusting teaching to take account of the results of assessment;
> • a recognition of the profound influence assessment has on the motivation and self-esteem of learners, both of which are crucial influences on learning;
> • the need for learners to be able assess themselves and understand how to improve;
>
> At the same time, several inhibiting factors were identified. Among these are:
>
> • a tendency for teachers to assess the quantity of work and presentation rather than the quality of learning;
> • greater attention given to marking and grading, much of it tending to lower the self-esteem of learners, rather than to providing advice for improvement;
> • teachers not knowing enough about their learners' needs.
>
> (Black and William 1998: 17)

Assessment for learning is based on the belief that everyone can learn and that formative assessment is a key strategy to help learners improve and develop. It can be contrasted with summative assessment which, historically, was based on the notion that there was a limited pool of talent with innate ability which had to be identified and selected. Assessment for learning does not necessarily involve comparison with other learners.

Assessment for learning is an essential element of preparing and planning teaching and learning. It might be more appropriate to talk of formative 'activities' rather than formative 'assessment'. Teachers should plan a range of activities and methods to allow all learners to know the what, how and why of assessment and to give them opportunities to progress towards their goals. The planning requires that feedback, the most powerful tool to improve learning, is central to learning. Planning should allow for interaction between teacher and learners so that the pace and delivery of the session can be adjusted to match the learners' progress.

Interaction between teachers and learners means that much assessment for learning is carried out informally by using activities such as listening; observing learners' work and their non-verbal communication; questioning, particularly higher order questions; discussions; dialogue and reflection. Questioning is a vital skill for teachers to develop, particularly as an element of formative assessment. While lower order, recall-type questions might be useful for checking learning, higher order questions which require learners to think are much more effective as part of formative assessment. You should refer to the use of Socratic questions outlined in Chapter 12. Assessment for learning is closely linked to notions of active learning and deep learning.

## Importance of feedback in formative assessment

Feedback is the most important aspect of formative assessment. Teachers can receive and give feedback in a variety of ways (you will find it useful here to link back to Chapter 3). Research suggests that immediate oral feedback is the most effective, provided it is developmental and makes learners extend their thinking and learning to a higher level. In this respect, the use of feedback is very much like the ideas of 'scaffolding' and the zone of proximal development we discussed in Chapter 5. Learners, in dialogue with teachers, can see where they want to get to but initially may need help in the form of questions, prompts and pointers to get there. Black and William's research suggests that formative assessment based on high quality feedback has the greatest effect size (i.e. effect on improvement) of any techniques used in education.

Feedback is important not only for the learners' development but also for teachers to be able to respond to learners and to 'fine tune' their teaching while it is in progress. Ecclestone makes this point quite clearly:

> From a pedagogic perspective, assessment activities cannot be understood as formative unless evidence from feedback is actually used to adapt teaching and learning activities, either there and then or in future planning. This iteration between feedback, whether from students' written work or their answers to classroom or tutorial questions, can therefore be minute-to-minute as teachers and tutors think on their feet and respond to individuals or groups during classroom sessions or tutorials, or more considered as teachers plan new activities and lessons.
>
> (Ecclestone 2010: 35)

Ecclestone's research suggests that while the principles and practices of formative assessment are generally well understood by academics and teacher educators, there is probably less understanding of it amongst teachers in the lifelong learning sector. There is evidence to suggest that, rather than using the potential of formative assessment to improve motivation and the quality of learning, it can become little more than a way of coaching learners to complete summative assessments. She argues for more extensive staff development and support for teachers to understand the 'spirit' of formative assessment and to develop it so that learners can become more independent and critical learners.

> **Activity**
>
> Consider the range of assessment techniques you use with your learners.
>
> To what extent are they formative?
>
> Are there any teaching and learning methods you use that you consider to be 'formative activities'?

## Summative assessment

Summative assessment is the assessment *of* learning. It is usually carried out at the end of a course of learning or at specific points in a learning programme, such as at the end of a module or unit, or phase test. Summative assessments are nearly always formal – a test, examination, an oral, essay, assignment – and are used to see if learners have acquired the skills and knowledge required by the specifications or at that particular stage. Summative assessments may be used to decide whether a learner can or should go on to the next stage and, in this sense, are sometimes referred to as 'high-stakes' assessments.

Summative assessments are important, as discussed earlier, because they lead to the production of grades and the gaining, or otherwise, of qualifications. We know that this process of qualification and grading is important for learners and many other interested parties. However, we need to remember the emotional aspects of assessment and the design of assessment, particularly to do with validity and reliability – all these aspects will be examined shortly. Weeden et al. (2002: 19) suggest:

> Summative assessment is a snapshot judgement that records what a [learner] can do at a particular time. It is concerned with providing information about a [learner] in a simple summary form which can be used to review progress, can be passed to a new teacher or school [or university or employer] or can certificate achievement in a formal way. This function probably dominates most teachers' views of assessment.

It would be wrong, however, to suggest that formative and summative assessment are opposites – A-level candidates, for example, will be judged and graded by summative assessment, but their success and the quality of their learning is likely to be improved if formative assessment is the basis of the teaching and learning.

## Ipsative assessment

Ipsative assessment is a form of self-assessment that allows learners to measure their own progress without comparing themselves to others or reference to standards set by external bodies. As a trainee teacher you will probably have carried out an initial audit of your skills, knowledge and attributes and produced a personal action plan with self-defined targets. When you review your targets you can assess the distance you have travelled and develop new targets as appropriate. For our own learners, particularly those who have not been successful in their previous education, ipsative assessment can be a powerful method of increasing self-esteem and confidence because it emphasises success rather than failure. This form of assessment works best when it is based on thorough initial assessment and the identification of clear learning goals and targets supported by an ILP.

## Norm referencing and criterion referencing

When discussing forms of assessment, the word 'referencing' means what is the referent of the learner; in other words what is he or she compared to. In the case of ipsative assessment (see above) learners are compared to and judged against their own previous performance.

## Norm referencing

Norm referencing has traditionally been, and to some extent continues to be, the main method of assessing and grading learners. You will almost certainly have experienced it at some point in your education. The most obvious example of this type of assessment is a formal, externally marked examination such as A-level, the results of which will have been published and have had significant consequences for your continued learning and your career prospects.

In a system of norm referencing, judgements – and grades – about an individual's performance in an assessment are made by referring to, or comparing against, another group of learners. This other group could be the class, the school or college, or the whole cohort entered for that assessment. It is based on the notion that in any given group of learners there will always be some who are very able and will get the highest marks, some who are not able and would fail, and a range of people in the middle. The examination system would have grade boundaries and a pass/fail boundary and, consistently, roughly the same numbers of students would be allocated within each grade. This system can encourage learners, and employers and universities, to perceive themselves as a 'pass' or a 'fail'.

Norm-referenced systems are relatively simple systems which are competitive and, implicitly or explicitly, suggest that the pool of talent is fixed and will not vary greatly in any given cohort of learners. The main function of the assessment in this system is to identify the high-fliers and to grade all the entrants. Such systems are still popular with governments because they can produce statistics and league tables, and with employers and further and higher education institutions because they facilitate selection. Given that schools and colleges are competing for learners, grades based on norm-referenced systems are an essential part of their marketing, recruitment and funding.

## Criterion referencing

Criterion referencing grew in part from a desire to move away from norm referencing and ranking, with their connotations of passing or failing, to an emphasis on what students can actually do. In criterion (criteria is the plural) referencing, learners are assessed against predetermined standards not with reference to their competitors. The standards prescribe the knowledge, skills and understanding that learners need in that subject or vocation. Criterion referencing assumed a more specialised form in competence-based assessment, as we shall see later.

A comparison with the driving test is often used to explain criterion-referenced assessment. All candidates for the driving test know what the criteria for success are and they are judged against them; if they fail they can work to improve and retake the test to see if they have met the criteria. If a norm-referencing system was used to assess drivers, a certain percentage of the population would never be able to pass the test. Criterion referencing is generally considered to be fairer since it removes the competitive element and the assumption that there will always be roughly the same proportion at each grade. To ensure fairness and equal opportunities, criteria should be written in a clear and unambiguous manner so that all learners can understand them. In BTEC courses, criteria clearly state what learners must be able to do or to produce in order to gain a pass, merit or distinction. It would be mistaken, however, to suggest that all assessments are either purely norm referenced or criterion referenced. Even A-level examinations have some criteria built in to them and the GCSE when it was introduced was said to be a criterion referenced system which would motivate learners. Neither should we assume there is any system which is completely objective and without bias from the assessor or some other influence. As James Atherton (2011) points out:

> All assessment is ultimately subjective: there is no such thing as an 'objective test'. Even when there is a high degree of standardisation, the judgement of what things are tested and what constitutes a criterion of satisfactory performance is in the hands of the assessor.

## Some principles of assessment

### Validity

When we set assessments for our learners we and they need to be sure about what we are actually assessing or measuring. An assessment can be said to be valid if it measures what it actually sets out to measure. For example, does a task assess the quality of a learner's written skills when (unless specified in the assessment criteria) it's an assessment in engineering? Tummons (2011: 38) provides a handy definition of a valid assessment as being 'an assessment which covers the course as a whole, uses appropriate real-life methods, is most suitable to the subject or vocational area and helps predict how the learner will perform in the future'.

'Face validity' is concerned with the extent to which an assessment looks like an assessment in that subject or vocational area. In examinations, for example, we expect clear, error-free papers in accessible and unambiguous language. Other aspects of validity relate to the extent to which the assessment reflects what is set out in the specifications and the extent to which the assessment measures the range of skills, knowledge and understanding outlined in the specification.

## Reliability

Reliability is closely linked to validity but the emphasis is more on the accuracy and consistency of its application. Would the assessment produce roughly the same results if used at a different time and a different place with a similar group of learners? One way in which we can ensure reliability is by a process of moderation or cross-marking based on all assessors using the same standards and criteria.

## Transparency

Transparency is essentially about the extent to which learners understand the assessment and to which it matches the learning outcomes. Learners don't like to be taken by surprise by being assessed on something they didn't expect, or don't understand or they just haven't covered. When designing assessments we must be sure that the task is aligned with the learning outcomes and the assessment criteria. Learning outcomes should be presented clearly and unambiguously to the learners and the links between the outcomes and the assessment criteria should be made plain to them, markers and internal and external verifiers.

Torrance et al. (2005) warn, particularly in the area of vocational assessment, that too much transparency can lead to a situation which goes beyond assessment *for* learning to a situation of assessment *as* learning. In other words, there is a danger that we can provide learners with so much clarity, explanation and assistance that they will succeed, but succeed at what? A balance needs to be struck between providing clarity of task and criteria with the possibility of challenge and discovery.

## Authenticity

Authenticity in assessment has two meanings. First, it is concerned with how closely the assessment mirrors the real world, particularly in relation to vocational assessment. If we are assessing students in catering, is the assessment in an authentic catering setting using the latest equipment and techniques? Ideally, the assessment should be undertaken in a workplace using a work-based assessor.

The second aspect of authenticity refers to the originality of the work produced by the student. Is it their own, have they had any help with it, or have they copied it? Given the ubiquity of the internet and its access by learners, can we be sure that work has not been plagiarised? Plagiarism is most likely to be presented in written work, so perhaps we need to consider whether a written piece is always the most appropriate form of assessment.

## Sufficiency

Here we are concerned with whether the quantity and coverage of the assessment tasks and activities are sufficient to provide evidence that the learning outcomes have been met. Sufficiency is particularly important in the assessment of competence-based courses such as NVQs and GNVQs. In such programmes the emphasis is on learners collecting evidence and assembling portfolios which are judged by assessors and assessment decisions made. You may have seen portfolios that comprise small mountains of material lovingly indexed and cross-referenced by the candidate as evidence of their competence. While we would wish to applaud candidates' organisational and presentational skills, there is always a danger that the collection of evidence and portfolio building becomes an end in itself. The question is 'Do we need all this?' Is the evidence the minimum necessary to demonstrate competence and to ensure coverage of all the units and the performance criteria?

## Fairness

Fairness is about ensuring that every person being assessed has an equal chance of a good and fair assessment. Some learners may feel that a teacher has a bias against them and, consequently, they are unlikely to do well in assessments. Anonymous marking is a possible solution to this concern. Additionally, of course, we need to ensure that learners with disabilities or particular needs have the necessary adjustments and allowances made in order for them to participate fully and equally in the assessments.

## Competence-based assessment

### Background to competence-based assessment

Competence-based assessment could be described as a more specialised and vocationally related sibling of criterion-referenced assessment. Wolf (1995) outlines the development of competence-based assessment from its mainly American origins, through its development in the 1980s and the establishment of the National Council for Vocational Qualifications (NCVQ). National vocational qualifications (NVQs) are based on a system whereby each vocational area is broken down into outcomes or units of competences, within which there are elements and performance criteria which describe specifically what a learner must be able to do. The process involves learners (or candidates) generating and collecting evidence, usually in a portfolio, which is then judged by an assessor against the outcomes.

There are several advantages to this form of assessment. First, given that it is a criterion-referenced system anyone who is able and meets the criteria successfully can achieve the qualification. Second, being vocational qualifications they are assessed in the workplace, hopefully with the latest technology and equipment, by assessors who are experts in the field. Finally, they are based on specific and transparent learning outcomes.

There are some downsides however, not least, the sheer bulk of portfolios and consequent difficulty of assessing them. In addition, the procedure involving assessors, internal and external verifiers and auditable evidence can be extremely onerous and bureaucratic. Others have argued that it is not realistic to disaggregate all work into a set of overarching competences. As Wolf (1995: 17) points out, NVQs are based on:

> the fundamental assumption that, for each industry, there exists a single identifiable model of what 'competent' performance entails. The idea that, for each role, there exists such an agreed notion of competence, which can be elicited and command consensus, is fundamental to any assessment system of this type.

Given these caveats, however, we must accept that competence-based assessment, like summative assessment, is a reality and that we have to design and implement it in the most efficient way and to encourage learning rather than merely collecting things.

## Assessing NVQ – practical considerations

### Underpinning knowledge

Early critics of NVQs claimed that there was little in the way of teaching and learning and that the process merely accredited skills which people were already carrying out. Hence the question 'Do we teach on NVQs?' The answer is, obviously, yes. If we expect candidates to demonstrate, for example, knowledge and practice of health and safety in a working environment, they have to learn about it first – legislation, safe working procedures – and then be observed and assessed doing it in the workplace. In short, they need the 'underpinning knowledge'.

### Generating evidence

Evidence to support competent performance can come from a number of sources:

- *Accreditation of Prior Learning and Experiential Learning (APEL)*. A system of APEL recognises that a learner might not have a specific qualification in a skill or subject but they have gained experience from previous work or life experience. This might take the form of references, letters of commendation, a diary or a logbook from a previous workplace signed by a line manager.

- *Accreditation of Prior Learning (APL)*. These two terms are often confused and used interchangeably. A claim for APL is based on the accreditation and certification of prior learning. So, for example, in previous post-compulsory teacher training courses someone with a City and Guilds 7407 Stage 2 could claim APL and join the second year of a Certificate in Education.

- *Naturally occurring evidence and direct observation*. This kind of evidence is based on candidates' performance in the workplace; the things that they naturally do as part of their working routines. Some of this will be the result of acquiring, then applying the underpinning knowledge. This might also include the production and collection of products or artefacts, for example, a letter produced by a candidate on a business administration course.

- *Performance on assignments*. Assignments and projects may be partly or wholly related to the candidate's type and place of work. The best kinds of projects are those that integrate theory and practice and provide opportunities to apply learning in the workplace. In addition, they should integrate functional skills development. An example would be in business administration where a candidate has been studying the Data Protection Act and is able to research the ways in which the employer complies with the Act. Giving a presentation on this could also entail the development of key skills in communication and IT.

*   *Photographic, video, audio or other electronic recording.* Learners, trainers and assessors are encouraged to use a range of assessment and evidence. Photographs of things produced by the candidate, candidates working with customers, receiving awards, can all be offered as evidence. Similarly, video and audio recordings may be provided. This is much easier than it was a decade ago because of the development of digital technology, although it's easier to edit out the 'bad' bits!

*   *Questioning.* Questioning is a useful method for assessors to check underpinning knowledge and to authenticate the validity and authenticity of evidence. Higher order questions allow candidates to demonstrate their thinking skills and ways in which they have applied and adapted theory in practice.

*   *Indirect evidence.* This includes items such as witness statements attesting to candidate's performance and skill development in the workplace, certificates, awards, references.

As mentioned earlier, NVQ portfolios can become unwieldy and be very time consuming to assess. QCA guidelines on generating and collecting evidence emphasise that portfolios should 'minimise bureaucracy and reduce the burden of assessment without compromising quality' (QCA nd). In addition, the guidelines urge candidates and assessors to use a range of assessment techniques and wherever possible to develop 'evidence-rich' integrated projects and activities which avoid an 'element by element or pc (performance criteria) by pc approach to collecting evidence' and also reduce the overall amount of evidence collected.

The final point is important because competence-based assessment can be extremely reductionist and lead to performance criteria being 'ticked off' without recognising the connections between them or understanding the framework into which all the elements fit. All forms of work are holistic, connected activities, not just a collection of competences. Major integrated projects follow best practice in teaching and learning in that they require learners to make connections and see the 'big picture'. It is important that candidates and assessors develop a 'helicopter vision' of the elements and performance criteria for each unit and are aware that the working day or the assignment can provide a range of valuable evidence.

## Assessment methods

It has been said that education is built on three pillars: what is taught (curriculum); how it is taught (pedagogy); and how it is assessed (assessment). For learning and teaching these three elements must be aligned and kept in balance. Many have argued that our education system is distorted by an over-emphasis on assessment and that, to a great extent, what we teach is what we test.

When considering assessment methods we must decide what is the most appropriate method (or methods) for our learners in order to meet the aims and learning outcomes of the course and the needs, abilities and styles of our learners. There is evidence to suggest that we are still too reliant on the use of written forms of assessment. This doesn't suit all people and there are equal opportunities issues for those who have dyslexia or sight problems. Equally, the type of assessment might affect learners' perceptions of particular courses. Torrance et al. (2005) carried out significant research in the assessment of learning in the learning and skills sector and vocational learning. In one of their conclusions they point out:

> Assessment methods *per se* do not directly affect learners' choice of award or likelihood of success, but the association of certain awards with methods which employ extensive writing (coursework assignments, exam essays) does. Thus for example, practical tests and/or multiple choice tests are seen as acceptable – and indeed unavoidable – across most groups of learners in the sector, especially younger trainees, but extensive written work is disliked and largely avoided except by A-level takers. Even in school and college-based AVCEs, the view is emerging that these are becoming too based on writing about the vocational field being studied, rather than engaging in the practical development of competence.
>
> (Torrance et al. 2005: 83)

It seems reasonable to suggest, therefore, that a significant task for professional development in lifelong learning is to widen our range and use of assessment methods.

The following overview of some assessment methods, indicating advantages and disadvantages in each case, is neither comprehensive nor detailed, but should serve as an introduction which you can follow up by further research and record and discuss in your journals. You will also see that many of these could also be described as teaching and learning methods and some of them are discussed in more detail in Chapter 6.

## Examinations

Examinations, especially externally set and marked, still form a significant proportion of assessment in post-compulsory education. Variations can include 'open book' or 'open notes' examinations in which students can rely less on memory.

### Advantages
Exams can help to focus learners because they know they have to work towards a specific goal. Externally marked exams don't provide any marking work for the teachers. Examinations are a simple summative form of assessment that produces grades and statistics.

### Disadvantages
The most obvious criticism of exams is that they are fear inducing for many learners and lead to grading based solely on the exam rather than a bigger picture of an individual's learning. I recently observed a group of students collecting their marked

exam scripts and listened to their comments. Every student looked first at the grade, then read the limited feedback in a couple of seconds; one remarked that he'd done well enough considering that he didn't like this module and had only revised the night before! I found myself wondering what benefit they had derived from the experience. Apart from the limited feedback, exams can lead to a surface approach to learning in which both teachers and learners are geared mainly towards the exam and what's needed to pass it.

## Essays

Many learners are assessed by essays because that form of assessment will be the basis of their final examination. So, in effect, the summative assessment structures the form of their ongoing assessment. Many are assessed by essays merely because they always have been.

### Advantages
Like exams, essays can be a very useful form of focusing learners and getting them to produce a snapshot summary of their learning at a particular stage. A written essay can also be a useful method to assess a learner's written skills and their ability to identify and summarise key points, to present arguments, to analyse and evaluate. Timed essays set in class are useful as preparation for exams and are easy to administer, although they create a marking burden. Essay performance gives a simple way to report predicted grades to exam boards.

### Disadvantages
Essays are a symptom of our reliance on written forms of assessment. While part of our job is to improve learners' ability to express themselves in writing, we do well to remember that in no situation other than an educational setting are people asked to write essays. Some people excel at essays and find it relatively easy to structure them and express themselves clearly. The danger here, of course, is that we might, even unconsciously, be marking learners on their essay writing skills rather than assessing their learning. Paradoxically, study skills support for essay writing may unwittingly reinforce the perception that the form is more important than the content. Equally, there is a possibility of a 'halo' effect by which the learners' achievements in previous essays will positively or negatively affect the marking of the current one. If I'm honest, I can recall looking at students' previous essay grades before marking the latest batch. Planned well and used judiciously, essays are a valuable element in an assessment package; used uncritically, they indicate teaching which is 'assessment oriented' rather than 'learning oriented'.

## Reports

### Advantages
Reports have the advantage that they are more 'real world' and likely to be part of learners' working lives. Reports can be clearly focused by providing guidelines as to their headings and style. Reports seem a natural follow-up to case study work or

experiments and the learning and skills can be extended by summarising and presenting the key findings to colleagues.

### Disadvantages

Like all written forms, reports have the disadvantage that they are time consuming for learners and teachers, so we need to ensure that the effort is equal to the value of them. Often learners are asked to write reports without a clear understanding of their form and purpose and the ways in which they are different from other written forms.

## Portfolios

You may have encountered the term portfolio in collection with NVQ, GNVQ or similar criterion-referenced systems. However, the term has long been in use in other disciplines, particularly in art in design where it generally means a 'portfolio of work'.

### Advantages

Portfolios give learners the opportunity to present a 'big picture' of themselves and their achievements and to show their development over a period of learning. They can be used both formative by and summatively, particularly in conjunction with learning journals and diaries. As indicated in the section on competence-based learning, portfolios allow the collection of a range of assessment evidence, including written, visual, audio and artefacts. Increasingly learners are presenting this range of evidence as e-portfolios.

### Disadvantages

The most obvious disadvantage of portfolios is that they can be difficult to assess, if only because of their bulk. There can also be problems with authenticity concerning the originality of the work submitted. As the word 'portfolio' has become widespread it seems to have lost its clarity. What exactly do we mean by a portfolio? Do our learners know what it means and why they are asked to produce them?

## Presentations

Presentations are frequently used, even stipulated, in assessment. The most common form involves research into a subject accompanied by a presentation to peers supported by printed and projected resources, followed by questions and discussion.

### Advantages

Presentations are invaluable for many reasons. Learners are very likely to present in some form in their working lives, if only at a job interview. Presentations are excellent for developing functional skills and confidence.

### Disadvantages

Teachers are generally very confident presenters and, consequently, we tend to forget some learners dread presentations and worry about them for weeks in advance. Another downside of presentations, particularly in large groups, is that they are time consuming. If you're going to have a whole session of presentations, try to vary the topic. Coffield (2009: 45) reports student frustration 'when, for example, a whole day was given over to hearing each member of the class make a 20–30 minute presentation on the same topic'. Some teachers, particularly those delivering A-levels who have extensive content to cover in a limited time, find the time spent on presentations outweighs their value.

## Displays and exhibitions

These can range from simple poster displays to a full-blown art and design exhibition with VIPs and free wine on the opening night.

**Advantages**
Displays and exhibitions can be good motivators for learners because they give them a chance to demonstrate their learning and skills to a wider public. This form of assessment can also develop teamworking and time management skills as well as publicity and marketing skills. For adult learners who may not have enjoyed success in education before, displays and exhibitions are good opportunities to share and celebrate success. In some cases, particularly, art and design, the work shown at the exhibition is assessed by external verifiers and examiners. At the less sophisticated end, simple poster displays give alternative ways of presenting and assessing work, particularly for learners with a visual preference.

**Disadvantages**
The main disadvantage of mounting exhibitions is the time and cost of preparing them (including the wine and nibbles on opening night!).

## Academic posters

Creating posters, or 'academic' posters as they are referred to in universities, is not only a method of assessment but also a resource and a learning and teaching method. It's worth spending some time on the planning and preparation so that the finished product looks attractive and professional and can be used on several occasions. As with any other communication, you need to consider the content and design in relation to the audience, purpose, message, and the effect or impact you want it to have. If you use a search engine and do an image search, you will find a wide variety of examples of academic posters. You might also want to find information and ideas for interactive posters. The University of Leicester has a tutorial on creating academic posters (www.connect.le.ac.uk/posters). The Edinburgh Napier University has a good webpage on creating posters (www2.napier.ac.uk/gus/writing_presenting/academic_posters.html).

## Learning journals, diaries and logs

These are not simply methods of assessment but are also strategies for learning and development. Many colleges and learning providers have programmes of personal development planning to help learners plan, monitor, self-assess and evaluate their learning in subject areas and in their wider skills development.

**Advantages**
Journals should be used to help learners reflect on their learning and to identify areas for improvement. This makes them invaluable in the development of independent learning, especially when used in conjunction with ILPs and as part of the Improving Own Learning Key Skill. Diaries and logs may also be used for assessment. One of their main benefits is that they provide continuity and structure for learners, making them not only look back on what they have just done but also look forward and plan for the next sessions.

**Disadvantages**
Journals, diaries and logs can be less valuable if learners don't understand why and how they should do them. There is a danger that they will be perceived merely as something to be done for the teachers but of little value to themselves.

## Informal methods of assessment

Teachers should make it apparent to learners that assessment is not always a formal and/or summative activity. Formative assessment, as previously discussed, can utilise a wide range of informal ways of assessing, checking and adjusting learning, including:

- discussion
- question and answer
- groupwork and activities
- quizzes
- gapped handouts
- observation
- reflection.

## Convergent and divergent assessment

When designing and delivering assessment techniques you should consider to what extent you wish to develop *convergent* or *divergent* responses in your learners. Convergent and divergent are not mutually exclusive; your assessments may be either or both, or a range in between the two.

*Convergent assessment* is relatively 'closed' or focused; that is one particular answer or solution to the problem. Multiple choice, computerised objective tests or short answer tests tend to be convergent. Convergent assessments are easier to mark, especially in computer-aided form, but can end up just as 'quiz' type tests which only measure learners' recall.

*Divergent assessment* tends to be more open and is aimed at generating a range of responses or alternative solutions to problems. Divergent activities are good for problem solving, creativity and generating ideas. Assessments and activities such as case studies and brainstorming sessions are divergent. Essays can involve divergent thinking and encourage learners to explore a range of ideas and theories.

## Giving feedback

Anecdotes of school are full of references to teacher feedback: 'could do better', 'must try harder', even just 'good' or 'fair'. Here's an example from my own school report for 1963 (Figure 9.1). One of my greatest achievements was to come top in composition and bottom in literature! My purpose in reproducing this is to demonstrate that limited feedback such as this is at best uninformative, at worst demotivating. Nothing in this indicates how improvements can be made, what 'fair' means or what 'good' means. Clearly this is a worst-case scenario but you will probably have seen a few examples from post-compulsory education which could 'do better'.

## What is feedback and what is it for?

Feedback is an essential element in effective communication between teachers and learners. This interpretation of feedback is used in the same way when we look at

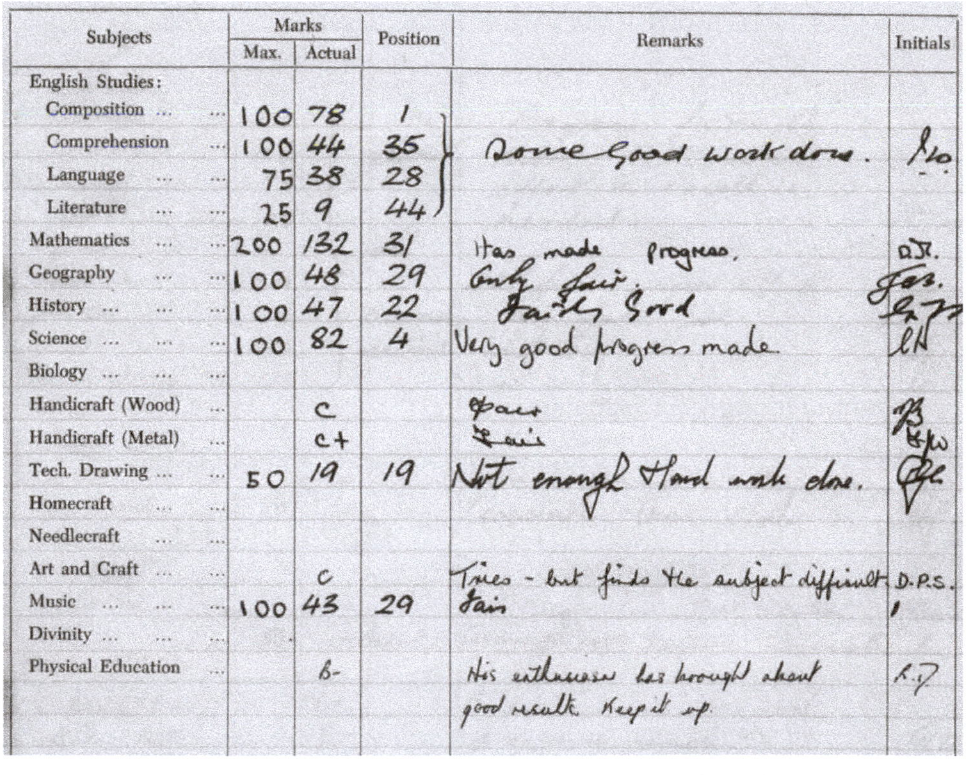

**Figure 9.1** School report.

assessment *for* learning. The willingness of learners and teachers to give and receive feedback is at the heart of formative assessment. Moorse and Clough (2002) state that assessment should involve learners, it is a two-way process. Feedback makes communication, teaching, learning and assessment into a two-way process. Feedback is one of the most powerful methods for improving learning. In this section I want to concentrate on the more specific meaning of feedback: the giving of information, advice and guidance to help learners improve using written and/or oral methods.

## Guidelines for giving feedback to learners

- Feedback should be positive. In both written and oral feedback teachers should indicate learners' achievements and areas of strength. The 'positive sandwich' is made up of two slices of positive, encouraging feedback, with a filling of specific reference to areas for improvement. In oral feedback, the positive element is reinforced by body language and tone of voice.

- Feedback should be targeted and identify specific areas for development in knowledge and skills.

- Feedback should be positive. In any area of life we feel better when people tell us that we have done something well; this is especially true of education and learning. However, students can soon become habituated to constant praise without any points for improvement.

- Feedback should be motivating and should encourage learners to want to do more. Limited or excessively critical feedback is demotivating.

- Feedback should be clear and unambiguous and, wherever possible, clearly related to learning outcomes.

- Feedback should take time. When learners have spent a lot of time on their work, cursory feedback or just a brief written comment is very dispiriting. Plan time to give whole-group feedback on general points, but also allow time for individual tutorials. You might think it's costly in time, but remember the power of feedback.

- If a student's work is a fail or a referral you must indicate precisely what they need to do in order to achieve a pass.

- Use feedback as 'scaffolding' to help them get to the next stage of their learning.

- Feedback should be part of a culture of high expectations. All learners can improve and we should expect them to. There is no point in 'labelling' learners as 'successes' or 'failures', 'academic' or 'not academic'. Think back to humanism in Chapter 5 – effective learning requires low threat (negative feedback can feel like a threat) with high challenge.

- When marking written work, don't return scripts covered in wounds inflicted by red pen, and avoid crosses and crossing out. When writing feedback remember that students can't hear you so be careful about the 'tone' of your comments.

- When giving grades in marked work, make sure that students know how to interpret their grades; share the criteria with them.

- In tutorial sessions or ILP reviews, feedback from individual pieces of work can contribute to an overall picture of the learner's progress and identify any general trends or areas for development.

## Emotional impact of assessment

One of the basic tenets of this book is that there is both an intellectual and an emotional component in learning. I would suggest that the emotional element has the greatest impact on learners' achievements. Nowhere is this emotional impact more pervasive than in the area of assessment. Assessment experiences have lifelong effects on people's lives and their life chances. Assessments of our performance are intimately bound up with our feelings about ourselves, our confidence and self-esteem. For many adults, their perceptions of themselves as 'successes' or 'failures', or as intelligent or not, stem in no small part from their experiences of assessment and the judgements made about them. In the lifelong learning sector we have to help learners and potential learners to change their self-concept even before they cross the threshold.

Anxiety about tests, it appears, begins quite early in life. Recent research suggests that the happiness and well-being of children begins to decline from Year 6, in part, it is suggested, because of the introduction of formal testing. With formal testing there is always the danger that the tests will become the end rather than the means and that learners – and teachers, managers, parents and politicians – will judge themselves solely on test results. Excessive formal, summative testing can reinforce young people's and adult's views of their abilities and the factors to which they attribute success or failure. This is particularly true of learners who are less able and who can't achieve success within the fairly narrow range of teaching and assessment they encounter.

---

**For your journal**

If you haven't already done so for your ILP, carry out an audit of the assessment methods you use. Ask yourself why you use them. Is it habit, because someone else suggested it, or because that's the way it's always been done?

What assessment methods have you not used? Could they be incorporated into your teaching?

In what ways have you given feedback to learners? How have they reacted to it and have there been signs of development?

Carry out some research with your learners; ask them what forms of assessment they find most helpful for learning.

**Journal extract: Philip**

Last week I set an essay on the sociology of the family. I was really rushed to get them marked and returned on time – I didn't want to keep them waiting. When I gave them back they didn't seem very interested and just stuck them in their files. I tried to go over some of the main points applicable to them all but there wasn't much discussion. My mentor said that my comments were too brief and that I hadn't really said how they could improve. She suggested that I should try individual tutorials to discuss their work. This is very time consuming. They need practice writing essays because they have to do them in the exam, but I'm not sure essays are always the best way.

## Further reading

Ecclestone, K. (2010) *Transforming Formative Assessment in Lifelong Learning*. Maidenhead: Open University Press.

Knight, P. (2001) *A Briefing on Key Concepts. Assessment Series No. 7*. York: Learning and Teaching Support Network (LTSN). This publication is intended for university teachers, but the 50 ideas for assessment might be very useful for those in lifelong learning.

Tummons, J. (2011) *Assessing Learning in Further Education* (3rd edn.) Exeter: Learning Matters.

## Websites

Qualifications and Curriculum Authority. Download copies of *Characteristics of Assessment for Learning* and *The 10 Principles of AfL*. www.qca.org.uk

UK Centre for Bioscience. www.bioscience.heacademy.ac.uk/ftp/Resources/gc/assess07-Keyconcepts%5B1%5D.pdf

# 10

# Functional skills and Skills for Life
Lynn Senior

**What this chapter is about**

- What are functional skills?
- Before functional skills
- Skills for Life
- 'Embedded' functional skills and Skills for Life
- Teaching and learning in functional skills
- Functional skills standards
- Assessment

**LLUK standards**

This chapter covers, at least, the following standards:
AS 1; AS 2; AK 2.1; AP 2.1; AK 2.2; AP 2.2; AS 3
BS 1; BK 1.1; BP 1.1; BK 1.2; BP 1.2; BS 3; BK 3.4; BP 3.4
CS 3; CK 3.3; CP 3.3; CK 3.4; CP 3.4

## What are functional skills?

The functional skills website on the Excellence Gateway (2012) defines these skills as: '. . . the essential English, mathematics and ICT skills that will enable learners to deal with everyday situations and practical problems in education, in work and in their everyday lives . . . these are vital skills that will enable learners to achieve, to progress and to develop their employability skills'. They were launched fully as a qualification in 2010 as part of the secondary curriculum, following a three-year pilot, and while predominantly aimed at post-14 are also available to younger learners. Functional skills qualifications are now widely available in schools, colleges, training providers and the workplace within England and are both stand-alone qualifications and integral components of apprenticeships, diplomas, GCSE and Foundation Learning Tier (FLT), available from entry level up to level 2, replacing both the Skills for Life and the key skills qualifications.

These skills qualifications were developed in response to employer requests that the future workforce needed to be able to compete globally, which meant having a workforce that was competent in what are seen to be key employment skills. Functional skills were conceived following the Labour government's '14–19 Education and Skills White Paper', produced in February 2005 and the 'Skills White Paper' from March 2005. The development was also in response to the realisation that it was possible for young people to achieve grade C in GCSE English and maths but still not have a satisfactory, functional knowledge of literacy and numeracy.

Functional skills are available at entry levels 1–3, levels 1 and 2 and they also exist as a stand-alone qualification, in addition to being an integral element of the 14–19 diploma. It was the intention of the then Labour government that functional skills would eventually replace key skills at levels 1 and 2. However, at the time of writing key skills are still very much in existence and can be undertaken in any approved centre, from schools and colleges to training providers. They are also offered by some employers, the armed forces and the Prison Service, as well as being one of the components of an apprenticeship. It was intended that functional skills should replace key skills in apprenticeships but the government has granted a temporary transitional extension until September 2012 during which functional skills and key skills can run in parallel.

One of the main differences between functional skills and previous qualifications is that they are not intended as discrete or 'add-on' but as part of an integrated curriculum. The intention, in short, is that learners should become 'functional' in life, learning and work. The Functional Skills Support Programme (2008) stated that functional skills should be recognised and promoted as essential for:

- getting the most from education and training
- the personal development of all young people and adults
- independence – enabling learners to manage in a variety of situations
- developing employability skills
- giving people a sound basis for learning.

Helping learners to become more 'functional' has significant implications for learning and teaching and will require the further development of existing practices including:

- focus on applied learning
- learner-centred approaches
- active learning and problem-centred approach
- partnership learning
- assessment for learning.

## Before functional skills

This whole area of 'skills', particularly those related to literacy, numeracy and ICT, can be confusing for the experienced teacher, let alone the novice. Various governments over the last 20 years have introduced a range of policies and initiatives aimed at overcoming the very real problem of poor literacy and numeracy, particularly in adults. Some of these initiatives are now discontinued, some remain and some are in transition.

### Basic skills

Basic skills are or were defined as 'the ability to read, write and speak in English/Welsh and to use mathematics at a level necessary to progress at work and in society in general' (Basic Skills Agency, www.archive.basic-skills.co.uk). By the mid-1990s there was no doubt in educational, economic and government circles that Britain had an unacceptably high number of people with poor or very poor literacy and numeracy. Not only was this recognised as a personal problem for each of these people, but it also had significant consequences for the economy. The government commissioned Sir Claus Moser to investigate the scale of the problem and make recommendations on how it could be tackled. His report, 'A Fresh Start', generally known as the Moser Report, was published in 1999 and painted a bleak picture of the national situation on literacy and numeracy. Moser's research suggested that seven million adults had literacy skills at or below those expected of 11 year olds; the situation regarding numeracy was at least as bad. Moser demanded a national strategy to reduce the numbers of adults with low levels of basic skills.

### Core or common skills

The term common skills can have several different meanings. In some cases common skills are the same as key skills, particularly in Scottish education.

In other areas, common skills and the common skills framework is used to describe the underpinning skills that a teacher working in the lifelong learning sector would need, commonly referred to as the *minimum core* and covering literacy, numeracy and ICT. Coverage of the minimum core is intended to provide a teacher with the minimum level of skills in language, literacy, numeracy and ICT that are essential to teachers who work in the lifelong learning sector.

### Key skills

Key skills were initially established following the Dearing Review of post 16-education (1996) and replaced what was previously known as core or common skills. They are defined as 'essential, generic skills which are the basis of all successful lifelong learning and development' (Scales 2008: 253). Six key skills exist at the time of writing:

- Communication
- Application of Number

- Information Technology
- Improving Own Learning and Performance
- Working with Others
- Problem-Solving.

Each of the skills is available at levels 1–4, with levels 2–3 attracting the Universities and Colleges Admissions Service (UCAS) points for application to university. To achieve a key skills qualification the learner must produce a portfolio of evidence and for the three main skills, Communication, Application of Number and ICT, also pass an externally assessed test.

## Skills for Life

Following the publication of the Moser report in 1999, the government launched the national Skills for Life strategy in 2001 which aimed significantly to improve the literacy, numeracy and language skills of adults in England. The original strategy included ICT but this was subsequently withdrawn. The strategy includes:

- *national standards* for literacy, numeracy and language which outline the range of skills and capabilities adults are expected to meet
- a *core curriculum* for each of literacy, numeracy and English for Speakers of Other Languages (ESOL) to clarify what should be taught to meet the national standards
- an *adult pre-entry framework* for literacy, language and numeracy for adults with learning difficulties and disabilities.

These documents are now available as part of the interactive core curriculum tool on the LSIS Excellence Gateway. This site also provides interactive pages and information for employability; embedded skills for life, and family learning. The documents provide advice and guidance on planning for teaching and learning skills for life with adult learners. According to the Excellence Gateway, the interactive online tool provides the following:

- promotes flexible and creative use of the curriculum content in a variety of learning contexts, including embedded learning
- enhances content and resources with additional guidance, exemplification and vocational material
- provides tools and features that will enable practitioners, including the wider embedded learning audience, to create effective personal learning experiences
- provides an online community where ideas and innovation can be shared and developed.

You can find the Skills for Life core curriculum documents and the interactive online tool at www.excellencegateway.org.uk/sflcurriculum.

## Minimum Core

The term Minimum Core refers to the knowledge, understanding and personal skills that all teachers should have to enable them to address the needs of their learners. The minimum core covers literacy, language, numeracy and ICT. Addressing the Minimum Core is a requirement of the generic Diploma in Teaching in the Lifelong Learning Sector (DTLLS). Part of the assessment criteria for this programme state that all teachers must demonstrate how they will develop the literacy, language and numeracy skills of their learners, through the specialist subjects that they teach. The minimum core is, essentially, about developing inclusive teaching and learning practices and helping learners to overcome barriers to learning. Information on the minimum core and details of how you as a teacher, who may not be a numeracy, ICT or literacy specialist, can undertake CPD to help you in this area can be found in many of the materials produced by the Centres of Excellence in Teacher Training (CETTs) that were developed to support the sector.

## The 'learning journey'

The 'learning journey' is a useful framework to understand and organise not only Skills for Life but also any programme of learning. It provides a structure for both learners and teachers. For Skills for Life the points on the journey could be as follows:

- Initial advice and guidance to help learners choose a learning programme.
- Initial assessment to discover the learner's skill levels.
- Diagnostic testing to provide detailed assessment of the learner's skill needs.
- An individual learning plan – agreed between learner and teacher and regularly reviewed together.
- Teaching and learning based around vocational or other learning contexts, using as far as possible embedded methods.
- Assessment for learning to help learners develop through structured, positive feedback.
- Summative assessment leading to the next stage in the learner's progression.

## 'Embedded' functional skills and Skills for Life

One of the key issues in both functional skills and Skills for Life is how they are taught. Should they be taught as an integral part of the learning programme or by separate provision? Increasingly, the consensus is that Skills for Life should be 'embedded'. The Skills for Life Strategy Unit defines embedding as follows:

> Embedded teaching and learning combines the development of literacy, language (ESOL), and numeracy with vocational and other skills. The skills acquired provide learners with the confidence, competence and motivation necessary for them to succeed in qualifications, in life and at work.

Recent research by the National Research Development Centre for Adult Literacy and Numeracy (NRDC; Roberts et al. 2005; Casey et al. 2006) suggests that embedding is preferable to stand-alone delivery, not only because it is more motivating and relevant for learners, particularly those on vocational courses, but also because it leads to increased retention and achievement. The NRDC's research indicates:

- On courses where skills were embedded retention was 16 per cent higher than non-embedded.

- On fully embedded courses, 93 per cent of those with an identified literacy need achieved literacy/ESOL qualification, compared to only 50 per cent on non-embedded courses

- For learners on fully-embedded courses 93 per cent of those with an identified numeracy need achieved a numeracy/maths qualification, compared to 70 per cent on non-embedded courses (Casey et al. 2006).

Research suggests that on programmes where the skills are embedded learners feel more motivated because they can see their skills being developed in a specific context in which they are interested. At a deeper level embedding helps learners to discover what it means to be a professional and:

> . . . learning what is worth knowing, how far they can draw on their existing expertise and what are the risks and challenges in taking on this new identity. This new professional identity is what motivates such learners and for young people this identity is often in contrast to their former experience as 'school pupils'. Teachers are both teachers and mentors. Learners are both 'doing things' and understanding the culture of their chosen jobs.
>
> (Roberts et al. 2005: 7)

Embedding these skills might seem the natural and obvious thing to do, particularly given what we know about 'situated' learning which is relevant to learners' interests and vocational areas. Quite simply, there are many courses in which numeracy is an everyday requirement, most notably in engineering or construction. Similar arguments also apply to literacy, language and ICT in vocational and other contexts. Providing embedded learning is a challenge for providers in terms of organisation and funding. The range of 'embeddedness' is a continuum but there are four main points along it:

1 *Non-embedded*. Skills and vocational learning/context are almost entirely separate.

2 *Partly embedded*. Skills and vocational learning/context are embedded to some degree.

3 *Mostly embedded*. Skills are mainly acquired and developed in context but some elements are separately taught.

4 *Fully embedded*. Learners experience their skills development and vocational learning as an integrated whole.

It should not be assumed that all learning must be integrated at all times. It may be appropriate on occasions, for example, to offer literacy support to business and administration students as separate provision so that they can develop the skills in writing letters and reports in a vocational context. It is vital that vocational teachers and Skills for Life teachers work together to plan and prepare schemes of work and learning activities and resources; vocational area staff should include Skills for Life staff in team and planning meetings. Vocational staff do not have to become literacy and numeracy teachers but they can learn about the barriers to skills development which their learners experience. Equally, Skills for Life teachers do not have to become plasterers or hairdressers but an understanding of the vocational contexts will better equip them to support learners and vocational staff and to develop learning and assessment materials which are set in a vocational context.

---

**Journal extract: Darren, training to teach Skills for Life (Literacy)**

I've been working with the hairdressing students on my placement for two weeks now and haven't felt particularly welcome. They're all at Level 1 and I've got to get them up to Level 2 but they're not really interested in writing. Talking – fine. Writing NO!

Up to now they've been working on standard worksheets on spelling, punctuation and grammar. Even I think these are boring. I visited the hairdressing team and discussed some ideas about connecting their written work to their vocational stuff more. They didn't seem particularly keen and didn't really think literacy was their business. But we started to work out a few ideas for the students to do some relevant written work. So far, we've come up with writing some publicity materials and adverts, plus some an idea for a short magazine piece about hairstyles and colours. At present the last idea seems to have grabbed the interest of most of them. Still a lot of spelling, punctuation and grammar problems but at least they're more interested and I've got some of their work I can talk to them about.

---

## Teaching and learning in functional skills

Functional skills should enable learners to solve problems in any given situation and therefore any activities that we provide should allow learners to make their own decisions and choices. Therefore, it is important that the variety of learning and teaching methods we use are designed to scaffold the learners and allow them to build their confidence as their skill level develops. The following learning and teaching methods are suggestions of the types of activity that could be used in the classroom.

### English

Functional English skills are, arguably, the easiest skills to embed in our everyday teaching. Embedded simply means to teach as part of the main subject rather than offering literacy or English as a discrete course. As teachers we regularly ask our learners to produce written accounts, make presentations on a given topic, and gather information from a range of sources. It is therefore a relatively simple task to apply the standards to the work we ask our students to complete. For example, if we are teaching travel and tourism we could set a piece of classwork that requires the learners to gather information on a range of destinations suitable for families with small children. They could be asked to collect data on temperature, number and type of beaches, hotels, activities available within a resort, children's clubs and prices of basic meals. Once they have the relevant information we could ask them to prepare fact sheets for the families, detailing appropriate information. This allows them to select relevant information from the range they have gathered. Following the completion of the fact sheets the learner could then make recommendations, with justification, about which destination would be the better option. Other examples of activities that you could consider might include the following:

- Completion of forms as part of a customer enquiry (role play).
- Completion of application forms as part of a work-related lesson.
- Responding to information provided over the telephone, e.g. taking a table booking at a restaurant, dealing with a customer complaint.
- Present an idea for a group event (beauty, business).
- Produce a leaflet or flyer for the company in which they complete the work experience.
- Interview members of staff/students about healthy eating (hospitality).

## Maths

Maths occurs in many parts of daily life, so again it should be relatively simple to embed functional maths into your teaching without the student realising that they are actually doing maths! Let's take unit 6 of the level 2 Diploma in Creative and Media, Creative Teamwork. As part of this unit the learner becomes involved in the planning and development of an event, which includes the production of a schedule or action plan for the event itself. As part of this the students could produce a cost plan for the implementation of the event, produce a schematic diagram that shows the layout for the event, with appropriate measurements and 3D drawings, produce break-even charts for ticket sales plus countless other numeracy based activities. Other examples of activities that you consider could include:

- Read bus or rail timetables.
- Draw schematic diagrams.
- Create 3D images.
- Measure out ingredients.
- Create a simple costing plan for an event or activity.
- Create graphs or pie charts comparing temperature or hours of sunshine.

## ICT

Many of our learners will already be familiar with a wide range of technology, including items such as mobile phones, i-Pads and i-Pods, not to mention the common types of software found on most personal computers, PowerPoint, spreadsheets, Word. In addition, most if not all students will be familiar with and using internet programs, blogs, wikis and social networking technologies such as Twitter and Facebook. As a functional skill ICT shouldn't be seen in isolation. If our learners are gathering information for a project, why not ask them to do it via the internet; if they are producing cost plans, make use of Excel or other spreadsheet software. If they are working on group activities and tasks, why not set up 'group emails' and 'wikis' for the purpose of the activity. Other examples of activities could include the following:

- Creation of simple forms to store data.
- Enter data into documents and edit.
- Use 'podcasts' to record group meetings.
- Produce PowerPoint presentations and handouts to support presentations.
- Produce a short promotional film or video for an organisation within the subject area.

**Activity**

Plan a session that integrates ICT functional skills into your subject. What opportunities for different ICT uses can you identify?

## Functional skills standards

The functional skills standards have been developed to define and differentiate the skill requirements and levels for each of the functional skills. The standards explain the difference between the different qualification levels and identify the key factors that will allow you to determine the learners' proficiency in that particular skill. Proficiency is assessed on the following:

- The complexity of situations and activities.
- The technical demand associated with these activities.
- A learner's level of familiarity with the task or activity.
- The level of independence a learner can use to complete the activity.

At the time of writing the functional skill standards include the areas of learning shown in Table 10.1.

**Table 10.1** Functional skills standards.

---

**Functional English**
Speaking and listening
Reading
Writing

**Functional Maths**
Process skills:
Choose an approach to tackle the problem, formulate a model using mathematics, use mathematics to provide answers, interpret and check the results, evaluate the model and approach, explain the analysis and results, apply and adapt this experience in other situations as they arise.

**Functional ICT**
Use ICT systems
Find and select information
Develop, present and communicate information

---

## Assessment

The assessment process for functional skills was developed by the QCA (now defunct) and ensures that the awarding bodies responsible for functional skills assessment take into account the application of the skill into a real life context. According to the latest information from Ofqual (2012: 2), assessment must:

- provide realistic contexts, scenarios and problems
- specify tasks that are relevant to the context
- require application of knowledge, skills and understanding for a purpose
- require problem solving.

For the most effective learning, teachers should be embedding functional skills into the curriculum rather than allowing them to be stand-alone and taught as separate entities. In other words, we should be making use of naturally occurring activities within the subject to help the learner develop the skills. However, at present functional skills tests are not contextualised and a learner needs to be able to apply his or her knowledge to any given situation. All of the major awarding bodies will have information for you to look at on the format and style of the tests and I would encourage you to look at your own awarding board information to enable you to prepare your students effectively if you do use embedding as your method of delivery.

Teachers and organisations can choose to enter the learner for assessment when they judge them to be ready at any time throughout the duration of the diploma qualification, or alternatively they can enter them at the end of the programme. My approach has been to enter learners halfway through their programme. This approach allows both teachers and learners to further identify any areas of weakness should the learner not succeed. This ensures that additional support and/or practice is provided in those areas to allow the learner maximum opportunity to succeed on the second attempt.

## CPD for functional skills

Whether or not functional skills are embedded within your curriculum area or treated as discrete subjects as a teacher you will need to ensure that your skills are up to date in line with the minimum core requirements of the lifelong learning sector (LLS). There are many activities that you can complete as part of your own CPD to update and refresh your skills. For example the Excellence Gateway (www.excellence.org.uk) has a section on CPD activities to enable teachers to better embed functional skills through a learner centred approach with the emphasis on the individual learners' needs and aspirations.

---

**For your journal**

Skills for Life and functional skills are a concern of all teachers in the lifelong learning sector.

To what extent does the delivery of skills affect your planning, preparation, delivery and assessment?

Do you consciously plan for skills development?

To what extent and in what ways have you embedded Skills for Life and functional skills into your planning and delivery?

How successful has this been and what have been the learners' reactions to the inclusion of these skills?

---

## Further reading

Senior, L. (2010) *The Essential Guide to Teaching 14–19 Diplomas.* Harlow: Pearson Education.

## Websites

Excellence Gateway:

- Skills for Life core curricula www.excellencegateway.org.uk/sflcurriculum
- Good Practice Guide for the initial skills check and assessment. www.repository. excellencegateway.org.uk/fedora/objects/import-pdf:16839/datastreams/PDF/content

- Overview of the learning journey. www.archive.excellencegateway.org.uk/pdf/Learning_Journey.pdf

Ofqual (2012) *Criteria for Functional Skills Qualifications.* www.ofqual.gov.uk/qualifications-assessments/89-articles/238-functional-skills-criteria

Skills Workshop. Free functional and skills for life resources. www.skillsworkshop.org/

# 11

# Behaviour for learning

**What this chapter is about**

- What is 'bad' behaviour?
- Reports – Elton, Steer, Ofsted
- Strategies to encourage positive behaviour
- 'Assertive discipline'
- Behaviour for learning
- The link between learning and teaching and behaviour
- Behaviour, motivation and emotional intelligence
- Enjoyment
- Adult learners' behaviour

**LLUK standards**

This chapter covers, at least, the following standards:
AS 1; AS 1.1; AP 1.1; AK 4.1; AP 4.1
BS 1; BK 1.1; BP 1.1; BK 1.2; BP 1.2; BK 1.3; BP 1.3 BS 2; BK 2.1; BP 2.1; BK 2.2;
BP 2.2; BK 2.3; BP 2.3; BK 2.5; BP 2.5 BS 3; BK 3.1; BP 3.1
CS 2; CK 2.1; CP 2.1
DK 1.2; DP 1.2

This chapter is called behaviour *for* learning because it isn't just about managing or 'curing' bad behaviour, it's about creating behaviour which is conducive to learning. 'Bad' behaviour is one of the issues which most concern new teachers in lifelong learning and in schools. The media and popular opinion tends to suggest that schools are populated by frightening and violent young thugs who terrorise their fellow learners and their teachers; for many people, the reputation of FE colleges is not much better. Having worked with 16–19 year olds as well as adults for more than 20 years, I have to say that the instances of extreme bad behaviour have been very few and that for most of the time most young people are pleasant, decent and want to learn.

The lifelong learning sector (LLS) covers a wide variety of learners from 14–16 year olds to senior citizens, with many different reasons and motivations for being there. Behaviour problems are generally associated with young learners, increasingly with 14–16 year olds in colleges, but adult education tutors would undoubtedly support the view that some adults can be difficult and demanding, indeed might exhibit 'bad' or 'challenging' behaviour. In this section there will be some discussion of the 14–16 and 16–19 groups specifically, but to a great extent the guidelines and advice on behaviour will be appropriate to learners of all ages.

## What is 'bad' behaviour?

When people talk of behaviour in schools and colleges, they generally tend to be talking about 'bad' behaviour, but there doesn't seem to be clear agreement about what constitutes bad behaviour. What do you think?

---

**Activity**

- List the kinds of behaviour that you consider to be 'bad'.
- What is it about these behaviours that makes them 'bad'?
- What are the consequences of these kinds of behaviour: (a) for you; (b) for the other learners?
- If you have done this activity as a group, do you all agree about what 'bad' behaviour is? In what ways are your views different?
- What words other than 'bad' might describe this behaviour and its consequences more accurately?

---

The suggested activity will almost certainly have revealed that we have different perceptions of learner behaviour and different thresholds of acceptability. One teacher might feel that groups should be run with military precision and with strict discipline and behaviour imposed on the learners. Another might prefer a noisy, physically active session in which learners have considerable freedom about how they behave and personal choice regarding how, what or even whether they learn. These two teachers – who I have lazily typified as 'the sergeant-major' and 'the hippy' – represent extreme views of attitudes towards behaviour and would probably regard each other's methods as anathema. As reflective teachers, we would argue that the most appropriate methods are those which are the most effective and that these will vary from teacher to teacher based on their understanding of their individual learners and groups and the context in which they are working. Those who work for large learning organisations, however, should consider the policies relating to behaviour and discipline and try, as far as possible, to have the same expectations of acceptable and appropriate behaviour.

Describing behaviour as 'bad' is imprecise and not very helpful in promoting positive behaviour. As we have seen, one teacher's 'bad' behaviour might be another teacher's free expression for students. Both of these would, almost certainly, agree that there are behaviours which are 'challenging' or 'disruptive' even, to use a term from schools, describing some learners as having emotional and behavioural difficulties (EBD). In essence, they would agree that for them some kinds of individual or group behaviour cause concern and are not conducive to learning and achievement. Given that there are differing perceptions of behaviour and thresholds of acceptability, we have to consider carefully just how 'bad' is the bad behaviour. Incessant talking, inappropriate comments or rudeness are extremely irritating but not life threatening, and often happen just because there is a room full of lively young people excited by each other's company. Teachers who respond disproportionately are in danger of escalating minor issues into major confrontations. The skill in teaching, as in personal relationships, is to recognise potential trouble spots and de-escalate them.

## A 'golden age' of behaviour?

Many people, especially politicians and those in the media, have a fondness for a 'golden age' somewhere in the past when everything was better than it is now. This is particularly true in discussions of behaviour in schools and colleges, which in the popular imagination has drastically declined and is taken as evidence of the moral collapse of youth in modern times. It seems likely that people have always thought this way, as these historical quotes suggest:

> I see no hope for the future of our people if they are dependent on the frivolous youth of today, for certainly all youth are reckless beyond words. When I was a boy, we were taught to be discreet and respectful of elders, but the present youth are exceedingly wise and impatient of restraint.
>
> (Attributed to Hesiod, eighth century)

> The world is passing through troublous times. The young people of today think of nothing but themselves. They have no reverence for parents or old age. They are impatient of all restraint. They talk as if they knew everything, and what passes for wisdom with us is foolishness with them.
>
> (Peter the Hermit 1274)

The Department of Education and Science (1989) report, *Discipline in schools* (known as the Elton Report), refers to a 1938 study of behaviour in 25 English girls' schools in which teachers complain about the number of difficult pupils they had to deal with and about persistent noise in the classroom (Department of Education and Science 1989: 64).

Aristotle, writing in the fourth century BC, was more understanding of young people in his recognition that life is, for many of them, exciting and full of possibilities:

'Young people are in a condition like permanent intoxication, because youth is sweet and they are growing.'

Despite moral panics about a decline in pupil behaviour, most recent reports (DfES 2005, 2009; Ofsted 2005) find little evidence to support this belief. As Watkins (2011: 3) remarks of his research in this area: '. . . There is no research which could provide us with evidence that pupil behaviour is becoming worse, or better for that matter.' There is still bad behaviour in schools and colleges, this is undeniable, but looking back to a mythical 'golden age' for solutions is a fruitless activity. We need to concentrate on the situations we face here and now.

## A definition of 'bad' behaviour

You might ask why we need to define bad behaviour; don't we just recognise when we experience it? As the activity above suggests, however, perceptions of what constitutes bad or disruptive behaviour are very subjective. The following defining characteristics are taken from the Learning and Skills Development Agency (2007: 2):

- Behaviour that disrupts routine teaching to an extent that challenges the teacher's resources and the concentration of other learners; this behaviour may not be violent, offensive or dangerous, simply disruptive.
- Behaviour that is offensive or violent, interfering with routine activity.
- Extreme passivity or non-engagement in learning.
- Intermittent patterns of attendance.

It is important to remember that the majority of bad or undesirable behaviour tends to be low level, as the following major reports have confirmed. The majority of research and reports into behaviour has been carried out in the context of schools; however, most of the conclusions are applicable to learning in post-compulsory settings.

## Elton Report 1989

This report was a major national investigation into behaviour in schools, prompted by media reports of declining behaviour in schools (Department of Education and Science 1989). It concluded that the key issue was constant low-level disruption and off-task behaviour. The key aspects of misbehaviour (going from the most frequent to the least) were identified as follows:

- talking out of turn
- work avoidance
- hindering other learners
- lateness
- unnecessary noise
- breaking rules

- out-of-seat
- verbal abuse of other pupils
- general rowdiness
- physical aggression to other pupils
- verbal abuse of teacher
- physical disruptiveness
- physical aggression towards teacher.

## Ofsted Report 2005

The Ofsted report *Managing Challenging Behaviour* (2005) stated in its main findings that 'the behaviour of the very large majority of pupils and students remained satisfactory or better'. They further state:

> The most common form of poor behaviour is persistent, low level disruption of lessons that wears down staff and interrupts learning. Extreme acts of violence remained very rare and are carried out by a very small proportion of pupils.
>
> (Ofsted 2005: 4)

## Steer Report 2005

The report *Learning Behaviour*, otherwise known the Steer Report, concluded:

> ... In our experience, where unsatisfactory behaviour does occur, in the vast majority of cases it involves low-level disruption in lessons. Incidents of serious misbehaviour, and especially acts of extreme violence remain exceptionally rare and are carried out by a very small proportion of pupils.
>
> (DfES 2005: 2)

## Steer Report 2009

This report, *Learning Behaviour: Lessons Learned*, noted that there had been no deterioration in standards since the 2005 report. Indeed, they state: ... 'There is strong evidence from a range of sources that the overall standards of behaviour achieved by schools is good and has improved in recent years' (DfES 2009: 5). This report sets out six core beliefs that underpinned its work:

- Poor behaviour cannot be tolerated as it is a denial of the right of pupils to learn and teachers to teach. To enable learning to take place preventative action is most effective, but where this fails, schools must have clear, firm and intelligent strategies in place to help pupils manage their behaviour.
- There is no single solution to the problem of poor behaviour, but all schools have the potential to raise standards if they are consistent in implementing good practice in learning, teaching and behaviour management.

- The quality of learning, teaching and behaviour in schools are inseparable issues, and the responsibility of all staff.

- Respect has to be given in order to be received. Parents and carers, pupils and teachers all need to operate in a culture of mutual regard.

- The support of parents is essential for the maintenance of good behaviour. Parents and schools each need to have a clear understanding of their rights and responsibilities.

- School leaders have a critical role in establishing high standards of learning, teaching and behaviour (DfES 2009: 3).

The references to parents in these core beliefs may not seem appropriate to all of the lifelong learning sector. However, for many young people in colleges the involvement of their parents is important and should be actively sought, but it is important to remember that it is the young person who is the focus of any discussion about their learning and development. For many young people in the lifelong learning sector the involvement of employers is also a key relationship.

### House of Commons Education Committee 2011: Behaviour and Discipline in Schools

This report notes problems of data collection on behaviour in schools and states that it is difficult to reach 'any evidence-based or objective judgement on either the state of behaviour in schools today or whether there has been an improvement over time' (2011: 3). The report concludes that much of the Elton Report, particularly the low-level nature of bad behaviour, remains valid today, although some of this behaviour is 'brushed aside'. While affirming the generally positive picture of behaviour in schools, the authors of the report surmise that previous reports have tended to draw on evidence from head teachers more than from practising classroom teachers, giving a somewhat rosier picture.

### Prevention is better than cure

There are many things you can do to create a learning climate which will encourage positive behaviour, particularly at the session planning stage. Television childcare experts emphasise the importance of structure and routine in children's lives and I would suggest this desire for structure extends to learners of all ages. There is considerable evidence to support the view that youngsters in schools do not like lessons which are badly planned and they do not feel sure about they are doing or do not have enough to do.

Bad behaviour cannot be completely eliminated but there is much that can be done to reduce it considerably. The following ideas and suggestions can contribute to improvement. Individually, they might not make a noticeable difference but if they are applied in combination and practised regularly and consistently by all staff – supported and actively promoted by management – things will improve.

## Structure and planning of sessions

In Chapter 8 we considered how to plan and structure sessions. You might want to refer to this in conjunction with the points which follow.

### Arrival

Wherever possible, arrive before your learners. This is important for several reasons. First, it demonstrates that you are a professional who starts the session promptly, that you are prepared and that you have similar expectations of your students. Second, difficult groups will know from the outset that you are running 'a tight ship' and monitoring their behaviour. Wherever possible greet the learners at the door as they arrive, using their names. Most importantly, early arrival gives you time to set up your resources and materials for the session and ensure that everything is working. If you have to spend five or ten minutes of the lesson sorting things out, learners will feel cheated that they've made the effort to arrive on time but you're not ready for them. In addition, you can prepare the environment by adjusting the light and temperature if necessary; arranging the furniture in a way that best suits this group, and making the place look tidy and businesslike. The room should be safe; check there are no trailing wires, dangerous equipment or electrical hazards.

### Establishment or opening phase of the lesson

This sets the tone of the whole session. Establish your authority from the outset and don't begin until you have silence and attention. Signal clearly the session is going to start, either with a firm clear statement or an agreed understood signal, such as a clap of the hands. Once you have silence and full attention, get straight into the lesson and don't wait for latecomers. Provide an overview of the session – what it's about, why you're doing it and what the learners will be doing. Begin with a bang – set a question or pose a problem – and try to get people interested and engaged straight away.

### Transitions

There should be smooth transitions between the different sections and the transitions should not leave any gaps which learners can exploit and pursue their own agenda. When you move from one section or topic to the next, briefly recap what has been done and state clearly what will happen next. Above all, keep them busy with appropriately challenging tasks. Don't allow too long for student activities and tell them clearly how much time will be allowed. If you consider your own attendance at staff development sessions, I am sure you will have 'messed about' if there wasn't enough to do or tasks were allotted too much time for completion; there's no reason why the same shouldn't apply to your learners.

### Ending

Plan so that you finish on time. Finishing too early sets a bad precedent and your learners will come to expect it every time. Don't overrun a session, even if it's been a great one; learners need their breaks. Having summarised the session, give a brief overview of the next and how it will link to the session just completed. Thank the learners for their attention and their activity, remind them of when and where the next session is and of any materials or equipment they will need.

## Strategies to encourage positive behaviour

This section provides some brief guidelines for developing positive behaviour. These cannot be applied to all learners at all times and as a reflective teacher you will need to develop a repertoire of techniques to draw on according to who you are working with. In the lifelong learning sector we are encouraging independent and active learning so it is important that our learners take responsibility for their actions and behaviour. We should aim to develop behaviour *for* learning. This emphasises the positive relationships we make with learners, rather than controlling and reprimanding them. Much of the following will apply to 14–19 year olds; some will be useful when working with adult learners

### Rules and routines

As stated earlier, people like structure. Establishing and implementing appropriate rules and routines is part of providing structure. When establishing these we should remember that both learners and teachers have rights and responsibilities which have to be balanced.

- If you work for a college or large learning organisation there will be policies and procedures relating to student behaviour. It is part of your job to know and apply these consistently. It makes life easier for teaching colleagues if these procedures are applied equally.
- You will want to develop your own rules and routines with your own learners. As far as possible, these should be discussed and agreed with them, be age-appropriate and applied consistently. You could even draw up a contract which is printed and displayed.
- Your rules and routines will include behaviours that are unacceptable, for example: mobiles switched off; no inappropriate language, particularly racist or sexist; no lateness, unless explained and agreed.
- Remember that it is more effective to recognise and reward positive behaviour rather than reprimand negative behaviour. Don't overdo it; too much praise can start to sound hollow and formulaic.
- Remember that learners have expectations of you; meeting these will go some way to developing positive behaviour. They expect well-planned and stimulating sessions; respect, politeness and fairness; professional, well-organised teachers; fair assessment; feedback on their progress and support in their development.

### Non-verbal communication (NVC)

Chapter 3 stresses the importance of NVC; you should revisit that section. Here are some specific examples related to behaviour.

### Eye contact

- Eye contact can be used positively to show that you are listening and interested in your learners.
- It can also be used to control learners who are behaving inappropriately. A prolonged look will generally change behaviour, if only briefly. Too much eye contact can, however, be confrontational.

### Posture

- Adopt a confident and assertive posture. You have legitimate authority within the classroom and you should not be frightened to appear in control.
- Vizard (2007: 61) recommends that you should '. . . stand upright with a straight back . . . avoid standing and stooping slightly with your head down and your leg bent as it creates an impression of lack of confidence'. He also suggests you should avoid closed body language such as folded arms; an open posture with feet slightly apart is a more confident posture.

### Movement

- Move around the classroom. 'Patrol' the classroom and be vigilant for signs of disruption if you have lively, challenging learners. There shouldn't be any 'no-go' areas for teachers in the room.
- When students are engaged on a task, standing and watching from the back of the room can be a good control position.
- Movement is not just about control, however. It is also about being there to offer support, especially during individual and group activities.

### Proximity

- Use personal space carefully and appropriately.
- In some cases it will be effective to move into an individual's space in order deliver or reinforce sanctions.
- Regular invasions of learners' space can be threatening and confrontational. If there are confrontations, don't 'square up' to people or invade their space face to face. It's better to stand back a bit and at right angles to the person.

### Voice and voice qualities

- Shouting is rarely appropriate, even if a learner has raised their voice to you. You should aim to keep calm and speak slowly and clearly to avoid escalating the tension.
- Speak clearly and at an appropriate pace and give clear instructions. Learners get frustrated when they can't hear or understand you.
- Try 'voice matching' and keep the volume and intonation at a pace which you expect from your students. This will avoid a situation becoming a 'shouting match'.

### Politeness and respect

- Teachers should model good behaviour; this includes basic politeness such as saying 'please' and 'thank you'.

- Learners deserve respect. We demonstrate this by fairness and politeness and by listening to them and showing that we value them as individuals.
- Use learners' names. It shows respect and affirms relationships. 'No-naming' is impersonal and implies that you can't be bothered getting to know people.

### Relationships
- Practise 'self-calming'. In a confrontation, the first person who needs to keep calm is you.
- Criticise the behaviour, not the person. Making personal comments, such as 'You're an extremely rude person' attacks the whole person. Be clear that you disapprove of what they've done or said, not of them.
- Use praise and reward regularly to recognise and encourage positive behaviour and achievements. You know how bad it feels when a manager consistently criticises you but rarely congratulates you on a job well done; it's the same for learners.
- Try using unconditional positive regard. This means that whatever the behaviour you maintain standards of respect and politeness with the individual and recognise their value as a person even if you disagree with their behaviour. I once had a tutee at college who had major attendance and punctuality problems and was an attention seeker in class. During our tutorial sessions I was consistently calm and polite, used his name, listened to him and was calm and reasonable. It was hard work but we avoided confrontations and eventually it paid off, partly because he felt I was treating him as an adult.
- Don't be frightened of saying sorry to a student if you feel you've overreacted to a situation. Dixie (2011: 8) says:

> We all get things wrong occasionally and, if you are trying to encourage a high level of reflectivity among your students, it is important to apologise to them when you get it wrong. When I say apologise, I do not mean in a fawning, sycophantic manner – that would be seen by many students as a sign of weakness.

### Rooms and spaces
- Depressing looking rooms and student spaces have a depressing effect on students. If you have any influence with estates colleagues, try to get rooms decorated in bright colours.
- As far as possible, try to create learning spaces that are bright, clean and tidy.
- Have recent displays of student work and relevant posters and other visual material in rooms and recreational spaces. Get students involved in creating displays. Unfortunately, some modern teaching spaces don't encourage wall displays, so you might need to find alternatives; perhaps they could make a YouTube video.
- Increasingly, schools and colleges are recognising the advantages of creating more open and interactive learning spaces which are technology rich and have flexible seating and working arrangements. This encourages a more cooperative and student-centred atmosphere.

## 'Assertive discipline'

In general terms the notion of assertiveness recognises that both parties in social encounters have rights which need to be recognised if their interactions are going to be mutually successful. A continuum of behaviours might look like this:

Non-assertive/passive          Assertive          Aggressive/hostile

Being assertive is not like being aggressive. Being assertive means being clear about what you feel, about what you want and how it can be achieved. It requires open and confident verbal and non-verbal communication and the ability to communicate calmly without hostility. Aggressive behaviour intimidates others and doesn't recognise their rights. It leaves them feeling hurt, humiliated or resentful; the most extreme form is bullying. Non-assertive behaviour means that you don't state your feelings or say clearly what you want. You tend to regard yourself as less important than others and don't recognise your own rights. It's bad for your self-esteem because you often feel that you have compromised yourself to please or appease others.

The assertive discipline approach was developed by Canter and Canter in 1976, based on providing clear, firm and non-hostile communication. It recognises that teachers and learners have rights.

## Teachers' rights

- A legitimate right to teach.
- A professional right and responsibility to establish rules and procedures which define acceptable behaviour.
- The right and responsibility to teach learners consistently to follow the rules.
- The right to ask for assistance and be supported by the organisation.

## Learners' rights

- The right to learn and develop appropriate behaviours and to be responsible for limiting their own inappropriate.
- Recognition of and support for appropriate behaviours.
- A structured environment in which they know in advance the consequences of appropriate or inappropriate behaviour.

A passive or non-assertive teacher might respond to inappropriate behaviours or make requests in a manner and tone which sounds meek or weary and resigned but irritable. This style often involves rhetorical questions such as 'Why are you doing that?' or 'Do you think that's clever?' Passive teachers are more likely to state the possible consequences of inappropriate behaviour but don't follow it up consistently, frequently allowing a 'second chance'.

An aggressive teacher uses hostile language, threats and anger. They often humiliate and ridicule learners who then feel belittled or resentful. They tend to chastise the person not the behaviour and attack learners' feelings of self-worth. I had some teachers like this when I was at school. Their style, underpinned by the ever-present threat of corporal punishment, was successful in that it left us docile, silent and scared but unsuccessful in that we were not in an emotional state for learning. Iron control was considered a success; learning a possible but not necessary outcome.

The key to assertive discipline is firm, fair, clear, consistent but non-hostile communication and actions based on agreed, possibly negotiated, guidelines and structure. Assertive teachers clearly state what they expect and don't get into arguments about the fairness or otherwise of rules.

## The teachers' voice

Canter (2010) emphasises the importance of developing and using the right 'teacher voice'. He states:

> Teachers who have not developed their voice often speak in a meek or non-assertive manner, which communicates to their students that they are not confident in their ability to lead the classroom. They are almost asking the students for permission to be the teacher.
>
> (Canter 2010: 9)

The teacher's voice, in summary, has the following characteristics:

- an assertive tone – it is decisive, self-assured and firm
- it fills the room – it uses volume appropriately to reach every corner of the room so that there are no 'dead spaces'
- it never speaks over learners – teachers never begin speaking until the students have stopped and are ready to listen
- it does not get into arguments with learners.

## Is assertive discipline appropriate for young people and adults?

The use of the assertive discipline model might seem authoritarian or inappropriate to teachers working with young people and adults in the lifelong learning sector. A reflective teacher will know about this model and will use it appropriately, but, particularly when they have worked with a group of adults for some time, they will know when it is appropriate to be more relaxed and communicate with learners in an equal and adult manner. However, the notion of assertiveness is an important one for both teachers and learners to understand and use if their interactions, and the learning, is to be successful.

### Behaviour for learning

Clearly, there are times when behaviour will have to be managed or controlled and teachers will need to have a range of strategies at their disposal in order to deal with specific behaviour issues and difficult situations. These, however, are not sufficient in themselves to create a positive atmosphere for learning. Ellis and Tod (2009: 46) criticise what they see as the 'separation of learning and behaviour'. They suggest that the representation of behaviour in schools has concentrated on bad behaviour which needs to be stopped or removed before learning can occur. As a consequence teachers may feel that they have to acquire and use a whole range of techniques to 'manage' behaviour which are separate from the skills and techniques needed to positively encourage learning for all. This model suggests that the more behaviour management techniques teachers acquire, the more effective they will become at stopping bad behaviour so that learning can begin.

Ellis and Tod (2009: 53) emphasise the importance of 'learning behaviour' and point out the two meanings of this phrase. The first relates to learning about behaviour and the appropriateness of different kinds of behaviour. The second, more importantly, refers to the types of behaviour that are conducive to learning and apply to all pupils. We are encouraged to adapt a 'behaviour for learning approach': '. . . It encourages a shift away from concern with stopping unwanted behaviour towards the promotion of effective learning behaviours' (Ellis and Tod 2009: 65).

## What are effective learning behaviours?

A systematic review of the relationship between learning theories and behaviour in school contexts (Powell and Tod 2004) found that learning behaviour is influenced by cognitive, affective and social factors and is an interaction of how learners think, feel and act. The key positive learning behaviours we should seek to develop in our learners are as follows:

- engagement
- collaboration
- participation
- communication
- independent activity
- responsiveness
- self-regard
- self-esteem
- responsibility.

The researchers grouped learning behaviours under three headings: the 'product' of learning (on-task); the 'participation' in group learning (for example, participation in engagement communication and collaboration); and the 'person' (self-esteem, self-regard, self-efficacy) (Powell and Tod 2004: 9).

### Product (on-task) learning behaviours

These behaviours relate to learners' motivation and self-discipline and their ability to be engaged and to stay on task. This links to Guy Claxton's notion of 'resilience' (see below). Positive influences on on-task behaviour are:

- focusing on learning improvements and personal mastery of skills rather than performance goals
- promoting on-task discussion between learners
- checking that tasks are understood by learners
- providing structured tasks that are supported by communication with teachers.

## Learning behaviours for participation

Participation recognises the importance of the social aspect of learning. Effective participation can be encouraged by, for example:

- encouraging dialogue and discussion between learners and between learners and teachers
- fostering effective communication
- discouraging competitive learning contexts and encouraging positive interpersonal relationships.

## Person-centred learning behaviours

These learning behaviours relate to the learners' 'relationship' with themselves and their self-esteem and their beliefs about their ability to learn and improve. The following are some key points in developing person-centred learning behaviours:

- developing learning and teaching which encourages motivation and self-discipline
- helping learners to recognise barriers to their own learning and to overcome these
- encouraging 'learning to learn'
- developing a sense of 'agency' and self-efficacy in learners whereby they feel that they can have some control over their own learning and development.

## The link between effective teaching and learning and behaviour

All the major reports outlined earlier in this chapter make clear that there is a direct relationship between the quality of teaching and learners' behaviour. The 2009 Steer Report concluded that 'consistent good quality teaching is the most significant factor in raising standards and reducing low level disruption. Learning, teaching and behaviour are inseparable issues for schools' (DfES 2009: 17).

It is important for teachers and managers in the lifelong learning sector to take a 'total' approach to their curriculum and to consider not only the range of their provision but also their teaching and learning methods, assessment methods, student support, learning facilities and resources.

## A learning and teaching policy

Many people working in the sector complain that there are too many policies covering a plethora of different issues and that many of these policies sit on shelves, unread, just in case an inspector should call. Policies are no good without actions; they should be developed collectively and understood and used by all. A learning and teaching policy should clearly set out the principles of learning, teaching and assessment which form the basis of the activities of teachers and learners. Such a policy is also a key document in creating an inclusive learning environment. The 2009 Steer Report provides an example of a teaching and learning policy, the introduction to which includes these key principles:

- There is no known ceiling to learning – intelligence can be developed.
- Each student must know what to do in order to improve and how to do it.
- Every student has the right to be successful and the ability to achieve.
- Our job is to create learning, not process and record what we find.

The sample policy goes on to specific principles and support for: learning and teaching: assessment, inclusion and supporting learning. You may find it useful to follow this up to look for ideas to support and own teaching and continuing professional development. You can find it online at: www.education.gov.uk/publications/eOrderingDownload/DCSF-Learning-Behaviour.pdf.

## Effective lifelong learning and building learning power

We have already considered the importance of behaviour for learning and the necessity to encourage effective 'learning behaviours' in our students. In his book *Building Learning Power*, Guy Claxton (2002) asserts his belief that we should be creating environments where young people (and, I suggest, people of all ages) can build their belief in themselves as learners and develop the positive attitudes and abilities necessary to become lifelong learners. To this end he proposes 'The Four R's of Learning Power' as the fundamental principles of learning and the 'Learning Power Palette' which describes the ways in which teachers can develop learning power. The following sections are taken directly from his book, which is well worth following up.

### The four R's of learning power

**Resilience – being ready, willing and able to lock on to learning**
- Absorption – flow, the pleasure of being rapt in learning.
- Managing distractions – recognising and reducing interruptions.
- Noticing – really noticing what's out there.
- Perseverance – 'stickability', tolerating the feelings of learning.

**Resourcefulness – being ready, willing and able to learn in different ways**
- Questioning – getting below the surface, playing with situations.
- Making links – seeking coherence, relevance and meaning.
- Imagining – using the mind's eye as a learning theatre.

- Reasoning – thinking rigorously and methodically.
- Capitalising – making good use of resources.

### Reflectiveness – being ready, willing and able to become more strategic about learning
- Planning – working learning out in advance.
- Revising – monitoring and adapting along the way.
- Distilling – drawing out lessons from experience.
- Meta-learning – understanding learning and yourself as a learner.

### Reciprocity – being ready, willing and able to learn alone and from others
- Interdependence – balancing self-reliance and sociability.
- Collaboration – the skills of learning with others.
- Empathy and listening – getting inside others' minds.
- Imitation – picking up others habits and values.

These four R's of learning power, Claxton suggests, can be promoted by the methods that teachers use and the ways in which they interact and work with their learners. The components of the 'Learning Power Palette' are as follows.

### Explaining – telling students directly and explicitly about learning power
- Informing – making clear the overall purpose of the classroom.
- Reminding – offering ongoing reminders and prompts about learning power.
- Discussing – inviting students' own ideas and opinions about learning.
- Training – giving direct information and practice in learning.

### Commentating – conveying messages about learning power through informal talk, and formal and informal evaluation
- Nudging – drawing individual student's attention to their own learning.
- Replying – responding to students' comments and questions in ways that encourage learners to learn.
- Evaluating – commenting on difficulties and achievements.
- Tracking – recording the development of students' learning power.

### Orchestrating – selecting activities and arranging the environment
- Selecting – choosing activities that develop the four R's.
- Framing – clarifying the learning outcomes behind specific activities.
- Target setting – helping students to monitor their own learning power targets.
- Arranging – making use of displays and physical arrangements to encourage independence.

**Modelling – showing what it means to be an effective learner**

*   Reacting – responding to unforeseen events, questions, etc. in ways that model good learning.

*   Learning aloud – externalising the thinking, feeling and decision-making of a learner-in-action.

*   Demonstrating – having learning projects that are visible in the classroom.

*   Sharing – talking about their learning careers and histories.

(Claxton 2002: 69)

## Behaviour, motivation and emotional intelligence

This section draws mainly on Daniel Goleman's work (1995, 1998) on emotional intelligence and in particular on two concepts relating to motivation – optimism and flow. In addition, you will be able to make links between these ideas and the elements of 'learning behaviours' discussed earlier.

### Optimism

Why some people tend to be optimistic and others pessimistic is a complex issue, drawing on arguments relating to nature and nurture and questions of human nature. I think we can safely assume that no one is born either an optimist or a pessimist; it is learned behaviour and, as such, can to some extent be unlearned. Pessimism is often the result of repeated negative messages to an individual from significant others, leading to a general belief that things tend to go badly. Optimism, on the other hand, is likely to have a similar origin in messages received but this time positive and resulting in a general feeling that things will go well, even if there are setbacks. If as teachers we can start to change the messages people receive, we can, even if only to a small extent, help learners to develop a more optimistic view of life and, consequently, their ability to succeed and do well. Optimism is related to success in learning and, it is claimed, is more likely to lead to achievement than skills and knowledge alone. Referring to the work of the psychologist Martin Seligman, Goleman writes:

> Seligman defines optimism in terms of how people explain to themselves their successes and failures. People who are optimistic see failure as due to something that can be changed so that they can succeed next time around, while pessimists take the blame for failure, ascribing it to some lasting characteristics they are helpless to change.

(Goleman 1995: 88)

There are clear links here to learners' previous negative experiences and particularly their experience of assessment. Those who have been repeatedly tested and failed can easily conclude that there is something fundamentally wrong with their ability to learn and, consequently, conclude that any future efforts will be equally fruitless. Psychologists use the term *self-efficacy* to describe the belief individuals have that they can take control over their lives and change them. Teachers are not psychotherapists or social workers, but it should be abundantly clear that part of our role is to help learners feel good about themselves and to believe that they can achieve. Optimism breeds hope.

## Flow

Have you ever been so involved in a task that time seems to fly by and you feel completely absorbed in your work? If so, you've experienced 'flow', and it's almost certain that every living human being can experience flow given the right task and the right environment. If we ask ourselves what the 'right' tasks are and what the 'right' environment is, we already know the answers. The right tasks are those which learners not only perceive to be interesting and relevant but also are at a level which is challenging but they feel they can reach with application and effort. The right environment is one in which they feel such challenges but feel supported and emotionally safe: that is safe from negative feelings like disapproval, humiliation or failure. Goleman (1998: 106) asserts:

> Flow is the ultimate motivator. Activities we love draw us in because we get into flow as we pursue them. . . . When we work in flow the motivation is built in – work is a delight in itself.

This might sound too idealistic a notion for learners in the lifelong learning sector but you will have seen learners experiencing flow and how motivated they become. The more motivated and involved in their work learners become, the less likely they are to engage in disruptive behaviour. The challenge, therefore, is to find tasks and methods which are most likely to bring this about. You can read more about this in 'Flow: The Psychology of Optimal Experience' (1990) by Mihaly Csikszentmihalyi. This book makes clear the link between flow and enjoyment, which takes us to our next section.

## Enjoyment

Coffield (2009: 17), writing advice for students, exposes what he refers to as 'five false ideas about learning'. The first of these is that 'learning is fun and always should be'. Having some fun while you learn seems quite a reasonable expectation, but there will be many occasions when learning is difficult, challenging and even disturbing because it makes you question your accepted ideas and assumptions. As a mature student, I recall studying a philosophy module which was intellectually stimulating, occasionally fun but for a short period of time very unsettling. Fortunately no permanent damage was done and my thinking was enhanced by the experience. Rather than expecting, and planning for learning to be fun, a more realistic aim might be for time at college and school to be enjoyable.

Gorard and Huat See (2011) carried out research into enjoyment at secondary schools across a range of settings and concluded that most students nearing the end of their secondary education did not enjoy their schooling. One of the main reasons for this was that only 38 per cent of year 11 students found their lessons interesting.

## Positive influences on enjoyment

This research suggests some positive factors which enhance enjoyment. These include:

- students being allowed to work at their own pace
- discussing things with staff and other students
- good facilities and resources supported by specialist staff
- being treated as 'emerging adults' by teachers
- opportunities to work in small groups
- being able to address teachers by their first names
- receiving individual attention
- autonomy in learning
- variety in teaching and learning.

This last point is supported by the report's conclusions about variation and imagination in the planning and delivery of sessions. The authors suggest:

> Overall, there was an appreciation of innovation and preparation in learning activities. Some students said that they enjoyed lessons that involve physical activities like getting them to move around or acting out a scene. Others like practical work, debates, dramatisations or just the unexpected. The key underlying message is that young people enjoy lessons where there is variation in delivery and activity.
>
> (Gorard and Huat See 2011: 680)

## Negative influences on enjoyment

Some of the negative factors related to enjoyment of school included:

- abusive behaviour by a minority of their peers
- frustration at time wasted by lessons disrupted by bad behaviour
- passive teaching
- unimaginative lesson delivery
- inaudible teachers
- teachers who avoided eye contact and continued with the session unaware that learners were not following them.

In relation to the final point the authors state:

> The experiences which were widely perceived to undermine enjoyment were passive pedagogy, such as listening to a teacher for lengthy periods, copying, note taking and having to sit still for a prolonged period. The lack of enjoyment in

passive learning was widely made by students. Many students did not like the classic style of lesson . . .

(Gorard and Huat See 2011: 683)

Learners' complaints about passive pedagogy and unimaginative delivery are not uncommon. In the past, learners frequently appeared unhappy with teachers who merely read out to them and required them to take notes, or having to listen to prolonged periods of teachers talking. Technology has done much to liberate us from passive learning and teaching but too frequently, especially in the inappropriate use of PowerPoint presentations, learners are confronted with an unreasonable number of densely packed slides which teachers read out to them. This kind of passivity can easily lead to low-level disruption.

## Some thoughts on adult learners' behaviour

> **Activity**
>
> In what ways can adults show difficult or challenging behaviour?
>
> To what extent do you think adult behaviour problems are the same in cause and effect as younger learners?
>
> Discuss any examples of 'bad' adult behaviour you have experienced in classes you have taught or been a learner in.

Traditionally, adult participation in education and learning was voluntary. If an adult attended a mature students course or access to higher education programme, a Workers Educational Association (WEA) class, or a non-vocational evening class they were there because they wanted to be and had actively chosen to participate. This still holds true for much adult education, but increasingly there are adult learners whose participation is not entirely voluntary and who might even feel coerced into training or learning – perhaps through compulsory staff development or attendance at courses in order to maintain benefits. Whether the participation is voluntary or compulsory, adults can still exhibit difficult or challenging behaviour. Jenny Rogers (2007) discusses some ways in which adult learners can be challenging in their behaviour. These are:

- anxiety
- memories of school
- challenge to beliefs
- differing expectations.

To a great extent, we have already discussed adult anxieties and memories of school at various points and concluded that we need to make positive attempts to understand their previous experiences and make learning a more positive experience for them.

Adult learners have had more experience of the world and more time to develop views and opinions; some of these may be very firmly held and any challenges to them can be unsettling for the learners. Putting forward ideas and concepts backed by research and evidence will not necessarily cause a sudden change in learners' viewpoints. Adults are no less immune than youngsters from the belief that their experience of the world is a reliable guide to the way the world actually is. The important thing is not to mock or dismiss learners' views and ideas out of hand; patience is required to get people to challenge their own perceptions. Critical thinking inputs can help here by encouraging learners to look at issues dispassionately and objectively.

Adult learners might arrive with preconceived notions of how teaching and learning should happen; this usually results from their previous experience of education and training. For many adults, active and student-centred learning is a novelty and many complain that they have come to 'be taught'. Graduates with experience of lecture-dominated teaching may find it difficult to imagine that other kinds of teaching and learning are possible. I can recall at least one trainee teacher who insisted that her subject (engineering) could only be taught by lecturing and teacher input. Fortunately she became more reflective and began to employ a much wider range of methods to suit her learners in FE colleges.

Rogers and Horrocks (2010: 206) emphasise the importance of tact and sensitivity when dealing with 'problem' adult learners and the need for teachers to adapt strategies based on their understanding of their own learners. These authors identify some 'types' of challenging students.

## Persistent talkers

These are students who monopolise discussions and are always first to answer questions, thereby denying others the opportunity to contribute. In such cases teachers need to be assertive and, while acknowledging the value of their contributions, suggest that they should let others participate. If the pattern of behaviour persists, it may be necessary to have a one-to-one discussion with the learner.

## The monomaniac

This learner has a particular theme or issue which they raise consistently regardless of whether or not it is relevant to the context. It may be a particular belief or opinion that they feel the need to state or it may be a life experience to which they constantly turn the discussion. I had an adult teacher trainee who had been made redundant from the mining industry and, understandably, felt very bitter. His constant references to his experience became tedious and annoying for his fellow students. As with the 'persistent talker', a personal discussion might be necessary. Alternatively, as Rogers and Horrocks (2010: 207) suggest, they could be given an opportunity to discuss the issue in session, provided they don't return to it.

## The quiet participant

This person is not necessarily a 'problem' or disruptive, it's more the case that they may be denying themselves the opportunity to participate and to develop their confidence. Tact and sensitivity are paramount in such cases because we don't want to lose someone who has probably invested a lot of emotional energy in just being there. It might be appropriate to engage the person in conversation during a break, possibly involving fellow learners. You could perhaps encourage them to start participating in groupwork where they feel less under the 'spotlight'. There is nothing wrong with being quiet, but many people may want to participate and just need encouragement.

## The alternative expert

This person frequently reminds the group that they are more knowledgeable than the teacher and relishes every opportunity to display this knowledge. This can be unsettling, even threatening, for the teacher. No teacher knows everything and in every group of learners there will individuals who are very knowledgeable in particular subjects or topics. People with special knowledge and relevant experiences are very valuable in adult learning groups, but like the persistent talker or the monomaniac they need to be managed and to recognise the boundaries of their knowledge.

### Case study: Barrie, training to teach English

*The setting*
The class is made up of 23 learners studying GCSE English on a university 'Access to Higher Education' programme. The classroom provides a safe and friendly learning environment. Groupwork is an integral part of the programme so the tables are organised to facilitate this, being placed in sets of five to accommodate five learner groups. The positive nature and good behaviour of the students suggests a motivated, focused group of engaged learners, enthusiastic and intent on achieving. Albeit, with one exception.

*The learner*
Student 567 has been diagnosed with sensory neural deafness and suffers from severe auditory impairment. She finds it hard to follow speech even with a hearing aid and communicates largely through British Sign Language (BSL) and Sign Supported English (SSE) which allows the use of some signs alongside spoken English in order to clarify meaning. She has a support worker in class fluent in BSL.

*The behaviour*
Despite this support, Student 567 became increasingly withdrawn and reluctant to participate in group activities. Her interaction with peers was minimal and indicated that she was struggling with a profound sense of social isolation. Her attitude and behaviour in class took a turn for the worse and she became a disruptive presence. She

demonstrated signs of frustration and agitation: she fidgeted in her seat, was very slow to settle at the beginning of class, pushed pens off her desk, sometimes 'accidentally', sometimes deliberately. She would attempt to disengage other learners in her proximity by demanding their attention or by borrowing their equipment without their consent.

*Actions taken*
In an attempt to improve the situation I have adopted a teaching practice which I hope will facilitate her learning within the group. I never shout at her, or any other student in the class and I make sure I have her attention by maintaining good eye contact. I keep background noise to a minimum and speak clearly but normally, in plain English, and never exaggerate lip patterns. When addressing her directly, I avoid looking at her communicator and use natural facial expressions, gestures and body language. I remain patient and friendly and avoid suggesting 'It doesn't matter' if Student 567 fails to understand my last sentence. If a sentence is not understood, I try to rephrase it or, as a final measure, I write it down. I now give handouts in advance of the lesson and give Student 567 plenty of reading time. I use PowerPoint to provide a strong visual resource and to back up spoken information. I ensure the classroom has good lighting and acoustics. I have implemented a series of short 'learning breaks' for Student 567 of no more than a minute in length. These breaks have already benefited Student 567 and her fellow learners, both in terms of increased focus and prolonged attention spans.

*Consequences*
Student 567 seems more at ease and less prone to disruption. Fidgeting has stopped and gradually her participation in the group has become more evident. In order for this beneficial change in behaviour to continue, additional time should be allocated to allow for preparation, planning, reading, research, composition and proof reading both for myself and for Student 567.

## Further reading

Canter, L. (2010) *Assertive Discipline: Positive Behaviour Management for Today's Classroom.* Bloomington, IN: Solution Tree Press.
Rogers, A. and Horrocks, N. (2010) *Teaching Adults* (4th edn). Maidenhead: Open University Press. See especially Chapter 8, 'The Adult Learning Group'.
Vizard, D. (2007) *How to Manage Behaviour in Further Education.* London: Paul Chapman.
Watkins, C. (2011) *Managing Classroom Behaviour.* London: ATL. Available online at: www.atl.org.uk/Images/Managing%20classroom%20behaviour%20-%202011.pdf

## Websites

Behaviour2Learn: Supports the development of positive behaviour in classrooms and schools by providing practical resources, videos and information for trainee and newly qualified teachers. www.behaviour2learn.co.uk/

# 12

# Wider skills for learning

**What this chapter is about**

- Using questions
- Thinking skills
- Personal, learning and thinking skills (PLTS)
- Employability
- Relevance
- Threshold concepts

**LLUK standards**

This chapter covers, at least, the following standards:
AS 1; AK 1.1; AP 1.1 AS 2; AK 2.2; AP 2.2; AS 3; AK 3.1; AP 3.1
BS 1; BK 1.3; BP 1.3; BS 2; BK 2.1; BP 2.1; BK 2.3; BP 2.3; BK 3.2; BP 3.2
CS 2; CK 2.1; CP 2.1; CS 4; CK 4.2; CP 4.2
DS 1; DK 1.1; DP 1.1; DK 1.2; DP 1.2

This chapter is a collection of loosely connected ideas and topics around the general theme of wider learning – for teachers as well as for learners. The chapter title refers to wider 'skills' for learning and includes, for example, a section on 'thinking skills'. Many people argue against using 'skills' in relation to thinking or questioning and I am quite happy for them to do this. It is true that the word 'skills' has become so widely used in so many different contexts that we might ask whether it retains any real meaning. It is used to describe literacy and numeracy in the context of 'basic' skills or 'functional' skills; to refer to the technical skills of a plumber, hairdresser, painter or pianist; and more abstract intellectual skills such as might be used when analysing a poem or doing accounts.

Lucas and Claxton (2009: 10) believe we need to broaden our understanding of 'skills' from the technical to 'more personal and subtle sensibilities, attitudes and values'. They favour the use of the term 'dispositions' which implies not just 'possessing' skills but also knowing when to use them. So, in the context of this chapter we might consider not just understanding the skills of questioning but knowing what kinds of questions to ask and, for teachers, using questions which make learners think rather than just testing what they know. Similarly, with regard to employability, it means going beyond CV writing and interview practice to the wider skills of reflection, evaluation, planning and development, and thinking about the kinds of learning and teaching which will encourage these.

## Questioning

Questioning is one of the most important skills in teaching and learning. Given the importance of using questions it is surprising that much teacher training in post-compulsory education treats this skill in a cursory manner. There is evidence to suggest that learners at all levels find teachers to be poor users of questions. Reflective practitioners are aware of their use of questioning and constantly seek to improve their practice.

## Importance of using questions in teaching and learning

Effective questioning helps learners to develop a fuller understanding of what they are learning and to promote deep and lasting learning. Questioning is fundamental to creating an active learning environment, for connecting learning, for checking learning and, above all, in developing interaction between teachers and learners.

> Good learning starts with questions, not answers.
> Asking good questions is the basis for becoming a successful learner. If children [and adults] aren't asking questions they're being spoon-fed. That might be effective in terms of getting results, but it won't turn out curious, flexible learners suited to the 21st century.
>
> (Claxton 1990: 27)

Ted Wragg's research (1984) suggests that teachers in schools ask up to 400 questions a day, which represents about 30 per cent of their total teaching time. However, only about 8 per cent of these could be considered as higher order questions, that is, questions which stimulate, for example, thought, analysis and evaluation. The majority of questions by far were concerned with management and control issues ('Are you listening?') or recall of information ('Who was Juliet's boyfriend?'). In lifelong learning, we could assume that there will be fewer issues relating to management and control of discipline and behaviour, although in some further education colleges there are increasing numbers of 14–16 year olds, some of whom might exhibit challenging behaviour. Can the same assumption be made about the use of higher order questions in the lifelong learning sector (LLS)?

The skilled and appropriate use of questions is frequently taken for granted, yet it should be a key element in the continuing professional development of teachers and a regular feature in the reflections and evaluations of trainee teachers. One of the underlying assumptions of this book is that learning is best when it is active, enquiring and involves the learners in discussion and higher order thinking. 'Teaching by asking' is at least as important as 'teaching by telling'.

## Why do teachers ask questions?

There are many reasons why teachers use questions. Some questions are used consciously and purposefully such as checking learning or encouraging discussion; others may be less apparent such as developing learners' confidence. However, research and observations suggest that teachers frequently used questions merely as a matter of course without being clear about their purpose or effect. The following categories suggest and explore some reasons for using questions.

### Gain attention or check that learners are paying attention

Even the most well-behaved groups will sometimes need to be brought back on track or kept focused by an appropriate question. Questions can be used to simultaneously keep people on task and check understanding: for example, rather than merely asking 'How are you getting on?' it might be more appropriate to ask 'Can you show me what you've discovered so far?' A question can be used to signal the end of groupwork activities and to summarise findings: for example, 'So, what suggestions have you come up with?'

### Reinforce and revise learning

Sometimes teaching by repetition and reinforcement – such as learning dates, formulas, procedures, lines from poems or plays – is necessary and appropriate. We want learners to repeat or reinforce knowledge and ideas, particularly those which are used regularly. Bloom's taxonomy (see Chapter 4) provides a very useful framework for asking questions at the appropriate level. At the base of Bloom's taxonomy are Knowledge and Comprehension and questions at this level would, for example: ask learners to name parts of the human body; identify the key components of a computer; repeat a formula; or recall a line from a poem. After recalling the line from the poem, learners might subsequently be asked higher level questions regarding the meaning or interpretation of the poem or why the poet used that particular combination of language, metre and rhyme. Questions at this level are generally referred to as recall questions.

### Check on student learning and understanding

Effective teaching and learning always includes checks on learning and understanding. It's no good just ploughing on with your session plan unless you have ascertained whether or not learners have grasped particular points. Questions to check learning need to be specific and to assess specific points which have been covered. Vague questions such as 'Did everybody get that?', or, worse still, 'All wright?' or 'OK?' will often be met with silence and averted eyes. Even 'Are there any questions?' is unlikely to get a helpful response, if any, because it's too easy just to answer yes or no, and many learners will not want to put their heads above the parapet and admit that they don't understand. Questions to check learning need to be more specific such as 'So, can you tell me what is the main ingredient of hollandaise sauce?' or 'Give me an example of a metaphor in this passage.'

### Diagnose learners' difficulties and adjust and re-present as necessary

This develops from the above point. Sometimes it becomes clear from learners' responses to questions that the level of the knowledge, ideas and material is wrong and the teacher will need to reflect and adjust the content and, or, the delivery. This kind of thinking on your feet is to be expected of a reflective practitioner and relates to Schon's idea of 'reflection in action', hopefully followed by 'reflection on action' in which the lesson is evaluated and conclusions drawn for subsequent planning.

### Check level of previous learning and introduce new topics

Verbal questioning is one of the most effective methods of ascertaining learners' prior knowledge, either at the first meeting of a new group or at the introduction of a new module or unit. It's generally more interesting as well as more active for learners to be asked to discuss what they already know rather than for the teacher to just tell them things. For example, instead of starting a sociology module on the family with some rather dry information and theory, it would be far more effective to ask learners 'Why do most people tend to live in families?' or 'In what ways are families different?' Such discussion, if skilfully handled, will almost inevitably raise some of the key issues of the module.

Alan Pritchard makes the point that 'learning is a process of interaction between what is known and what is to be learnt' and that it is important to activate prior knowledge. In a passage which applies equally to adult learners as to children, he suggests:

> Effective approaches involve what is sometimes referred to as 'elicitation'. This is the process of drawing out from the children [and learners of all ages] what they already know, even if they do not realise that they know it. By careful questioning, a teacher can draw out . . . ideas, facts, and notions which can be of direct relevance to the topic the teacher wishes to introduce and develop.
>
> (Pritchard 2009: 106)

### Create a communication climate in which learners know that asking questions is encouraged and expected

As we saw in Chapter 3, one of the main determinants of successful learning is the establishment of a positive communication climate. One way we can develop such a climate is by the skilful and encouraging use of questions in our learning sessions. Questions that confuse, humiliate, discourage, or fail to challenge learners will contribute to a climate in which they will switch off and not want to contribute to the sessions. This kind of climate is more likely to produce a passive learning situation where learners are not encouraged to discuss ideas and knowledge or to create their own meanings. For many adult learners such passive, teacher-centred learning was the norm in school and asking questions was not encouraged – possibly discouraged. It is vital that we create an atmosphere in which learners feel that it is acceptable, indeed desirable, to ask questions, whether it's for information and ideas to be repeated or clarified, or whether it's to stimulate discussion and enquiry, or to promote thinking skills and deep learning.

### Develop learners' confidence

The lifelong learning sector – especially further and adult education – has a tradition of giving second chances to people who have 'failed' in their previous encounters with education and, consequently, had their self-esteem and confidence knocked. Many learners need help in developing their confidence in speaking, suggesting and testing ideas, giving examples and, above all, asking questions. You can help to break the cycle of failure and flagging self-esteem by the ways in which you ask and respond to questions. Adjust the level of questions to suit the abilities and level of your learners; give them opportunities to answer and have their answers valued. Make sure that you acknowledge every learner's answers positively and, wherever possible, build on them by extending and developing with further questions and answers. Even when answers are wrong, let people down gently and don't humiliate them.

### Provide motivation

All learners, whatever level they are working at, need to be motivated. The best way to do this is by giving them regular opportunities to demonstrate their learning and feel a sense of achievement. Questions give learners the opportunity to succeed, demonstrate learning and get the positive feelings that go with it. However, it is important to get the level of questioning right and to avoid too many closed questions (see below) or too many recall questions. The sense of achievement is heightened when learners have successfully responded to higher order questioning, particularly when they have solved a problem or reached a conclusion.

### Develop discussion

Discussion is a technique widely favoured by learners at all ages and levels. The initiation and development of discussion requires the use of well-structured and considered questions. We shall see later how linked questions can be used to develop discussion and draw ideas from learners and help them develop thinking skills.

### Contextualise and connect learning

Questions give learners opportunities to put their learning into context and to connect it to existing learning. In a music class learners can put music theory into practice by relating it to their favourite music by asking, for example, 'What's the chord sequence in that song? How can I develop something similar in my composition?' Similarly, in a health and social care group learners might be asked questions to relate their learning to their own experience or to items in the news.

**Develop higher level thinking skills and encourage a problem-solving approach to learning**

Questioning is one of the main methods of developing thinking skills. The use of higher order questions, as opposed to simple recall and comprehension, makes learners apply, analyse and evaluate their learning. Thinking skills are not only for learners. Kerry (2002) refers to the 'thinking teacher', that is one who has 'a curious mind; one that investigates problems rather than accepts the solutions of others', in other words a 'questioning teacher'. Kerry also refers to questions being used to 'think aloud and make the intuitive leap'. Learners can be encouraged to suggest ideas and hypothesise, particularly in relation to problem solving. However, they need to feel confident that they can ask questions or provide answers which seem initially to be incorrect or even 'off the wall'. Such thinking frequently turns out to be original and creative.

## Levels of questions

The level of questions can be located anywhere on a range from lower order, which requires learners to *remember*, to higher order questions, which require learners to *think*. Bloom's taxonomy of educational objectives (cognitive domain) is useful not only for writing learning objectives but also for framing questions. Some examples of questions at each of Bloom's levels are as follows:

- *Knowledge:*      What are the main components of a computer?

  In what year was the Russian Revolution?

- *Comprehension:* Can you explain what a modem does?

  Can you describe that in a different way?

- *Application:*     What happens when you put salt on ice?

  How does physical exertion affect blood sugar levels?

- *Analysis:*        What do the results of your experiment tell you?

  How has this poet used metaphor to affect the reader?

- *Synthesis:*       How can we use our analysis of film in making this video?

  How can we combine these ideas?

- *Evaluation:*      In what ways could you improve this piece of work?

  How effectively does Hardy use language to evoke nature?

Effective questioning requires teachers to consider the level of questioning in relation to the learners' abilities and prior learning; their confidence and motivation; level of learning, and the session objectives. It would be wrong to assume that higher order questions can only be put to higher level learners. All learners can respond to higher order questions if they are expressed unambiguously and develop clearly from previous recall and lower order questions.

## Types of questions

Not all questions are the same or serve the same purpose. We can distinguish between three basic types of question:

- closed
- open
- linked (or Socratic).

### Closed questions

Closed questions generally only have one correct answer or can be answered with a simple 'yes' or 'no'. Closed questions don't require the answerer to develop the response or take the discussion any further; they put the initiative back on to the questioner. At a simple, light-hearted level, an example of a closed question would be 'Do you come here often?' A simple yes or no answer is sufficient and nothing further needs to be said – end of encounter!

Closed questions have a place in teaching and learning, for example, in checking learning and understanding. 'Who developed penicillin?' is a useful question to check knowledge, but without further questions it's not going very far. Too many closed questions are likely to switch learners off because they feel unchallenged and not able to engage with the learning at a higher level. Closed questions tend to be *convergent*, that is, intended to solicit an already known answer.

### Open questions

Open questions may have several possible answers rather than one correct answer, or perhaps even no answer. They require the answerer to provide more than just a one-word or phrase response. Open questions are generally higher order questions which require learners to think and to develop deep rather than surface learning and discussion. Open questions tend to be *divergent* in that they can open up discussion and the development of ideas. If we develop the penicillin example further, we could ask learners questions such as 'What were the effects of penicillin?' or 'To what extent is penicillin still effective today?' or 'Why is penicillin becoming less effective?' Research suggests that effective teachers use more open questions than less effective teachers. Open questions are the key to building linked sequences of questions, sometimes known as Socratic questions.

### Linked or (Socratic) questioning

Two thousand five hundred years ago, Socrates practised his philosophy by engaging participants in a series of questions to test their assumptions and to extend their thinking. He believed that people already knew a great deal and that his task was to draw the knowledge from them by rigorous and linked questioning. Socrates never wrote anything down but his dialogues were recreated by Plato, his pupil, who featured Socrates as a character in works such as *The Republic*. In our learning sessions we may not necessarily be discussing the big questions which concerned Socrates and his pupils, such as virtue and democracy, but we can still use Socratic questioning to get students thinking through ideas and testing their assumptions and their reasoning. An example of a series of linked questions might look something like this example from a media studies class:

*Teacher:*   Jason, why is there a cliffhanger at the end of a soap opera?

*Jason:*   To make sure people keep watching.

*Teacher:*   Good. Zaheera, why is it important that people keep watching?

*Zaheera:*   To maintain high viewing figures.

*Teacher:*   Yes, right. So, Kylie, why do TV companies need high viewing figures?

*Kylie:*   To attract advertisers.

*Teacher:*   So, why is it important to attract advertisers?

*Kylie:*   Because they pay to advertise.

*Teacher:*   Precisely; income. Sean, what do the TV companies do with the income?

*Sean:*   Make more programmes.

---

**Activity**

Write a script similar to the above using a series of linked questions which could happen in one of your classes.

Clearly, the success of these linked questions depends on learners giving the 'right' answers or answers which will generate further questions. Using open questions will help to generate a dialogue.

---

## Developing higher order questions

Robert Fisher is one of the leading figures in developing philosophy for children. Fisher's key work *Teaching Thinking* (2003) is based on the belief that philosophy is an active questioning process which is open to all and concerned with real, everyday issues of life, as opposed to the academic tradition in which philosophy is the preserve of the educated few. The Philosophy for Children movement was originally developed by Matthew Lipman at Montclair University (USA). Fisher quotes Lipman's opinion regarding the 'decline' of children's natural desire to learn: 'Why is it that children of four, five and six are full of curiosity, creativity and interest, and never stop asking for further explanations, by the time they are eighteen they are passive, uncritical and bored with learning?' (Lipman 1982: 27). Clearly, Lipman is expressing an opinion but he does underline a widely held belief that as children grow and mature they lose their natural desire to question, explore and play with ideas. Whether this change is the result of maturation, teenage angst or the supposed deadening effects of formal education, we cannot be sure. However, in lifelong learning we have the opportunity to use, or to reawaken adult learners' desire to enquire and explore ideas by the ways in which we as teachers use questions.

## Thinking skills

Let's begin this section with some activities to make you think. Consider the following questions and, if possible, discuss them with colleagues or fellow trainees.

1    What are the differences between:
     •    information
     •    knowledge
     •    thinking?
2    What does 'thinking' mean? What are you doing when you think about something?
3    Can you describe the way you think? How similar or different is your way of thinking from other people's?
4    What are the differences between thinking about what you did on your holidays and thinking to solve a problem?

In considering these questions you've been involved in 'metacognition', that is thinking about thinking, particularly your own thinking. Metacognition is one of the most powerful methods of improvement for learners and teachers.

## What are thinking skills?

We all think more or less all of the time. Much of our thinking involves random, unstructured thoughts, daydreams, reminiscences and just general ideas popping into our heads. This kind of thinking is effortless and frequently serves no particular purpose – sometimes it is a source of pleasure, sometimes anxiety.

Thinking skills are centred on more deliberate, purposeful, structured thinking processes which are learned and developed through application and practice. When we talk about thinking skills we are usually referring to a range of higher order thinking processes. Fisher (2006: 25) suggests: 'Such processes include remembering; questioning; forming concepts; planning; reasoning; imagining; solving problems; making decisions and judgements; translating thoughts into words and so on.'

McGuiness (1999) says that thinking skills include:

•    collecting information
•    sorting and analysing information
•    drawing conclusions from information
•    'brainstorming' new ideas

- problem solving
- determining cause and effect
- evaluating options
- planning and setting goals
- monitoring progress
- decision making
- reflecting on one's own progress.

Clearly, the thinking skills outlined by Fisher and McGuiness coincide with a number of teaching and learning methods and processes discussed elsewhere in this book. For example, these kinds of thinking skills can be applied to learners devising and monitoring their own projects, using their ILPs to identify their strengths and ways to improve, and working out the ways in which they learn most effectively.

## Why are thinking skills important?

Thinking skills are important for two main reasons: first, for their benefits to the economy and society; second, their impact on learners and teachers. Developing thinking skills is an important element in employability.

The importance of developing skills for the needs of the economy in an increasingly competitive world is beyond question. We have always needed the skills of literacy and numeracy, that's basically why the 1870 Education Act made schooling compulsory. Without a fully skilled workforce we can't compete. We rightly recognise the skills of literacy, numeracy and ICT for individual and economic success, but we live in a rapidly changing world in which these 'basics' on their own will be insufficient. They need to be matched by the development of the kinds of higher order, transferable skills outlined above because individuals in an 'information society' will be unable to 'store' sufficient knowledge in their memories for the future and the rapid rate of information increase will require them to develop higher order skills which are transferable to other contexts.

Guy Claxton (1999) writes persuasively about 'information' and argues against the simplistic view of learning as the 'application and manipulation of information'. You will be familiar with learners whose first instinct on being given a task to complete or being asked to find information is to use a search engine to trawl the internet. While this method will yield much useful, reliable and accurate information, it will most likely bring forth a greater amount of material of doubtful and unreliable origin. Thinking skills approaches would require learners to justify their use of the internet as well as to demonstrate judgement in selecting and evaluating information sources. As Claxton points out:

> Info-evangelists . . . seem to talk as if the endless accumulation of up-to-the-minute information were the answer to all the world's ills . . . . Access to avalanches of information, loosely connected by threads or casual associations, does not of itself bring about the transformation of that information into knowledge or wise

judgement, nor the development of the requisite skills and dispositions for doing so. It is the business of education to foster the development of the ability to select, integrate and evaluate theories and opinions, not to drown in information.

(Claxton 1999: 224)

From the learners' and the teachers' point of view the development of thinking skills has many benefits. The most obvious is that it improves achievement. The Cognitive Acceleration through Science Education (CASE) programme developed at King's College, London develops thinking skills in schools through science education. The most recent evidence suggests that students in schools using this at Key Stage 3 achieve 19 per cent more A–C grades in GCSE science than those using traditional methods. Significantly, the CASE science students achieve 16 per cent more A–Cs in English and 15 per cent more in maths, suggesting that students have transferred their thinking skills to other subjects.

The importance of the thinking skills approach is underlined by Geoff Petty (2009) with his idea of the 'content trap'. He suggests that: 'Weak teachers spend almost all their time teaching content; thinking skills are relatively ignored. They teach the easy stuff and ignore the hard. Teaching both skills *and* content gets much better results.' One can possibly understand that busy teachers in colleges, training providers and schools feel that they only have time to teach to the exam or test and that wider skills and higher order thinking are luxuries they cannot afford, but thinking skills programmes integrated across the curriculum seem to improve results and, most likely, will make the experience more active and enjoyable for learners and teachers.

## How can thinking skills be developed in the lifelong learning sector?

Learning is lifelong, not just an activity which happens at specific times in our lives and in certain places such as school, college, workplace or training courses. It is a natural human activity which we do all the time, particularly at times of change such as when we start a new job or a new relationship or, on a simpler level, when we buy a new piece of technology. Learning on a simple level is about working things out; it requires the conscious application of thinking, adaptation and development. Formal learning in formal situations has traditionally been based on the acquisition of knowledge and, to a great extent, our examination system reinforces this view of learning: that is, learning as a body of knowledge which you own rather than as a set of skills which you use and refine. Thinking skills go beyond the acquisition of knowledge. In formal learning situations we need to recognise and develop our higher order skills through learning which makes us think and construct, test and justify our learning. Some of the best practice in FE colleges and adult learning (for example, reflection and evaluation, discussion, collaborative groupworking) has been based on these principles for a long time and is, in many ways, ahead of schools in the development of thinking skills.

Thinking skills can and should be taught but the main question is how. There are two main approaches – either by specifically designed thinking skills courses or by embedding thinking skills activities across the curriculum using teaching and learning techniques chosen to encourage higher order skills. As with key skills the best practice, I feel, is via the embedded route. This approach is sometimes referred to by thinking skills experts as 'infusion', but this is the first and last time I will use the term; I'll stick with 'embedding'.

This section will consider a range of techniques and ideas for developing thinking skills for learners and teachers. Many of these ideas are underpinned by the active and constructivist learning principles discussed throughout this book and some, especially questioning and problem-based learning, have already been considered in detail in their own right. However, developing a thinking skills approach to learning and teaching is not just a matter of acquiring some new techniques; it's more an attitude of mind based on enquiry, curiosity and, to some extent, risk taking.

**Using Bloom's taxonomy**
Bloom's taxonomy (see Chapter 4) is a framework that can be used to develop thinking skills, especially the higher order elements – analysis, synthesis and evaluation. Using the taxonomy in your session planning will encourage you to include higher order activities and develop thinking skills. Share the taxonomy with your learners. Get them to identify when they are using particular elements of it and, especially, get them to evaluate their learning either through written evaluations or discussions and presentations. This can happen in each session through a debriefing at the end.

**Debriefing**
A debriefing at the end of each session, or at the end of an extended task over several sessions, is one of the most valuable ways to get learners to reflect on and evaluate their learning. It also provides an excellent method of linking forward to the next session. Here are some tips for debriefing:

- Get learners to restate the 'big picture': what was the task or what was the problem they set out to solve?
- Ask them to explain their methods and activities. Ask them to explain and justify choices of method and ways of working.
- Ask them to describe methods they rejected and explain their reasons.
- Use higher order questions to help learners connect and extend their thinking.
- Ask them to identify methods they have used and skills and knowledge which can be transferred to other learning.
- If it's a debriefing at the end of a major project make it a more intensive activity. Learners could give presentations and take part in discussions.

**Discussion**
We have seen the benefits of using discussion in Chapter 6. A thinking skills approach can help to improve the quality of discussion. A particularly useful method is in Edward de Bono's *Six Thinking Hats* (1985) which is designed to get learners to discuss and analyse ideas and problems from different perspectives. If, for example, a learner proposes an idea which is really 'off the wall' and derided by fellow learners it can be evaluated using this method with individual learners 'wearing' a particular hat and using the approach that goes with it. The six thinking hats are as follows:

1   *White hat* is neutral and objective and encourages the wearer to consider the facts.

2   *Red hat* is emotional and involves the expression of subjective points of view and feelings.

3   *Black hat* urges a careful and cautious approach and looks for the weakness in an idea.

4   *Yellow hat* is positive and optimistic and recognises the benefits of the idea. It's the 'let's go for it' hat.

5   *Green hat* is the creativity hat. It encourages new ways of thinking and alternative approaches.

6   *Blue hat* encourages metacognition, thinking about the thinking involved and the use and control of the other hats.

A similar approach, frequently used in business, is the SWOT analysis in which learners consider the Strengths, Weaknesses, Opportunities and Threats of a particular proposal.

### Reflection and evaluation

Encourage learners to reflect on and evaluate their work. In art projects learners are frequently asked to explain the 'history' of their work up to the current stage and explain, for example, the influences on their work; how they modified and adapted ideas in the light of experience; how they want their work to develop and what research and experimentation will be necessary. You might be able to adapt this approach with learners in different subjects. Learning logs can be a useful way to record and reflect on learning. You can apply the same principles as outlined in Chapter 2, particularly 'reflection in action' and 'reflection on action'.

### Thinking circles and 'café philosphique'

In a thinking circle, groups of learners and teacher/s are given a written or visual stimulus as a starting point for discussion. The idea of the 'café philosophique' conjures visions of French philosophers in black poloneck jumpers vigorously debating and exchanging ideas through a thick fog of cigarette smoke; this is a great idea but you should omit the cigarettes. This is much more informal than a debating society or seminar so don't do it in a classroom; find somewhere more relaxed where people can lounge around and get drinks and food. Doing it using a blog is far less effective because it lacks the immediacy of response, the passion and the social contact. It's a great format for discussing 'big issues'. *The Philosopher's Magazine* has examples on their website. Scientists can develop a 'café scientifique'. We are all affected by science but very few of us will become scientists; the 'café scientifique' is where scientists can explain and justify their views to non-scientists.

### What if?

This is sometimes referred to by historians as 'counterfactual' history, what would things be like now if history had been different? The clichéd example is what the world would be like if the Nazis had won World War II. This method is not just for history; English literature students could explore what would have happened if

Bathsheba Everdene hadn't sent Farmer Boldwood the Valentine card in *Far from the Madding Crowd*; travel and tourism students could consider what the world would be like if planes hadn't been invented; engineers could speculate about engineering if there was no such thing as steel. These activities might begin with instant unsupported speculation but learners must research and justify their speculations and make imaginative connections.

### Reading images

This is a technique which I and many other media teachers have employed successfully. A photograph or image is a frozen moment in time. It's a good thinking skills exercise to imagine and explain what happened immediately before and after that moment; where it is and who the people are. You can use the concepts of 'denotation' and 'connotation' here. Denotation requires learners to describe what they see; for example, a man with a gun and a child crying. Connotation is about interpretation and how the image makes you feel: the man with the gun could either represent a threat or protection; the child may be crying because it is frightened or relieved to be protected. Learners' interpretations of the image will be affected by where and when they think the image is set.

### Making connections

Learning is essentially about making connections. There are many methods and techniques which teachers use to encourage learners to connect ideas and to discover relationships. Here's one that I use. I produce a set of about ten cards, each with a single word or phrase, which are or can be connected in various ways. For example, a set might include the following:

- smoking
- freedom
- taxes
- health
- poverty
- age
- illness
- the economy
- regulation
- work.

Learners then take the cards, fix them to flipchart sheet and draw connecting lines between any two or more cards and explain and discuss their connections. In the list above they might agree that smoking is bad for health but that the taxes from cigarettes go towards the health service. Smokers might be poor but cigarette manufacturers make profits which they pay tax on. Should people have the freedom to smoke? As the session develops, learners can add new cards which they use to make further connections. The teacher's role is to push the learners to explain ad justify their connections and to speculate about others.

**'Beat the teacher'**

In this method teachers challenge learners to ask them questions on their specialist subject area. Any questions they cannot answer go into a bank of unanswered questions which learners can then follow up, report back and discuss the sources of the answers. This kind of activity reminds all involved that while they may be experts in their subjects, teachers don't know everything.

The methods outlined here are intended as a kind of 'starter pack' for thinking skills activities. I urge you to try some of these techniques and to follow up further methods and ideas, not only because they are more effective but also because they are more fun.

## Personal, learning and thinking skills (PLTS)

Personal, learning and thinking skills (PLTS) were developed as part of the generic learning on the 14–19 diplomas which were introduced form 2008. The framework for PLTS was set out by the Qualifications and Curriculum Authority (2007), which no longer exists. The framework makes specific reference to the development of young people's skills but it can also serve as a comprehensive framework for learners of all ages, including those not on diploma courses.

### Independent enquirers

Young people process and evaluate information in their investigations, planning what to do and how to go about it. They take informed and well-reasoned decisions, recognising that others have different beliefs and attitudes.

### Creative thinkers

Young people think creatively by generating and exploring ideas, making original connections. They try different ways to tackle a problem, working with others to find imaginative solutions and outcomes that are of value.

### Reflective learners

Young people evaluate their strengths and limitations, setting themselves realistic goals with criteria for success. They monitor their own performance and progress, inviting feedback from others and making changes to further their learning.

### Teamworkers

Young people work confidently with others, adapting to different contexts and taking responsibility for their own part. They listen to and take account of different views. They form collaborative relationships, resolving issues to reach agreed outcomes.

## Self-managers

Young people organise themselves, showing personal responsibility, initiative, creativity and enterprise with a commitment to learning and self-improvement. They actively embrace change, responding positively to new priorities, coping with challenges and looking for opportunities.

## Effective participators

Trainee teachers frequently acknowledge the difficulties they have in developing open and linked questions and I am sure most experienced teachers would agree that it is a skill which needs conscious reflection and practice supported by examples and role models. Fisher (2003) gives examples of the types of questions that he believes are 'invitations to better thinking' (see Table 12.1).

**Table 12.1** Examples of questions to develop higher order skills.

| | |
|---|---|
| **Questions that seek clarification** | |
| 'Can you explain that?' | *Explaining* |
| 'What do you mean by . . .?' | *Defining* |
| 'Can you give me an example of . . .?' | *Giving examples* |
| 'How does that help . . .?' | *Supporting* |
| 'Does anyone have a question to ask?' | *Enquiring* |
| **Questions that probe reasons and evidence** | |
| 'Why do you think that . . .?' | *Forming an argument* |
| 'How do we know that . . .?' | *Assumptions* |
| 'What are your reasons. . . .?' | *Reasons* |
| 'Do you have evidence . . .?' | *Evidence* |
| 'Can you give me an example/counter-example?' | *Counter- examples* |
| **Question that explore alternative views** | |
| 'Can you put it another way?' | *Restating a view* |
| 'Is there another point of view?' | *Speculation* |
| 'What if someone were to suggest that . . .?' | *Alternative views* |
| 'What would someone who disagreed with you say?' | *Counter argument* |
| 'What's the difference between those views/ideas?' | *Distinctions* |
| **Questions that test implications and consequences** | |
| 'What follows from what you say?' | *Implications* |
| 'Does it agree with what was said earlier?' | *Consistency* |
| 'What would be the consequences of . . .?' | *Consequences* |
| 'Is there a general rule for that?' | *Generalising rules* |
| 'How could you test to see if it was true?' | *Testing for truth* |
| **Questions about the question/discussion** | |
| 'Do you have a question about that?' | *Questioning* |
| 'What kind of question is that?' | *Analysing* |
| 'How does what was said/the question help us?' | *Connecting* |
| 'What have we got so far/can we summarise?' | *Summarising* |
| 'Are we any closer to answering the question?' | *Concluding* |

*Source:* Fisher (2003)

## Questioning skills

Questioning in teaching and learning is frequently taken for granted, but it is a skill which needs conscious development if we are to become effective teachers. The following summary outlines some of the most important questioning skills:

- Create an appropriate climate in which learners will want to ask questions.
- Express questions clearly. Avoid over-long and complex structures; try not to use two-part questions.
- Use appropriate volume and speed of speech – ensure that learners can hear you.
- Ensure that the content and language of questions are appropriate to the learners. This entails knowing your learners; one way we get to know our learners is by questioning them.
- Avoid questions which are too easy or too difficult for that group. Be prepared to ask differentiated questions with learners of different abilities in the same group.
- Put questions into context and provide necessary background information.
- Make sure you pause and allow learners thinking time – teachers can get nervous if answers don't come immediately. You could consider using collaboration in which pairs of learners work together to provide an answer.
- Use prompts and provide clues to help learners get to the answers. Questions can be part of the 'scaffolding' process which provides initial support for learners to reach new heights in their learning.
- Use follow-up questions to extend thinking and make greater cognitive demands on learners. Encourage learners' thinking skills by using higher order questions. Develop linked questions.
- Involve the whole group, not just a 'favoured few'. Distribute questions around the group and use people's names to invite them in. When a learner asks a question, ensure the whole group is listening.
- Acknowledge and give praise to learners' answers, even if they are not what you were looking for or expected.
- Never make light of or disregard learners' responses. Make them feel that their contributions are valued.
- Remember the importance of non-verbal communication – especially, smiles, eye contact, tone of voice – in encouraging learners.

**Activity**

What's wrong with these questions?

- 'What did I just say?'
- 'Don't you think you ought to know this?'
- 'Did everyone get that?'

- 'Can you have this done before Easter?'
- 'In what ways was the situation in Iraq a disaster?'
- 'Why is daytime television so poor?'
- 'How many of you know the answer to this?'
- 'What are the government's reasons for the extension of academy schools and how have people argued against them?'

**For your journal**

Take some time to reflect on your use of questions in your teaching:

- Do you consider why you use questions?
- Do you use a range of question types, for example, open or closed, questions to extend thinking and develop discussion?
- Are your questions clearly stated and well structured?
- How well do you learners respond? Does it vary from group to group?

Young people actively engage with issues that affect them and those around them. They play a full part in the life of their school, college, workplace or wider community by taking responsible action to bring improvements for others as well as themselves.

## Some ideas for integrating PLTS into your teaching

PLTS will not be effective if they are treated as a 'bolt-on' extra. They need to be planned in right from the start and this means using learning and teaching methods which necessitate the application and development of these skills; teacher-dominated transmission teaching will not do. Well-planned project ideas also provide opportunities for the development of functional skills. Here are a few starter ideas for embedding personal, learning and thinking skills into your teaching.

### Health and social care
Organising a 'Healthy Life' exhibition would offer a wide variety of opportunities for developing PTLS, functional skills and employability. The spider diagram in Figure 12.1 suggests a few; you will be able to think of many more.

### Engineering
Engineering offers many opportunities for problem-based learning and the development of PLTS. Learners could be encouraged to identify and analyse an engineering

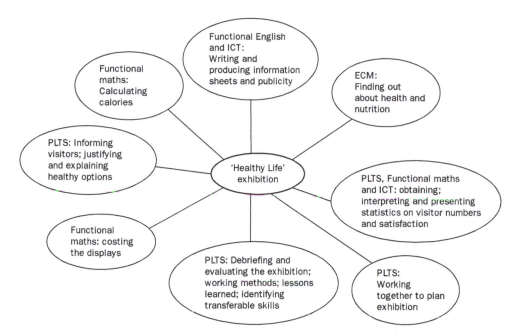

**Figure 12.1** 'Healthy Life' exhibition – combining functional skills and PLTS.

problem and plan, research, produce, analyse and evaluate their solutions. Such a project would involve all elements of the PLTS framework.

### Creative and media

Media planning and production projects, for example, the development of an advertising campaign, can be structured around PLTS and functional skills. In media projects it is particularly important for learners to match the campaign to the needs and lifestyles of the target audience and to create products in the appropriate style, tone and presentation to suit that audience. It's pretty much what teachers have to do for learners!

## Employability

> An educational system isn't worth a great deal if it teaches young people how to make a living but doesn't teach them how to make a life.
>
> (Anonymous)

It could be argued that employability, or employability skills, has always been at the centre of education but is more explicitly referred to in current educational discourse. The debate concerning education for the economy versus education of the 'whole person' is not new. I would argue, however, that this is a false division. The most important elements of success in work and life are the kinds of learning experiences that people have and their belief in themselves as learners. The attitudes, abilities and skills of being a good learner are the same as those of a good employee or, indeed, self-employed person. Many young business people report that for them the old distinctions between work, life and learning are blurred.

The Foster Report (2005) made clear recommendations regarding the future and purposes of further education: '. . . Perhaps our most crucial recommendation is that colleges should sharpen their focus and direct the main force of their effort towards improving employability and supplying economically valuable skills' (Foster 2005: 3). The political focus has for some time now been shifting towards the development of employment skills in education, particularly since the Leitch Report in 2006. One of the difficulties is what is meant by 'employability skills'. As Martin et al. suggest: 'Definitions of employability skills range from a vague notion of having something to do with preparing for a first job, through to very precise lists of specific skills, and on to employability being seen as a learning process' (Martin et al. 2008: 7). The UK Commission on Employment and Skills (UKCES 2009: 10) provides a far more general definition of employability skills as 'the skills that almost everyone needs to do almost any job'.

## What do employers want?

When asked what skills and qualities they want in new young employees, employers suggest a wide range of generic skills in addition to job-specific skills. These employer 'wish lists' usually include the following:

- communication skills
- teamworking skills
- problem-solving skills
- literacy skills
- numeracy skills
- general IT skills
- timekeeping
- business awareness
- customer care skills
- personal presentation
- enthusiasm/commitment
- enterprising.

## UKCES model of employability skills

The UK Commission on Employability and Skills (UKCES) is a social partnership of large and small employers, trades unions and the voluntary sector which is concerned with fostering economic growth and creating jobs. In 2009 they published *The Employability Challenge* which set out their ideas on developing employability skills in education. A key component of this report is their model of employability

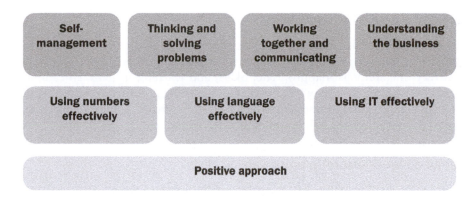

**Figure 12.2** UKCES model of employability skills.

skills, which integrates personal skills and functional skills as part of a framework for learning and teaching (See Figure 12.2).

In detail, the UKCES model has these elements:

- a foundation of *positive approach*: being ready to participate, make suggestions, accept new ideas and constructive criticism, and take responsibility for outcomes.

This foundation supports three functional skills:

- *using numbers effectively* – measuring, recording measurements, calculating, estimating quantities, relating numbers to the job.
- *using language effectively* – writing clearly and in a way appropriate to the context, ordering facts and concepts logically.
- *using IT effectively* – operating a computer, both basic systems and also learning other applications as necessary, and using telephones and other technology to communicate.

These functional skills are exercised in the context of four personal skills:

- *self-management* – punctuality and time management, fitting dress and behaviour to context, overcoming challenges and asking for help when necessary.
- *thinking and solving problems* – creativity, reflecting on and learning from own actions, prioritising, analysing situations and developing situations.
- *working together and communicating* – cooperating, being assertive, persuading, being responsible to others, speaking clearly to individuals and groups and listening for a response.
- *understanding the business* – understanding how the individual job fits into the organisation as a whole; recognising the needs of stakeholders (customers and service users, for example); judging risks, innovating and contributing to the whole organisation (UKCES 2009: 10).

## Developing learners' employability

As with functional skills and thinking skills the main debate around employability skills concerns the most effective strategies for learning. This is another case where the 'delivery' metaphor is inappropriate. Skills, and learning in general, cannot be 'delivered' to learners as if they were packages. Learning is something that happens within each person; it isn't something which is 'done to them'. Fundamentally, there are two possibilities: embedded or non-embedded (discrete).

### Non-embedded, or discrete, employability skills

In this strategy, employability skills are provided in discrete sessions and not contextualised within the programme of study or set within, for example, a work-based project. Such discrete provision might include: preparing a CV; interview preparation; customer awareness or communication skills. Similarly, functional skills might be delivered as free-standing maths, English or IT classes.

There isn't necessarily a problem with this strategy. It might be appropriate on occasions for some learners to have stand-alone sessions, particularly when it comes to acquiring the basic knowledge and skills. However, most research suggests that learning these kinds of skills is most effective when it is embedded within a realistic context. Another problem with this approach is that it can be seen as 'remedial', implying that the learners have some kind of deficit which needs to be 'fixed'. In times of full employment, many of these skills would have been learned naturally and normally within work.

### Embedded employability skills

By far the most effective way of developing learners' employability and other skills is through the embedded route whereby they are planned and learned in context and are, as far as possible, such an integral part of learning that learners don't necessarily recognise them, although when reflecting on their progress they can identify them and see how much they have learned.

Earlier in this chapter we looked at learners creating a 'Healthy Life' exhibition as a way of developing their PLTS and functional skills. Such activities almost naturally encourage the development of employability.

### Importance of work experience and employer involvement

The specialised diplomas which were introduced for vocational learners in 2008 required that colleges and schools developed their programmes in conjunction with local employers. Whatever the future for the diplomas, this still seems a positive notion.

It is important for young people to have work experience not only in order to become familiar with that particular business or profession, but also for the opportunity to understand and develop the wider aspects of employability such as timekeeping, reliability and communication. In addition, learning can be enhanced when employers are involved in developing learning experiences and assessments and take part in assessing the learners. UKCES (2009: 20) emphasise the motivational aspect of employer engagement in learning and how young people feel more positive about seeing their learning in real-life settings.

## 'Making mistakes'

It is clear that for our economic and social development, innovation, creativity and risk taking are crucial to success. Innovation, creativity and development have always been preceded by people thinking up ideas and solutions to problems, trying them out, improving them and learning by mistakes. UKCES emphasise the importance of learners having the opportunity to make mistakes and operating on a trial and error basis in which they can reflect on their learning and recognise the positive and negative consequences of their actions.

This approach to learning, often referred as 'learning by doing' and specifically shown in Kolb's learning cycle (see Chapter 2), seems natural and normal, but we have to ask to what extent it is at odds with the exam and league table culture prevailing in our schools and colleges. Teachers and managers can easily feel that their job is to fill the learners with exactly what they need to pass examinations and tests and that there is little room for experimentation and possible failure. Failure is not a bad thing; telling someone they are a 'failure' is. Bloomer (1997: 60), writing about the curriculum, in this case the A-level curriculum states:

> Creativity and novelty, whether of a demonstrably practical or theoretical form, can become stifled, since, while credit can be given to successful risk taking, much less is given to failed risk taking and often none at all is given for the act of risk taking itself. Taken together, these observations suggest that the 'safest' preparation for examinations is for students to stockpile dependable, 'correct' course knowledge, to rehearse that knowledge and to dispatch it in its most unambiguous form. The cost of this is that 'non-essential' course knowledge is discarded, that complex or contentious knowledge is simplified and that creativity is abandoned because of its risks.

## Employability – a curricular process?

We are rightly encouraged to provide opportunities for our learners to develop their employability. Unfortunately, we may feel that we don't have time to do this as well as to train people for the specific skills of their jobs or getting them through exams – we might feel, in short, that employability is a luxury we can't afford. This may be true if you offer employability skills as discrete packages of learning. However, it may be more realistic and effective to consider ways in which employability can be developed within an integrated curriculum. The key to this is to offer a broad range of learning activities that encourage deep learning, thinking skills and problem solving. Employability is best considered as a learning process. Knight and Yorke have researched and written widely on employability in universities and their conclusions are equally applicable to the lifelong learning sector. They state:

> We take it as a premise that there is no necessary conflict between employability and traditional academic values. Good teaching and learning practices can serve both kinds of end . . . a concern for employability is not inimical to good learning, but is supportive of it.
>
> (Knight and Yorke 2003: 4)

## Helping your learners to find their way in to your subject

One of the most important tasks for a teacher is to invite learners in to their subject, not only to become familiar with the content and skills but also to help them to understand it at a deep level and develop ways to think and talk about it. Some teachers are very welcoming, others less so. This is not just a matter of the teacher's personality or style, it's something we can all develop. If you recall learning in any subject or discipline at any stage of your life, but particularly within an educational institution, you will remember that you didn't know everything at once. Some elements, a few key concepts, some key words might have been familiar to you, but the big picture will have been indistinct and potentially alienating. You will also, no doubt, recall gradual realisation and piecing together of a more complete understanding. Teachers can help learners to do this; we can help them find 'ways in'.

In Chapter 5 we considered some of the theoretical underpinning of effective learning, particularly the use of advance organisers to help learners understand the 'big picture' and constructivist learning theory which emphasises the role of previous learning and the development of personal understandings and schemas. Here, we will look at how we can make learning more relevant and how we can use 'threshold' concepts.

### Relevance

Students will find it easier to get into a subject if they can see its relevance. How does it relate to real life? How does it relate to their previous experience and can teachers help them to make connections? Learners often feel that they are thrown in at the deep end of a subject rather than being given an opportunity to splash about in the shallow end and gradually develop the confidence to move up. In some areas of learning, for example, maths, science and engineering, teachers may have been used to filling up learners with content prior to applying and analysing it. Kember et al. (2008: 254), writing of first year teaching at university, suggest:

> It was not just that the abstract theory aroused little interest, it was also hard to understand in many cases. Without seeing an application which put the theory in context it became hard to grasp the meaning. It was also difficult to frame suitable questions to advance understanding.

If students' first experiences of a subject are of seemingly unconnected bits of theory and unusual terminology, they are likely to feel confused and demotivated. Supplying reasons and contexts for learning from the outset will increase motivation. Relevance can be established by, for example:

- using real-life examples
- drawing cases from current issues
- giving local examples
- relating theory to practice.

In subjects such as sociology and health and social care, new students will probably know about a range of social issues but will be unfamiliar with the concepts and language which the subject specialism uses to understand and discuss these things. Northedge (2003: 173) gives an example of how we can begin with the familiar and use it as a way into the subject and its language and concepts. The first step is to capture students' attention and establish a common focus for understanding and meaning making. He illustrates this by an example from a social work training in which students are introduced to and discuss a case study of two homeless drug users. By this everyday, 'common-sense' discussion students can relate to a real-life scenario and start to tease out some of the key issues. The discussion would not necessarily include subject-specific language and concepts. The second step leads from familiar to subject specialist discourse by discussion and questioning and the introduction of specialist concepts. A further advantage of this process, implicit in Northedge's work, is that students can develop their critical thinking skills as they move from 'common-sense' understandings and opinions to more rigorous and objective, academic understandings. Northedge's ideas seem to challenge conventional wisdom that students need to acquire theory and content before they can apply it to problems. Sometimes introducing problems first can be a stimulating introduction and increase motivation to develop the understanding of theory.

## Threshold concepts

Threshold concepts are particularly associated with the work of Meyer and Land (2003, see also Land et al. 2008) who suggest that 'threshold concepts may be a way of overcoming the "over-stuffed curriculum"'. They state: 'A tendency among academic teachers is to stuff their curriculum with content, burdening themselves with the task of transmitting vast amounts of knowledge bulk and their students of absorbing and reproducing this bulk.' This may be true of vocational teachers as well as academics concerned to give their learners everything they need for the assessments. Focusing on threshold concepts can help teachers to identify what is fundamental to the students' grasp of the subject. Three of the key features of threshold concepts are that they are:

- *transformative* – they make a difference to who we are and how we perceive the world. They change our ways of understanding.
- *irreversible* – once understood they are unlikely to be forgotten. Teachers can find it difficult to recall a time when they didn't understood these concepts and therefore may not find it easy to empathise with students who are struggling with them.
- *integrative* – they help students to make connections. As Cousin (2006: 4) points out: 'mastery of a threshold concept often allows a learner to make connections that were hitherto hidden from view.' There is a clear link here to constructivist theories of learning.

'Socialisation' is an example of a threshold concept from sociology. Initially difficult for students to grasp, once mastered it provides a basis for understanding much of sociology. It is transformative, irreversible and integrative. Stokes et al. (2007: 436) provide examples of threshold concepts in other disciplines:

- economics – opportunity cost, elasticity.
- pure mathematics – complex numbers, limits.
- electrical engineering – frequency response.
- statistics – sampling distribution.
- computer science – object-oriented programming.
- law – precedence.

---

**Activity**

Can you identify any 'threshold concepts' in your subject specialism?

For example, in sociology and media studies, 'ideology' can be a really difficult concept to grasp. Equally, using concepts such as 'horsepower' or 'torque' in motor vehicle courses can be challenging.

In what ways can you help your learners to understand these concepts? Don't be frightened of 'dumbing down'; use a picture, a diagram or a model.

---

## Further reading

Bowkett, S. (2006) *100 Ideas for Teaching Thinking Skills*. London: Continuum. An accessible book with lots of ideas for developing thinking skills.
Cousin, G. (2006) An introduction to threshold concepts, *Planet*, 17 December. Available at www.gees.ac.uk/planet/p17/gc.pdf (accessed 11 December 2011).
Lucas, B. and Claxton, G. (2009) *Wider Skills for Learning*. London: National Endowment for Science, Technology and the Arts (NESTA). Available at www.nesta.org.uk.
McGregor, D (2007) *Developing Thinking; Developing Learning. A Guide to Thinking Skills in Education*. Maidenhead: Open University Press.
Martin, R., Villeneuve-Smith, F., Marshall, L. and McKenzie, E. (2008) *Employability Skills Explored*. London: Learning and Skills Network.

## Websites

Robert Fisher's website on teaching thinking and creativity. www.teachingthinking.net/.
*The Philosopher's Magazine* has a section on 'café philosophique' and some interesting and amusing debates, a recent example, 'Shakespeare vs. Britney', considers questions of what art is. www.philosophersnet.com.

# 13

# Continuing professional development

**What this chapter is about**

- Synthesis – bringing it all together
- What is effective learning and teaching?
- Continuing professional development
- The 'dual professional'
- Evaluating your sessions and being observed

**LLUK standards**

This chapter covers, at least, the following standards:
AS 1; AK 2.1; AP 2.2; AS 2; AK 2.1; AP 2.1; AS 3; AK 3.1; AP 3.1; AS 4; AK 4.2;
AP 4.2; AK 4.2; AP 4.2; AK 4.3; AP 4.3; AS 5; AK 5.2; AP 5.2; AS 6; AK 6.2; AP 6.2;
AS 7; AK 7.2; AP 7.2; AK 7.3; AP 7.3
BS 1; BK 1.1; BP 1.1; BK 1.2; BP 1.2; BK 1.3; BP 1.3; BS 2; BK 2.6; BP 2.6
DS 1; DK 1.1; DP 1.1; DS 3; DK 3.1; DP 3.1; DK 3.2; DP 3.2

## Synthesis – putting it all together

At various points throughout this book I have encouraged you to make connections between the different elements of teaching and learning and to consider the effects they have on each other. Competence-based systems of learning and assessment can all too frequently break things down into their constituent elements but forget to put them back together; they forget the 'big picture'. A great car is a more than just the sum of its parts; its gearbox, transmission, steering and aerodynamics are designed as individual parts but they are also designed to work together so that the whole of the car is greater than the sum of its parts. Great teaching is the same and good teachers ensure that all the elements are aligned to meet the needs of the learners. Good teaching and effective learning is creative – it is a synthesis of, at least, knowledge, skills, methods, theory, experience and reflection.

**Activity**

Ron, our fictional teacher from the discussion case study, is meeting a group of young learners for their first (all day) session in a further education college. They have come from various local schools but none of them has enjoyed learning or had any significant achievements. Now that Ron is a wiser and more experienced teacher, he knows that he can make a difference to these people and, hopefully, re-engage them in learning. He knows that getting it right in this first session is vital to success.

This first session has two purposes. The stated, explicit purpose of the session is to induct them and carry out initial assessments – potentially a dull and anxiety-inducing experience. The implicit but far more important purpose of this session is to show the learners that they will have a different experience in college; that they will be respected and treated more like adults than in school; that teachers will have high expectations of them and provide challenging but achievable learning activities; that they will be listened to and their experiences valued; that the learning environment will be emotionally safe and, in short, to make them want to keep coming to college and learning.

Going back over all that you have read and learned so far, consider each of the following and discuss how they can contribute to making a better learning experience for them:

- communication
- learning theories
- planning
- teaching and learning methods
- motivation
- assessment
- resources
- inclusive learning.

## What is effective learning and teaching?

What do we mean by effective teaching and effective learning? Effective for whom or for what? Effective teaching could be teaching that gets results. In an assessment-driven system, teachers who produce the best results are highly valued – rightly so. Good results mean better reputation and more secure funding and future for the organisation and its teachers. Better results mean more people progressing to higher levels of learning. Conversely, effective teaching in an assessment-driven system can mean a narrowing of the curriculum and content and an emphasis on transmission-based teaching; at its worst, teaching to the test. Good teaching that produces good results does not necessarily produce lifelong learners. Teaching that gets results is also, we are told, good for the economy and society. People need skills to get on in their lives and work and the lifelong learning sector (LLS) can provide these skills. But does it also produce lifelong learners?

Another view is that good teachers create frameworks in which people can learn, rather than just be taught. Effective teaching encourages learning. This is why the best teachers are always a bit subversive. They acknowledge the importance of results for learners and institutions and strive to improve them, but they also know that creating excitement and enthusiasm for learning is the greater prize.

## Hay McBer model of teacher effectiveness

There are many analyses and models that attempt to describe effective teaching. One of the most useful is provided by the Hay McBer (2000) *Research into Teacher Effectiveness*. The report was commissioned to provide a framework to describe effective teaching in schools, but with a few modifications and provisos it is equally useful for teachers in the lifelong learning sector. Figure 13.1 shows the three main interlinked components of the model: teaching skills, professional characteristics and classroom climate. Each element breaks down into categories and subcategories which constitute a valuable toolkit for teachers to evaluate their effectiveness.

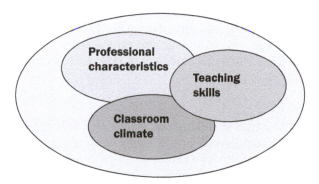

**Figure 13.1** Hay McBer's three measures of teacher effectiveness.

## Teaching skills

Teaching skills has six categories (I have omitted the 'homework' category):

1  *High expectations.* Effective teachers have high expectations of all their learners which they communicate to them and support them in achieving. These expectations will be differentiated to meet the needs of all learners.

2  *Planning.* Effective teachers set clear frameworks and objectives and share them with their learners.

3   *Methods and strategies*. Effective teachers use and develop a variety of teaching and learning methods to meet the needs of a wide range of learners. They use active learning methods to develop higher order skills and encourage learning.

4   *Management and discipline*. Effective teachers establish a physically and emotionally safe and secure learning environment. They set boundaries, often in negotiation with learners, in which inappropriate behaviour is censured and appropriate behaviour is recognised and encouraged.

5   *Management of time and resources*. Effective teachers are skilled managers of time and resources to maximise learning. Learning sessions are clearly structured and make full use of time.

6   *Assessment*. Effective teachers use a wide range of methods to check understanding and assess learning. They consciously use teaching, learning and assessment methods which are based on assessment *for* learning.

All of these elements combine to create well-structured sessions which flow and keep learners on task.

## Professional characteristics

The Hay McBer report states:

> Professional characteristics are deep-seated patterns of behaviour which outstanding teachers display more often, in more circumstances and to a greater degree of intensity than less effective colleagues. They are how the teacher does the job, and have to do with self-image and values; traits, or the way the teacher habitually approaches situations; and, at the deepest level, the motivation that drives performance.
>
> (Hay McBer 2000: 14)

This statement should be read in conjunction with the LLUK Standards Domain A: Professional Values and Practice which provide the underpinning values for those teaching in the lifelong learning sector. The professionalism cluster has five elements: professionalism; planning and setting expectations; thinking; relating to others; leading.

### Professionalism
*   *Respect for others*. This is the core value and is based on respect for all learners and colleagues (teaching and non-teaching). It is closely linked to valuing diversity and inclusive practice.
*   *Challenge and support*. These are related to high expectations of learners and to helping all learners develop their self-esteem as well as their learning.
*   *Confidence*. Effective teachers are confident in their role and their self-image as professionals. They are emotionally intelligent, positive and believe in success.
*   *Creating trust*. Effective teachers are consistent and fair. They keep their word and don't betray the trust of learners or colleagues.

### Planning and setting expectations

- *Drive for improvement.* Teachers in lifelong learning set targets and measure them against internal and external data and benchmarks.

- *Information seeking.* As well as seeking information about standards and achievement, effective teachers constantly seek to find out about their learners in order to meet their needs and provide differentiated learning.

- *Initiative.* Effective teachers use their initiative and take opportunities to deal with problems before they escalate. In addition, they seize opportunities to develop positive aspects of learning sessions in response to feedback from learners and unplanned events.

### Thinking

- *Analytical thinking.* This is related to reflection and evaluation. Effective teachers analyse their practice as a key to improvement.

- *Conceptual thinking.* Effective teachers are able to see patterns and links and to make connections. They provide the 'big picture' for themselves and their learners.

### Relating to others

- *Understanding others.* This relates to communication skills, emotional intelligence and recognising feedback. Effective teachers have insight into their learners and what motivates them and overcoming barriers to learning.

- *Impact and influence.* Effective teachers recognise and use their ability to impress and influence others – colleagues and learners – to produce positive outcomes.

- *Teamworking.* Effective teaching in the lifelong learning sector requires teachers to cooperate and collaborate with a range of people – learners, colleagues, managers, external bodies.

### Leading

- *Managing learners.* Effective teachers are adept at keeping their learners on task and engaged in learning.

- *Passion for learning.* This is self-evident really. They are committed to their subject area but above all committed to learning.

- *Flexibility.* Teachers in lifelong learning are flexible in their approach to learners and learning, as well as seeking opportunities to develop and extend their range of teaching and depth of learning.

- *Holding people accountable.* Effective teachers hold people, learners and colleagues, accountable. For learners, this means taking some responsibility for their own learning and developing independent learning.

## Classroom climate

It will be useful to read this section in conjunction with the *communication climate* section in Chapter 3. In the lifelong learning sector there is a wide variety of learning situations, including classrooms, laboratories, workshops and workplaces. In addition, some learning will happen in situations other than a conventional class, for example, NVQ assessment. Given the much wider range of learning situations than in schools, however, Hay McBer's guidelines for classroom climate are still useful. They are essentially about the ways in which 'effective teachers use their knowledge, skills and behaviours to create effective learning environments'. The key elements are as follows:

1  *Clarity.* There should be clarity about the purposes of the learning, the aims and objectives, activities and assessment. There should also be clarity about the 'big picture' and how the current learning fits in with and connects to previous learning.

2  *Order.* This isn't just to do with maintaining discipline. It's also about having a structured and businesslike attitude to learning sessions.

3  *Standards.* For many groups of learners it will be appropriate to have a set of standards relating to behaviour. These standards could be negotiated and contracted with learners.

4  *Fairness.* This means the degree to which there is an absence of favouritism. It also means avoiding bias, stereotypes and making assumptions about learners. It's about equality.

5  *Participation.* Effective teachers use methods to encourage and develop active learning. They provide opportunities for learners to participate by using discussion, higher order questions and similar activities.

6  *Support.* This is part of providing an emotionally safe environment in which learners can seek guidance and support as well as taking risks and learning from mistakes.

7  *Safety.* The degree to which learners feel that the learning environment is an emotionally and physically safe place, free as far as possible from fear-inducing factors.

8  *Interest.* Effective teachers strive to make the learning environment interesting, exciting and stimulating.

## Teaching and Learning Research Project (TLRP)

### Ten principles

These principles were developed from research undertaken by the Teaching and Learning Research Project (TLRP, 2007: 14) which analysed key findings from projects in primary and secondary schools. Their findings can just as easily be applied to the lifelong learning sector. Effective teaching and learning contributes the following elements:

1  *Equips learners for life in its broadest sense.* This is about developing learners as 'active citizens' who can develop their intellectual, personal and social resources. Much of learning in schools and colleges is prescribed and outcomes can be narrow. This principle requires us to look to the development of broader outcomes

such as lifelong learning and employability and, more broadly, equity and social justice.

2  *Engages with valued forms of knowledge.* Teachers in lifelong learning should have a thorough understanding of the subjects they teach so as to engage learners with the big ideas and key processes of those subjects. However, as Coffield (2008): 12) asks: '. . . Whose valued forms of knowledge? The government's? The tutor's? The student's? Experts in the field?'

3  *Recognises the importance of prior experience and learning.* This principle is a clear link with constructivist theories of learning and also with Malcolm Knowles' theory of androgogy (1978) which suggests that adult learners have considerable life experiences and want to have these recognised in their learning.

4  *Requires the teacher to scaffold learning.* 'Scaffolding' is an important educational concept which means that teachers can help learners by providing them with support structures to help them build their learning. These structures are gradually removed as the learning becomes secure.

5  *Needs assessment to be congruent with learning.* There are two aspects to this. The first is that assessment should advance learning and help learners to learn; in other words, formative assessment or assessment for learning. The second aspect echoes the concept of 'constructive alignment' in which learning outcomes and assessment objectives are matched and assessment has maximum validity (Biggs and Tang 2011).

6  *Promotes the active engagement of the learner.* Learners should be actively involved in their learning rather than passive 'consumers' of knowledge 'delivered' to them. This principle argues for the 'active engagement' of learners and the development of independence and autonomy by increasing their repertoire of learning strategies.

7  *Fosters both individual and social processes and outcomes.* The first aspect of this principle affirms the importance of the social aspects of learning, of people cooperating and collaborating. In constructivist theory this is also known as co-constructionism. The second aspect argues for giving learners a 'voice' and consulting them about their learning.

8  *Recognises the significance of informal learning.* Not all learning happens in the classroom or other educational settings. Informal learning which happens in, for example, homes and workplaces is significant and can fruitfully be linked to more formal learning. There is a link here to situated learning theory.

9  *Depends on teacher learning.* In terms of CPD this is the most important of these ten principles. Improvements in teaching and learning are clearly related to the need for teachers to continually develop, to enhance their knowledge and skills and develop their roles, particularly through classroom inquiry and action research.

10  *Demands consistent policy frameworks with support for teaching and learning as their primary focus.* This principle argues for consistent policy frameworks at institutional and systems level. For CPD this means that institutions and senior managers should recognise the fundamental role of teaching and learning in improving colleges and learning providers.

**Activity**

Consider how far these ten principles reflect your own practice as a teacher? Do they underpin the values and practice of your place of work?

Use these principles as a framework to consider your own CPD.

## Continuing professional development

According to the Institute for Learning (IfL): 'Continuing professional development means maintaining, improving and broadening relevant knowledge and skills in your subject specialism and your teaching so that it has a positive impact on practice and learner experience.' (2009: 4). The key word is *professional*. Teachers in the lifelong learning sector are encouraged to think of themselves as professionals, but people don't become professional or behave professionally just because they are told to. The essential characteristics of professionalism are autonomy, specialist knowledge and responsibility. There is an expectation that we will have specialist knowledge and that we are responsible people, but many teachers in the sector do not feel that they have autonomy in the ways in which they do their jobs. Teachers have a right to be professional but they also have a responsibility to be professional. Part of this responsibility is to engage in meaningful CPD not only to maintain their licence to practise, but also and more importantly because it benefits them, their organisation and above all their learners

### The dual professional

The IfL CPD model is based on the notion of the 'dual professional': that is being a subject specialist and also continually developing their understanding of the theory and practice of teaching and learning. It is important that those currently in the sector and those about to enter it understand the changing nature of teaching and learning and of lifelong learning. The purpose of teaching is learning. For many, however, teaching is still seen as a process of transmission of knowledge from an expert to students and the retention of this knowledge being assessed in some way. Clearly, the role of the expert subject teacher is vital to learning; learners want teachers who 'know their stuff'. Unfortunately, the 'stuff' teachers know goes out of date quite quickly. Consequently, teachers will have to become not only subject experts but people who can help learners to learn as well as being lifelong learners themselves. As Wells (1986: 222) says: 'At every level, students must be encouraged actively to take responsibility for their own learning, and this applies as much to teachers as learners as it does to the students they teach.'

### From 'sheep-dip' to personalised CPD

CPD on its own does not make a professional but the introduction of the IfL and the requirement for CPD offers some real possibilities for teachers to seize the initiative and take some control of their own CPD and possibly, as a consequence, become more professional. Villeneuve-Smith et al. (2009: 13) suggest that 'the move to professionalise the workforce changes everything – arguably for the better'.

Those who have been working in the sector for some time, particularly in FE, will be familiar with the 'sheep-dip' approach to staff development in which all teaching staff were 'invited' to attend mass training events, usually at the end of an academic year, which were chosen by others on their behalf. This in-service education and training (INSET) model has the attraction that it is relatively cheap, provides easily auditable evidence of training and causes minimum disruption to the organisation's main purpose – teaching and learning. There are undoubtedly good examples of effective INSET events, especially to provide an introduction to a major new initiative. Equally, there are probably as many bad examples which, while they may tick some boxes, are not good models of teaching and learning. Villeneuve-Smith et al. (2009: 6) ask:

> Have you ever sat through a badly taught training day on good teaching? Suffered death by PowerPoint on a programme for innovative uses of e-learning? Attended a didactically taught course on active learning? . . . it could be argued that good CPD should practise what it preaches. Why should the sector accept development activities that don't reflect in their delivery what you already know about good teaching and learning.

If personalisation, with its acknowledgement of learners as individuals located within specific contexts and with a wide range of needs and ways of learning, is the new mantra in the sector then surely the same should apply to teachers and their CPD. This conception of CPD, based on a professional dialogue about teaching and learning, reflects what the IfL is looking for. Indeed, the IfL review of CPD (2009: 11) urges: 'a broad interpretation of CPD beyond attendance at courses, workshops or formal study'; and 'a personalised approach to CPD; practitioners leading in their own CPD and using judgement and expertise to develop leading edge practice in teaching and training'.

The IfL CPD guidelines provide a comprehensive list of the kinds of activities that are in line with these principles, including mentoring new colleagues, peer observation and review, and action research.

Personalised CPD, by implication, should mean a move to more teacher autonomy and the recognition that professional teachers, in their specific contexts and subject disciplines, are best placed to recognise problems that need to be solved or to identify opportunities for improvement.

## Encouraging collaboration and the development of learning communities

There is a body of learning theory, social constructivism, which asserts that learners learn best in groups where they can share and develop ideas and contribute to solving problems. The same is true for teachers who, to use a clichéd old phrase, need peers and, possibly, colleagues from different disciplines, to 'bounce ideas off'.

Good teachers are also good learners; their CPD is based on learning. Coffield (2008) suggests two contrasting metaphors of learning that apply equally well to learners and teachers. The first is the *acquisition* metaphor in which learning is seen as gaining ownership of knowledge and skills, endorsed by certificates from examination boards or certificates of attendance at training events. This metaphor employs such key words as 'delivery' and 'transmission'. In contrast the *participation* metaphor, with its associated key words, 'community, identity, meaning, practice, dialogue, co-operation and belonging' (Coffield 2008: 8) suggests that learning results from participation in communities of practice which learn, share, develop and communicate within a common, shared context. This clearly relates to the IfL's belief in 'professional dialogue' and teachers researching into their own practice as the bases of meaningful CPD. Wells (1986: 221) refers to teachers as 'theory-builders':

> Every teacher needs to become his or her own 'theory-builder' but a builder of theory that grows out of practice and has as its aim to improve the quality of practice. For too long, 'experts' from outside the classroom have told teachers what to think and do. They have even designed programs that are 'teacher-proof' in an attempt to bypass teacher involvement in the same way that so many teachers have bypassed student involvement.

Wells' criticism of 'experts from outside' may bring to mind official advice and guidance and examples of 'best practice' which are considered to be transferable to any place of learning regardless of context. For some time now teachers in the compulsory sector have become accustomed to documents, CDs and DVDs demonstrating good practice arriving at their schools. The 'Gold Dust' resources are admirable examples of the kinds of materials that can be produced by groups of people working together and they are frequently usefully adapted by teachers in the sector. However, the physical versions of the 'Gold Dust' resources can often be seen on staffroom shelves in serried ranks and in pristine condition. The difficulty with such materials is that they seem to be produced in 'context-free' environments and as such may not easily translate to a particular teaching and learning environment.

The idea that learning materials, resources and methods which are successful in one place will therefore be successful in another is part of a wider culture of 'best practice'. An A-level teacher in a college sixth form centre, a literacy tutor in a young offenders' institution and a work-based learning assessor in a training provider could, no doubt, have interesting and useful discussions about what they do and how they do it and might learn much from each other. It seems unlikely, however, that they could develop a range of materials that would meet the needs of all or indeed any of their learners. The notion of 'best practice' is frequently extended to areas other than teaching and learning – to management, administration, funding and record keeping.

James and Biesta (2007) undertook a large-scale longitudinal research project, published as *Improving Learning Cultures in Further Education*, in which they develop a cultural approach to understanding learning. They argue for the transformation of learning cultures in further education based on their conclusions that all places of learning are particular and located in their own contexts and, while there will be many similarities, they are all unique:

The cultural approach also enables us to adopt a different and in our opinion more realistic way to understand and manage the improvement of teaching and learning. The essence of this approach is to work to enhance learning cultures, in ways that make successful learning more rather than less likely. Because of the relational complexity of learning, and of the differing positions and dispositions of learners, there is no approach that can ever guarantee universal learning success, however success is defined. Rather than looking for universal solutions that will work always, everywhere and for everyone, the cultural approach helps us to see that the improvement of learning cultures always asks for contextualised judgement rather than for general recipes.

(James and Biesta 2007: 37)

Even if you don't read the whole book, James and Biesta's conclusions, particularly the suggested 'principles of procedure' for transforming learning cultures in FE, will interest anyone who wants to improve learning and teaching. Their conclusions also provide a good contextual underpinning for considering your CPD in its widest sense.

Kathryn Ecclestone (2010) proposes a 'problem-based methodology' for CPD in which teachers formulate their own problems and questions in their own settings and undertake 'trial and error' approaches to resolving them. Such approaches might be regarded as expensive and uncertain but they are likely to be more effective than imported solutions. They have the added advantage of restoring, perhaps in small measure, teachers' professionalism and autonomy. Ecclestone (2010: 190) states that the problem-based methodology 'is an explicit, albeit small attempt to redress the balance in CPD back towards the imaginative criticism of autonomous professionals ... requiring teachers to identify practical problems that are genuinely meaningful to them (as opposed to being told what problems or questions to address in the latest policy initiative)'.

---

**Activity**

To what extent is your own CPD personalised?

Take some time to consider your own professional development and how much say you have had in deciding priorities and choosing your activities.

What would be your priorities for development? How would they benefit you, your learners and your organisation?

---

## Evaluating your sessions

There are probably as many session observation and evaluation forms as there are learning providers. Many of these will provide useful advice and guidance to help teachers improve, but some won't. You are probably working quite happily with a standard lesson evaluation format but if you're not and you need to create your own here are some suggestions.

## First impressions

This is an unscientific 'gut feeling' approach to evaluating sessions which needs to be backed up by a more analytical approach but makes a useful starting point.

- How did you feel at the end of the session?
- How do you think your learners felt?
- Was there a buzz about the session?
- What was the learners' non-verbal communication like? Did they look as if they were enjoying themselves?

## Some general questions to ask yourself

- What were you planning to do:
  - With whom?
  - How?
  - Why?
- What happened?
- What went well?
- What was effective? How? Why?
- What went according to plan/what didn't?
- What were the causes of difficulties/changes, etc.?
- What would you do again?
- What wouldn't you do again?
- What was unaccounted for/not planned for?
- How will your planning for the future change?

To the above you could add the kinds of questions that inspectors ask:

- Do they know *what* they are learning and *why* they are learning it?
- Were they learning? Were *all* of them learning? How do you know?
- How did you assess the learning and check understanding?
- What did you do to help those who weren't learning?

### A lesson observation and evaluation checklist

Checklists can assume mammoth proportions and as a result become just a box-ticking exercise. They should always be used as a basis for discussion with your mentor, tutor, colleague or with yourself. The checklist in Table 13.1 is intended simply as guide to the elements of an effective teaching and learning session.

**Table 13.1** Session evaluation and observation checklist.

**Planning**
- Scheme of work
- Session plan
- Aims and objectives – precise and SMART
- Structure and timings
- Variety of teaching and learning methods
- Differentiation planned in
- Resources and equipment prepared and ready
- Room layout appropriate

**Start**
- Prompt start
- Learning set in context
- Refers to/links to previous session
- Gets learners' attention before starting
- Purpose and content of session explained
- Structure provided
- Objectives shared (as appropriate)
- Registration
- Lateness challenged or managed
- ILPs reviewed (as appropriate)

**Communication**
- Appropriate use of voice: pace; pause; volume; variation
- Appropriate use nonverbal communication/body language
- Relationship/rapport established
- Appropriate level of language for learners
- Technical terms explained
- Avoidance of jargon
- Listening skills
- Learners' communication/feedback noticed and responded to

**Methods and strategies**
- Variety of methods used to stimulate and motivate learners
- Promotes inclusive learning
- Methods selected to suit learners, levels and tasks
- Whole group/small group/individual learning as appropriate
- Questions used to check learning
- Questions used to extend and develop learning
- Clear explanations provided
- Clear instructions provided

**Learning**
- Learners on task
- Learners involved
- Learners interested
- Learners understand
- Learners motivated
- Appropriate level for these learners
- Learning extended

(Continued)

**Table 13.1** Continued

---

**Resources**
- Appropriate resources selected/created
- Resources used competently
- ILT incorporated as appropriate

**Skills**
- Skills for Life embedded
- Key skills embedded
- Thinking skills planned in

**Behaviour management**
- Behaviour managed appropriately
- Positive behaviour recognised and rewarded
- Negative behaviour censured

**Monitoring and assessment**
- Range of methods used to check understanding
- Assessment *for* learning
- Assessments clearly explained
- Assessments relevant, fair and valid
- Developmental feedback provided

**Ending**
- Debriefing session (as appropriate)
- Main points summarised and recapped
- Learners given opportunity to apply and discuss learning
- Link forward to next session
- Crisp ending, on time

---

## Being observed

Observation of teaching and learning is part of the quality procedures in all learning institutions. Grading observations of teaching is a thorny issue and many teachers are wary about what the grades are used for, particularly at times when redundancies loom. Many colleges and providers give their teachers a numerical grade; others use particular words or phrases to describe performance such as excellent, very good, good, satisfactory, inadequate. Whatever system is in place, the main purpose of observation should be improvement rather than simply grading. Undertaken in the right spirit, observation should be supportive and developmental. The observation process should ideally involve:

- a time and date mutually agreed by observer and observee
- ample notice allowing the observee to prepare
- agreed and shared criteria and format for observation
- developmental feedback provided as soon as possible after the observation
- action planning for improvement following observation and feedback
- support for improvements.

Observers should be skilled in and preferably trained in observation procedures, particularly how to give sensitive and developmental feedback. If the relationship between observer and observee is positive, it might be a good idea to negotiate a focus for your observation. You could, for example, agree a focus on your classroom communication and interaction, or your use of questions.

## Peer observation

Peer observation is encouraged by many learning providers and can be a more supportive and less threatening activity than an observation by a manager or member of an observation team. The process of observation is voluntary and involves two or perhaps three colleagues agreeing to observe each other. There are obvious advantages on both sides: the observee can get useful advice and suggestions from their observer colleague; the observers can see different or novel approaches that they haven't previously been aware of.

### Aims of peer observation

The main aims of peer observation and development are:

- to contribute to a culture of teamwork and mutual support
- to reinforce reflective practice that leads to improved learning for students
- to encourage innovation with support from peers: a developmental approach.

### Objectives for peer observation

- Encourage CPD.
- Stimulate improvements in teaching and learning.
- Improve teachers', especially new teachers', confidence.
- Foster discussion and dissemination of good practice.
- Stimulate further research.

### Some principles and ideas for peer observation

- Should be voluntary.
- Should be non-judgemental.
- Should be supported by management but run by and for teachers.
- Each pairing/triad could have a specific, agreed focus.
- Peer observation could be supported by reading and research, perhaps even an action research project.
- Peer observation and review could take place across partnerships with schools, employers and training providers, particularly in diploma teaching.

## Reviews and appraisals

Everybody working in the lifelong learning sector will be required to have appraisals, usually with managers, of their performance and set agreed targets for development which meet the needs of the teachers and the learners but are also in line with the organisation's mission and objectives. New teachers may also have meetings with mentors to support them in their development and to review their progress. Without careful planning, preparation and a supportive framework, such meetings can seem to the participants little more than bureaucratic exercises; handled well, they should be valuable to the individual teacher and to the organisation. The following are some examples of development targets and activities which could emerge from reviews and appraisals:

- Upgrading subject-specific knowledge and skills.
- Work placement visits.
- Developing links with local employers.
- Developing links as part of employability initiatives.
- Further study for advanced qualifications.
- Becoming an external verifier or external examiner.
- Action research projects.
- Writing articles for journals or websites. These might be based around action research carried out with colleagues.
- Provide staff development sessions for colleagues in your subject specialism.
- Visiting conferences or training sessions.
- 'Cascading' information and ideas from attendance at conferences and training sessions.
- Become part of or set up learning communities, possibly in your subject area.
- Become a subject learning coach.
- Some organisations have advanced practitioner posts for experienced and excellent teachers.
- Develop new courses or curriculum areas in response to recognised need in the organisation, local business or community.

## Some ideas for subject-specific CPD

This section is intended to provide you with some general ideas for activities for subject-specific CPD activities. This is just a sample of some of the most usual activities. However, it is important that you consider the full range of possibilities within your specialism because there may be things you do as a matter of course which you don't consider to be CPD. I recall a trainee teacher of film and media studies who needed to teach French New Wave cinema – in discussion we decided that watching films was perfectly acceptable as CPD.

In its review of CPD, the IfL makes the point that CPD based on professional dialogue about teaching and learning is the most effective. It goes on to say: 'There is an over-focus on formal courses. Personalised CPD, such as peer coaching, is under-developed, yet research shows that this is the most effective' (IfL 2009: 11).

## Gaining qualifications

You might want to update your knowledge and skills by gaining a specific qualification in your subject area or to develop your range of expertise by studying for a qualification in a related discipline. If you are a subject specialist in, for example, a vocational area you could investigate a foundation degree. These are designed in conjunction with industry and employers to address skills gaps and to upskill the workforce. They include a wide variety of specialisms, for example: manufacturing management; sport studies; early years and childhood practice; multi-media design. Foundation degrees are equivalent to the first two years of an honours degree and you will have the opportunity to top up to a full degree.

You might also want to consider gaining a qualification in Skills for Life (literacy, numeracy or ESOL) as a Skills for Life specialist or as a vocational teacher who wants to work more effectively with Skills for Life specialists. You will, of course, need to be up to date with functional skills, especially in relation to the new diplomas.

Once you have begun studying, from PTLLS upwards, FE colleges and universities will be keen to offer a range of higher courses through first degree, masters and doctorate.

## Industrial updating

One of the strengths of FE has always been the experience that vocational staff bring with them from their previous work in business and industry. It is important for all learning providers to develop links with industry through placements, secondments and work shadowing. To facilitate such activity LLUK and Skills for Business have developed the Catalyst programme which aims to increase links between education, training and business. One of their services, Business Interchange, encourages the development of work experience placements for teachers and trainers.

## Examiner, verifier and assessor roles

Undertaking assessor and verifier roles are excellent opportunities to develop both elements of dual professionalism and give you the opportunity to see student work within your place of work or, as an external verifier, in other colleges and training providers. External work offers great opportunities for networking and sharing ideas. Further information on assessor and verifier awards is available on the main awarding body websites.

## Working with awarding bodies

The main awarding bodies offer a wide range of support, from downloadable documents to bespoke training programmes. You should check out the services available from the awarding body for your course; don't leave it to the course leader. If you are a new teacher it is especially useful to look at the subject specifications, past examination papers and examiners' reports. Awarding bodies provide training events, particularly when there are changes to courses or new specifications introduced. It is often the case that colleges and learning providers will send one representative to meetings and ask that person to 'cascade' the information – another excellent CPD opportunity.

## Giving presentations

Giving presentations to colleagues at work or in the wider setting of a conference are excellent opportunities for developing both sides of the dual professional. As mentioned above, you may be reporting back on a training session you have attended or you may be organising and running a staff development activity. As well as giving you an opportunity to research and develop your subject expertise, these events also challenge you to hone your presentation skills. The IfL points out that, 'the least frequent activities engaged in were research and contributions to journals and conferences.' (IfL 2009: 11)

## Writing

There are always opportunities for writing for a range of purposes and audiences, whether as printed documents or as online writing. These opportunities may be report writing to inform or persuade colleagues; writing articles for specialist journals or for more general publications such as the IfL's *In Tution* journal. Many specialist bodies and networks encourage and accept book reviews and articles from specialists; websites increasingly provide blogging opportunities. If you and your colleagues are involved in an action research project, you will need to write up the results and disseminate to colleagues and the wider subject community.

If you don't consider yourself to be a writer and you've got something to say, it's likely that other people will want to hear it. Just write, then get someone to help you with structure, grammar, spelling and the technical bits.

## Reading

Reading books, articles, reports and websites is a 'taken for granted' activity, but is frequently a legitimate and justifiable CPD activity. If you're teaching English literature obviously you will need to read the set texts but you can also benefit from reading other relevant books – fiction, history, sociology – to provide context. Specialists who are members of professional bodies will receive publications and journals which contain valuable advice, links and networking opportunities. Academic and specialist journals are easily available online now and colleges will have subscriptions and electronic access to organisations such as the British Education Index (BEI), the Educational Resource Information Centre (ERIC) and the EBSCO electronic journals service. Libraries can be a bit intimidating for the uninitiated – just go in and ask, the staff will want to help. The above activities are just a few suggestions for subject-specific CPD. The IfL CPD guidelines provide further examples which you might want to follow up.

## Subject-specific mentoring

Mentoring, especially subject-specific mentoring, is increasingly being seen in the lifelong learning sector as one of the most effective forms of CPD and personal development. Much has been published on mentoring and coaching. This section provides a brief introduction and signposts to more detailed sources are given at the end of the chapter.

Mentoring and coaching are frequently discussed as if they were interchangeable. MacLennan (1995) makes a simple distinction between a coach, someone you learn *with*, and a mentor, someone to you learn *from*. Whereas coaching can be seen more as a way to help someone to grow and help them to discover their talents and improve performance, mentoring is more concerned with learning from a more experienced practitioner. Pollard and Trigg (1997: 19) define mentoring as: 'the provision of support for the learning of one person through the guidance of another person, who is more skilled, knowledgeable and experienced in relation to the context of the learning taking place.'

## Role of the mentor and mentoring skills

Wallace and Gravells (2005: 4) provide a comprehensive discussion of the role and importance of the mentor, particularly the subject-specific mentor supporting trainee teachers. They identify the key responsibilities of a mentor as follows:

* to model good classroom practice
* to contribute to the assessment of the student teacher's classroom practice
* to *support* the student teacher's grasp of subject knowledge in terms of currency, breadth and appropriate structure for presentation to learners
* to *assess* the student teacher's grasp of subject knowledge in terms of currency, breadth and appropriate structure for presentation to learners.

In past industrial times a new recruit to a job often learned by 'sitting next to Nellie' and observing her skills and methods. This model worked well if Nellie was keen to pass on her skills and support new recruits. If, however, Nellie was an embittered and cynical worker and an unwilling teacher, her services would be less than useful. In a modern environment, a good and effective mentor needs to have or develop a variety of skills to support their mentees including:

* planning
* liaising
* demonstrating
* facilitating
* observing
* assessing
* guiding

- questioning
- listening
- reflecting.

Effective mentoring requires patience and empathy. You may recall learning a new skill and feeling uncertain of your suitability to do it and unable to assess your progress. A patient mentor guides and supports the mentee as they learn, as well as showing empathy for the new practitioner and remembering what it was like for themselves when they started.

## Subject learning coaches (SLCs)

The Subject Learning Coach Programme is part of the Teaching and Learning Programme which you can access through LSIS website. The role of the SLC is to act as a change agent within a particular subject specialism in an organisation to develop subject strategies, resources and best practice; to provide individual and group training; and to use peer coaching techniques to support the improvement of teaching and learning. The SLC programme is built around three interconnected 'enablers': teaching and learning resources; subject coaching networks; professional training programme.

## Teaching and learning resources

The 'Gold Dust' resources which have been available in physical form and were distributed to all learning providers are now available online. They provide a wide range of materials to support the development of teaching and learning (for example, using questions, developing active learning) in subject settings. The subject resources library includes:

- business
- construction and built environment
- creative and media
- engineering
- foundation learning
- IT
- land-based
- mathematics
- science
- society, health and development
- modern foreign languages.

### Subject coaching networks

Subject coaching networks are one-day regional events which take place at least twice a year. At these sessions participants can experiment with the teaching and learning resources and try out new approaches to teaching and learning in their subject area. In addition they provide networking opportunities and chances to practise coaching skills with peers. Currently, the subject networks are:

- adult learning
- business education
- creative and media
- construction and the built environment
- E2E (Foundation learning)
- society, health and development
- IT
- land-based studies
- modern foreign languages.

The LSIS STEM programme provides support and resources for science, technology, engineering and mathematics.

### Professional training programme
Professional training is provided through the Advanced Learning Coach (ALC) training programme. While SLCs work with colleagues at subject and team level to improve teaching and learning, the ALC programme is more strategic in focus and aims to develop participants to work with senior managers in developing organisational CPD and quality improvement plans.

## Conclusion – 'teacher artistry'

Educationally, we live in an age of frequent changes in policy, quality systems, audit trails, checklists, tickboxes and accountability. Accountability should be welcomed because we are in receipt of public money which should be spent wisely and well. Systems such as the observation checklist can contribute positively to accountability and improvement; used badly they reduce the art of teaching to merely a set of competences.

In her review of the research into teacher effectiveness, Alma Harris writes of the research tradition based on the notion of 'teacher artistry': 'Within this research tradition there is the central recognition that teaching involves creativity and is carried out in a highly personalised way' (Harris 1998). Professional teachers must work within and meet the demands of the organisations and systems of their profession, but they also have a personal, professional responsibility to reflect, learn, develop and be creative.

## Further reading

Institute for Learning (IfL, 2009) *Guidelines for your Continuing Professional Development*. London: Institute for Learning.

James, D. and Biesta, G. (2007) *Improving Learning Cultures in Further Education*. London: Routledge

Scales, P., Pickering, J., Senior, L., Headley, K., Garner, P. and Boulton, H. (2011) *Continuing Professional Development in the Lifelong Learning Sector*. Maidenhead: Open University Press.

Steward, A. (2009) *Continuing your Professional Development in Lifelong Learning*. London: Continuum.

Teaching and Learning Research Project (TLRP, 2007) *Principles into Practice: A Teacher's Guide to Research Evidence on Teaching and Learning*. London: Institute of Education. www.tlrp.org/pub/documents/Principles%20in%20Practice%20Low%20Res.pdf

## Websites

LSIS Excellence Gateway CPD pages. www.excellencegateway.org.uk/node/17221.

# Appendix
## National Qualifications Framework (NQF)

| | | | | |
|---|---|---|---|---|
| NVQ<br>Level 5 | | Key Skills<br>Level 5 | Level 5 | HE Level<br>8 – Doctorate<br>7 – Masters |
| NVQ<br>Level 4 | | Key Skills<br>Level 4 | Level 4 | HE Level<br>6 – Degree<br>5 – Diploma<br>4 – Certificate |
| NVQ<br>Level 3 | | Key Skills<br>Level 3 | Level 3<br><br>Advanced<br>A – level | |
| NVQ<br>Level 2 | Skills for Life<br>Level 2 | Key Skills<br>Level 2 | Level 2<br><br>Intermediate<br>GCSE A* – C | |
| NVQ<br>Level 1 | Skills for Life<br>Level 1 | Key Skills<br>Level 1 | Level 1<br>Foundation<br>GCSE D – G | |
| | Skills for Life<br>Entry 3 | | | |
| | Skills for Life<br>Entry 2 | | | |
| | Skills for Life<br>Entry 1 | | | |

# Bibliography

Adler, R., Rosenfeld, L. and Towne, N (1998) *Interplay: The Process of Interpersonal Communication* (7th edn.) New York: CBS.

Ainscow, M. and Booth, T. (2011) *Index for Inclusion: Developing Learning and Participation in Schools*. Bristol: Centre for Studies in Inclusive Education (CSIE). www.csie.org.uk/publications.

AOC/FENTO (2001) *Mentoring Towards Excellence*. London: FENTO.

Appleyard, N. and Appleyard, K. (2010) *Communicating with Learners in the Lifelong Learning Sector*. Exeter: Learning Matters.

Archer, M. (2002) Thinking about educational systems, in A. Pollard (ed.) *Readings for Reflective Teaching*. London: Continuum.

Argyle, M. (1994) *The Psychology of Interpersonal Behaviour* (5th edn). London: Penguin.

Atherton, J. S. (2005) *Teaching and Learning: Assessment*. www.learningandteaching.info/teaching/assessment.htm#Validity (accessed 29 January 2007).

Atherton, J. S. (2011) *Learning and Teaching: Reflection and Reflective Practice*. www.learningandteaching.info/learning/reflecti.htm (accessed 15 October 2011).

Ausubel, D. P. (1960) The use of advance organizers in the learning and retention of meaningful verbal material, *Journal of Educational Psychology*, 51: 267–272.

Becta (2009) *Pushing the Boundaries of Technology: Towards a Future Vision for the Innovative Use of Technology in FE Colleges*. Coventry: Becta.

Berliner, D. (2001) Teacher expertise, in F. Banks and A. Shelton Mayes (eds) *Early Professional Development for Teachers*. London: David Fulton.

Berlo, D. (1960) *The Process of Communication: An Introduction to Theory and Practice*. New York: Holt, Rinehart and Winston.

Biggs, J. (2003) *Teaching for Quality Learning at University* (2nd edn). Maidenhead: Open University Press.

Biggs, J. and Tang, C. (2011) *Teaching for Quality Learning at University* (4th edn). Maidenhead: Open University Press.

BIS (Department for Business, Innovation and Skills, 2011) *New Challenges, New Chances: Further Education and Skills System Reform Plan*. London: BIS.

Black, P. J. and William, D. (1998) Assessment and classroom learning, *Assessment in Education: Principles, Policy and Practice*, 5(1): 7–73.

Blakemore, S.-J. and Frith, U. (2005) *The Learning Brain: Lessons for Education*. Oxford: Blackwell.

Bloom, B. S. et al. (1956) *Taxonomy of Educational Objectives. 1: Cognitive Domain*. London: Longman.

Bloomer, M. (1997) *Curriculum Making in Post-16 Education*. London: Routledge.

Bowkett, S. (2006) *100 Ideas for Teaching Thinking Skills*. London: Continuum.

Bourdillon, H. and Storey, A. (2002) *Aspects of Teaching and Learning in Secondary Schools: Perspectives on Practice*. London: Routledge Falmer.

Brookfield, S. (1995) *Becoming a Critically Reflective Teacher*. San Francisco: Jossey-Bass.

Bruner, J. (1960) *The Process of Education*. Cambridge, MA: Harvard University Press.

Bruner, J. (1996) *Towards a Theory of Instruction*. Cambridge, MA: Harvard University Press.

Burton, G. and Dimbleby, R. (1995) *Between Ourselves: An Introduction to Interpersonal Communication* (2nd edn). London: Arnold.

Callaghan, J. (2004) Diversity, ILPs, and the art of the possible, *Reflect: The Magazine of the NRDC*, 1 October.

Canter, L. (2010) *Assertive Discipline: Positive Behaviour Management for Today's Classroom* (3rd edn). Bloomington, IN: Solution Tree Press.

Canter, L. and Canter, M. (1976) *Assertive Discipline: A Take Charge Approach for Today's Educator*. Santa Monica, CA: Canter and Associates.

Casey, H., Cara, O., Eldred, J., Grief, S., Hodge, R., Ivanic, R., Jupp, T., Lopez, D. and McNeil, B. (2006*) 'You wouldn't expect a maths teach to teach plastering'. Embedding Literacy, Language and Numeracy in Post-16 Vocational Programmes – The Impact on Learning and Achievement*. London: NRDC.

Centre for Educational Research and Innovation (CERI, 2007) *Understanding the Brain: The Birth of a Learning Science*. CERI: Paris.

Clarke, A. (2011) *How to Use Technology Effectively in Post-Compulsory Education*. London: Routledge.

Claxton, G. (1990) *Teaching to Learn*. London: Cassell.

Claxton, G. (1999) *Wise Up. Learning to Live the Learning Life*. Stafford: Network Educational Press.

Claxton, G. (2002) *Building Learning Power*. Bristol: TLO Ltd.

Coffield, F. (2008) *Just Suppose Teaching and Learning Became the First Priority*. London: Learning and Skills Network.

Coffield, F. (2009) *All You Ever Wanted to Know about Learning and Teaching but were too Cool to Ask*. London: Learning and Skills Network.

Coffield, F., Moseley, D., Hall, E. and Ecclestone, K. (2004) *Should We Be Using Learning Styles?* Norwich: Larning and Skills Research Centre.

Costa, A. L. (2001) *Developing Minds: A Resource Book for Teaching Thinking* (3rd edn). Alexandria, VA: Association for Supervision and Curriculum Development.

Cousin, G. (2006) An introduction to threshold concepts, *Planet*, 17 December. www.gees. ac.uk/planet/p17/gc.pdf (accessed 11 December 2011).

Csikszentmihalyi, M. (1990) *Flow: The Psychology of Optimal Experience*. New York: HarperCollins.

Cutting, R. (2009) Widening participation in adult education, in S. Gibson and J. Haynes (eds) *Perspectives on Participation and Inclusion*. London: Continuum.

Davison, J. (2008) Why we shouldn't have it all off pat, *Times Educational Supplement*, 14 March.

de Bono, E. (1976) *The Greatest Thinkers*. New York: GP Putnam.

de Bono, E. (1985) *Six Thinking Hats*. Harmondsworth: Penguin.

Department for Education and Skills (DfES, 2005) *Learning Behaviour: The Report of the Practitioners on School Behaviour and Discipline* (The Steer Report). London: DfES.

Department for Education and Skills (DfES, 2006) *Personalising Further Education: Developing a Vision*. London: DfES.

Department for Education and Skills (DfES, 2009) *Learning Behaviour: Lessons Learned* (The Steer Report). Nottingham: DfES.

Department of Education and Science (1989) *Discipline in Schools* (The Elton Report). London: HMSO.

Dewey, J. (1933) *How We Think*. New York: D. C. Heath.

Dewey, J. (1938) *Experience and Education*. New York: Macmillan.

Dewey, J. (1997) *Experience and Education*. New York: Simon and Schuster.

Dixie, G. (2011) It pays to say the hardest word, *Times Educational Supplement*, 18 November.

Driscoll, J. and Teh, B. (2001) The potential of reflective practice to develop individual ortho-paedic nurse practitioners and their practice, *Journal of Orthopaedic Nursing*, 5: 95–103.

Dweck, C. (2000) *Self-theories: Their role in Motivation, Personality and Development*. Philadelphia, PA: Psychology Press.

Eastwood, L., Coates, J., Dixon, L., Harvey, J., Ormondroyd, C. and Williamson, S. (2009) *A Toolkit for Creative Teaching in Post-Compulsory Education*. Maidenhead: Open University Press.

Ecclestone, K. (2010) *Transforming Formative Assessment in Lifelong Learning*. Maidenhead: Open University Press.

Ellis, S. and Tod, J. (2009) *Behaviour for Learning: Proactive Approaches to Behaviour Management*. London: Routledge.

Entwistle, N. (2000) Promoting deep learning through teaching and assessment: conceptual frameworks and educational concepts. Paper presented at TLRP Conference, Leicester, November.

Equality and Human Rights Commission (2011) "What equality law means for you as an education provider - further and higher education." http://www.equalityhumanrights.com/advice-and-guidance/new-equality-act-guidance/equality-act-guidance-downloads/ (accessed February 2012)

Field, J. (2011) Learning our way out of a crisis, *Adults Learning*, 23: 1.

Fisher, R. (2003) *Teaching Thinking*. London: Continuum.

Fisher, R. (2006) Thinking skills, in J. Arthur, T. Grainger and D. Wray (eds) *Learning to Teach in the Primary School*. London: Routledge Falmer.

Flanagan, F. (2006) *The Greatest Educators . . . Ever!* London: Continuum.

Foster, A. (2005) *Realising the Potential: A Review of Further Education Colleges*. London: DfES.

Freire, P. (1972) *Pedagogy of the Oppressed*. Harmondsworth: Penguin.

Furlong, J. (1998) Educational research: meeting the challenge of change. An inaugural lecture, Graduate School of Education, University of Bristol.

Gardner, H. (1993) *Multiple Intelligences: The Theory in Practice*. New York: Basic Books.

Geake, J. (2009) *The Brain at School: Educational Neuroscience in the Classroom*. Maidenhead: Open University Press.

Gibbs, G. (1988) *Learning by Doing*. London: Further Education Unit.

Gilbert, I. (2002) *Essential Motivation in the Classroom*. London: Routledge Falmer.

Gill, D. and Adams, B. (1998) *ABC of Communication Studies*. Cheltenham: Nelson.

Ginnis, P. (2002) *The Teacher's Toolkit*. Camarthen: Crown House Publishing.

Gleeson, D. and James, D. (2007) The paradox of professionalism in English further education: a TLS project perspective, *Educational Review*, 59(4): 451–467.

Goleman, D. (1995) *Emotional Intelligence*. London: Bloomsbury.

Goleman, D. (1998) *Working with Emotional Intelligence*. London: Bloomsbury.

Gorard, S. and Huat See, B. (2011) How can we enhance the enjoyment of secondary school? The student view, *British Educational Research Journal*, 37(4): 671–690.

Gorard, S. and Rees, G. (2002) *Creating a Learning Society?* Bristol: Policy Press.

Green, H., Facer, K., Rudd, T., Dillon, P. and Humphreys, P. (2005) *Personalisation and Digital Technologies*. www.futurelab.org.uk/research/personalisation.htm (accessed 29 March 2006).

Green, L. (2007) Freed from the pen, *Times Educational Supplement* 30 March.

Green, M. (2003) *Improving Initial Assessment in Work-Based Learning*. London: Learning and Skills Development Agency.

Grundy, S. (1987) *Curriculum: Product or Praxis?* London: Falmer.

Hall, E.T. (1966) *The Hidden Dimension: Man's Use of Space in Public and Private*. Garden City, NY: Doubleday.

Hargie, O. and Dickson, D. (2004) *Skilled Interpersonal Communication* (4th edn.). London: Routledge.

Harkin, J. (2006) Treated like adults: 14–16 year-olds in further education, *Research in Post-Compulsory Education*, 11(3): 319–339.

Harkin, J., Turner, D. and Dawn, T. (2001) *Teaching Young Adults*. London: Routledge Falmer.

Harris, A. (2001) Effective teaching: practical outcomes from research, in F. Banks, and Shelton A. Mayes (eds) *Early Professional Development for Teachers*. London: David Fulton.

Hart, S., Dixon, A., Drummond, M.J. and McIntyre, D. (2004) *Learning Without Limits* Maidenhead: Open University Press

Hay McBer (2000) *Research into Teacher Effectiveness*. London: Hay Group/DfEE.

Heath, H. (1998) Keeping a reflective practice diary: a practical guide, *Nurse Education Today*, 18: 592–598

Heinich, R., Molenda, M., Russell, J. D. and Smaldino, S. (1999) *Instructional Media and Technologies for Learning*. Upper Saddle River, NJ: Prentice-Hall.

Henry, J. (1994) *Teaching Through Projects*. London: Kogan Page.

Honey, P. and Mumford, A. (1986) *Manual of Learning Styles* (2nd edn). London: Peter Honey Publications.

Howard-Jones, P. (2007) *Neuroscience and Education: Issues and Opportunities, Commentary by the Teacher and Learning Research Programme*. London: TLRP. www.tlrp.org/pub/documents/Neuroscience%20Commentary%FINAL.pdf.

Howard-Jones, P. (2008) *Potential Educational Developments Involving Neuroscience that may Arrive by 2025*. www.beyondcurrenthorizons.org.uk/potential-educational-developments-involving-neuroscience-that-may-arrive-by-2025/.

Hughes, M. (1997) *Closing the Learning Gap*. Stafford: Network Educational Press.

Institute for Learning (IfL, 2009) *Guidelines for your Continuing Professional Development*. London: Institute for Learning.

James, D. and Biesta, G. (2007) *Improving Learning Cultures in Further Education*. London: Routledge.

Jones, C. A. (2005) *Assessment for Learning*. London: Learning and Skills Development Agency.

Jordan, A., Carlile, O. and Stack, S. (2008) *Approaches to Learning: A Guide for Teachers*. Maidenhead: Open University Press.

Keddie, N. (1971) Classroom knowledge, in M. F. D. Young *Knowledge and Control. New Directions for the Sociology of Education*. London: Collier Macmillan.

Kelly, A. V. (2009) *The Curriculum: Theory and Practice*. London: Sage.

Kember, D., Ho, A. and Hong, C. (2008) The importance of establishing relevance in motivating student learning, *Active Learning in Higher Education*, 9(3): 249–263.

Kennedy, H. (1997) *Learning Works: Widening Participation in Further Education*. Coventry: FEFC.

Kerry, T. (1982) *Effective Questioning*. London: Macmillan.

Kerry, T. (2002) *Explaining and Questioning*. Cheltenham: Nelson Thornes.

Knight, P. (2001) *A Briefing on Key Concepts. Assessment Series No. 7*. York: Learning and Teaching Support Network (LTSN).

Knight, P. and Yorke, M. (2003) Employability and good learning in higher education, *Teaching in Higher Education*, 8(1).

Knowles, M. S. (1978) *The Adult Learner: A Neglected Species*. Houston, TX Gulf Publishing.

Kolb, D. (1976) *The Learning Style Inventory*. Boston, MA: Mcber.

Kolb, D. A. (1984) *Experiential Learning: Experience as the Source of Learning and Development*. Upper Saddle River, NJ: Prentice Hall.

Land, R., Meyer, J. and Smith, J. (2008) *Threshold Concepts within the Disciplines*. Rotterdam: Sense Publishers.

Lasswell, H. (1948) The structure and function of communication in society, in L. Bryson (ed.) *The Communication of Ideas*. New York: Harper and Row.

Lave, J. and Wenger, E. (1990) *Situated Learning: Legitimate Peripheral Participation*. Cambridge: Cambridge University Press.

Lawrence, D. (2000) *Building Self-esteem with Adult Learners*. London: Sage.

Lea, J., Hayes, D., Armitage, A., Lomas, L. and Markless, S. (2003) *Working in Post-Compulsory Education*. Maidenhead: Open University Press.

Learning and Skills Council (LSC, 2003) *Successful Participation For All: Widening Adult Participation Strategy. For Consultation*. www.lsc.go.uk (accessed 19 April 2007).

Learning and Skills Development Agency (LSDA, 2007) *What's Your Problem? Working with Learners with Challenging Behaviour*. London: LSDA.

Lefrancois, G. (2000) *Psychology for Teaching* (10th edn). Belmont, CA: Wadsworth Thomson Learning.

Legge, K. and Harari, P. (2000) *Psychology and Education*. London: Heinemann.

Leitch, A. (2006) *Prosperity for All in the Global Economy: World Class Skills*. London: HM Treasury.

Le Versha, L. and Nicholls, G. (2003) *Teaching at Post-16: Effective Teaching in the A-Level, As and VCE Curriculum*. London: Kogan Page

Lifelong Learning UK (LLUK, 2011) *New Overarching Professional Standards for Teachers, Tutors and Trainers in the Lifelong Learning Sector*. London: LLUK.

Lipman, M. (1982) Philosophy for children, thinking, *The Journal for Philosophy for Children*,

Longworth, N. (2003) *Lifelong Learning in Action*. London: Kogan Page.

Lucas, B. and Claxton, G. (2009) *Wider Skills for Learning*. London: National Endowment for Science, Technology and the Arts (NESTA). www.nesta.org.uk.

Lucas, B. and Claxton, G. (2010) *New Kinds of Smart: How the Science of Learnable Intelligence is Changing Education*: Maidenhead: Open University Press.

McCarthy, M. (2006) Message understood?, *The Guardian*, 11 April.

McGregor, D. (2007) *Developing Thinking: Developing Learning*. Maidenhead: Open University Press.

McGregor, D. and Cartwright, L. (2011) *Developing Reflective Practice: A Guide for Beginning Teachers*. Maidenhead: Open University Press.

McGuiness, C. (1999) *From Thinking Skills to Thinking Classrooms: A Review and Evaluation of Developing Pupils' Thinking*. Nottingham: DfEE.

McLay, M., Mycroft, L., Noel, P., Orr, K., Thompson, R., Tummons, J. and Weatherby, J. (2010) Teaching in the lifelong learning sector, in J. Avis, R. Fisher and R. Thompson (eds) *Teaching in Lifelong Learning: A Guide to Theory and Practice*. Maidenhead: Open University Press.

MacLennan, N. (1995) *Coaching and Mentoring*. Aldershot: Gower.

McNair, S. and Quintero-Re, L. (2008) *CONFINTEA VI United Kingdom National Report: National Report on the Development and the State of the Art of Adult Learning and Education (ALE)*. Leicester: NIACE.

Marland, M. (2002) *The Craft of the Classroom: A Survival Guide* (3rd edn). London: Heinemann.

Martin, R., Villeneuve-Smith, F., Marshall, L. and McKenzie, E. (2008) *Employability Skills Explored.* London: Learning and Skills Network.

Marton, F. and Saljo, R. (1976) On qualitative differences in learning: outcome and process, *British Journal of Educational Psychology,* 46: 4–11.

Meyer, J. and Land, R. (2003) *Threshold Concepts and Troublesome Knowledge: Linkages to Ways of Thinking and Practising within the Disciplines.* Edinburgh: Teaching and Learning Research Project (TLRP).

Mezirow, J. (1991) *Dimensions of Adult Learning.* New York: Jossey-Bass.

Minton, D. (2005) *Teaching Skills in Further and Adult Education* (3rd edn). London: Thomson.

Moon, J. (1999) *Reflection in Learning and Professional Development.* London: Kogan Page.

Moon, J. (2004) *A Handbook of Reflective and Experiential Learning: Theory and Practice.* London: Routledge.

Moon, J. (2005) *Guide for Busy Academics No. 4: Learning Through Reflection.* York: Higher Education Academy.

Moorse, R. and Clough, L. (2002) *Recognition and Reward: Using Feedback for Learner Success.* London: Learning and Skills Development Agency.

Mortiboys, A. (2005) *Teaching with Emotional Intelligence.* London: Routledge.

Northedge, A. (2003) Enabling participation in academic discourse, *Teaching in Higher Education,* 8(2): 169–180.

Ofqual (2002) *Criteria for Functional Skills Qualifications.* Coventry: Ofqual.

Ofsted (2003) *The Initial Training of Teachers.* London: Ofsted.

Ofsted (2004a) *Why Colleges Fail.* London; Ofsted.

Ofsted (2004b) *Why Colleges Succeed.* London: Ofsted.

Ofsted (2005) *Managing Challenging Behaviour.* London: Ofsted.

Ofsted (2006) *Handbook for Inspecting Colleges.* London: Ofsted.

Ofsted (2009) *Handbook for Inspecting Colleges.* London: Ofsted.

Petty, G. (2009) *Teaching Today* (4th edn). Cheltenham; Nelson Thornes.

Pollard, A. and Trigg, P. (1997) *Reflective Teaching in Secondary School.* London: Cassell.

Powell, S. and Tod, J. (2004) *A Systematic Review of how Theories Explain Learning Behaviour in School Contexts.* London: EPPI Centre.

Powell, B., Knight, S. and Smith, R. (2003) *Managing Inspection and ILT.* Coventry: BECTA.

Prensky, M. (2001) Digital natives, Digital Immigrants, *On the Horizon,* 9 (5).

Pritchard, A. (2009) *Ways of Learning: Learning Theories and Learning Styles in the Classroom* (2nd edn.) London: David Fulton.

Qualifications and Curriculum Authority (QCA, 2001) *Assessment for Learning.* www.qca.org. uk/ca/5–14/afl/ (accessed 25 January 2007).

Qualifications and Curriculum Authority (QCA, 2007) *The Secondary Curriculum Review. Curriculum Lenses: The Personal, Learning and Thinking Skills Framework.* http://www.qca. org.uk/secondarycurriculumreview/lenses/skills/personal-learning/definitions. (accessed 15 May 2007).

Randle, K. and Brady, N. (1997) Managerialism and professionalism in the 'Cinderella service', *Journal of Further and Higher Education,* 49(1): 229–239.

Reynolds, B. (1965) *Learning and Teaching in the Practice of Social Work* (2nd edn). New York: Russell and Russell

Roam, D. (2008) *The Back of the Napkin.* London: Penguin.

Roberts, C., Baynham, M., Shrubsall, P., Brittan, J., Cooper, B., Gidley, N., Windsor, V., Eldred, J., Grief, S., Castillino, C. and Walsh, M. (2005) *Embedded Teaching and Learning of Adult Literacy, Numeracy and ESOL: Seven Case Studies.* London: NRDC.

Rogers, C. (1969) *Freedom to Learn: A View of What Education Might Become.* Columbus, OH: Charles E. Merrill.

Rogers, J. (2001) *Adults Learning* (4th edn). Maidenhead: Open University Press.

Rogers, J. (2007) *Adults Learning* (5th edn). Maidenhead: Open University Press.

Rogers, A. and Horrocks, N. (2010) *Teaching Adults*. Maidenhead: Open University Press.

Rollett, B. A. (2001) How do expert teachers view themselves?, in F. Banks and A. Shelton Mayes (eds) *Early Professional Development for Teachers*. London: David Fulton.

Rose, C. and Faraday, F. (2006) *The Journey towards Disability Equality: Responding to the Duty to Promote Disability Equality in the Post-school Sector*. London: Learning and Skills Network.

Rosenshine, B. (1971) *Teaching Behaviors and Student Achievement*. London: National Foundation for Educational Research.

Royal Society, The (2011) *Brain Waves Module 2: Neuroscience: Implications for Education and Lifelong Learning*. London: The Royal Society. www.royalsociety.org/policy/projects/brain-waves/education-lifelong-learning/.

Scales, P. (2008) *Teaching in the Lifelong Learning Sector* (1st edn). Maidenhead: Open University Press.

Scales, P., Pickering, J., Senior, L., Headley, K., Garner, P. and Boulton, H. (2011) *Continuing Professional Development in the Lifelong Learning Sector*. Maidenhead: Open University Press.

Schon, D. A. (1983) *The Reflective Practitioner*. New York: Basic Books.

Schuller, T. and Watson, D. (2010) *Learning Through Life: Inquiry into the Future for Lifelong Learning* (IFLL). Leicester: National Institute for Adult Continuing Education.

Schramm, W. (1973) *Men, Messages and Media*. New York: Harper and Row.

Senior, L. (2010) *The Essential Guide to Teaching 14–19 Diplomas*. Harlow: Pearson Education.

Shannon, C. E. and Weaver, W. (1949) *The Mathematical Theory of Communication*. Urbana, IL: University of Illinois Press.

Sharma, M. (2003) *Dyscalculia*. Skillswise expert column. www.bbc.co.uk/skillswise/tutors/expertcolumn/dyscalculia (accessed 21 April 2007).

Skidmore, P. (2003) *Beyond Measure: Why Educational Assessment is Failing the Test*. London: Demos.

Smith, M. K. (2011) What is praxis? *Encyclopaedia of Informal Education*. www.infed.org/biblio/b-praxis.htm (accessed 19 December 2011).

Standards Verification UK (SVUK, 2006) *New Professional Standards: Teacher/Tutor/Trainer in the Lifelong Learning Sector*. London: SVUK.

Stanton, N. (2009) *Mastering Communication* (5th edn). Basingstoke: Palgrave Macmillan.

Stenhouse, L. (1975) *An Introduction to Curriculum Research and Development*. London: Heinemann.

Steward, A. (2009) *Continuing Your Professional Development in Lifelong Learning*. London: Continuum.

Stokes, A., King, H. and Libarkin, J. (2007) Research in science education, *Journal of Geoscience Education*, 55(5): 434–438.

Stradling, B. and Saunders, L. (1993) Differentiation in practice: responding to the needs of all pupils, *Educational Research*, 35: 127–137.

Swan, M. (2006) Learning GCSE mathematics through discussion: what are the effects on students?, *Journal of Further and Higher Education*, 30(3): 229–241.

Teaching and Learning Research Project (TLRP, 2007) *Principles into Practice: A Teacher's Guide to Research Evidence on Teaching and Learning*. London: Institute of Education. www.tlrp.org/pub/documents/Principles%20in%20Practice%20Low%20Res.pdf.

Tomlinson, J. (1996) *Inclusive Learning – Principles and Recommendations. A Summary of the Findings of the Learning difficulties and Disabilities Committee*. Coventry: FEFC.

Tomlinson, J. (2003) Notes towards a definition of inclusive learning, *Learning and Skills Research*, 6(3): 5–7.

Torrance, H. and Pryor, J. (1998) *Investigating Formative Assessment: Teaching, Learning and Assessment in the Classroom*. Maidenhead: Open University Press.

Torrance, H., Colley, C., Garratt, D., Jarvis, J., Piper, P., Ecclestone, K. and James, D. (2005) *The Impact of Different Modes of Assessment on Achievement in the Learning and Skills Sector*. London: Learning and Skills Development Agency.

Tufte, E. R. (2006) *The Cognitive Style of PowerPoint: Pitching out the Corrupts Within*. Cheshire, CT: Graphics Press LLC.

Tummons, J. (2010) *Curriculum Studies in the Lifelong Learning Sector*. Exeter: Learning Matters.

Tummons, J. (2011) *Assessing Learning in Further Education* (3rd edn). Exeter: Learning Matters.

Tyler, R. W. (1949) *Basic Principles of Curriculum and Instruction*. Chicago, IL: University of Chicago Press.

UK Commission on Employability and Skills (UKCES, 2009) *The Employability Challenge*. London: UKCES.

Villeneuve-Smith, F., West, C. and Bhinder, B. (2009) *Rethinking Continuing Professional Development in Further Education. Eight Things You Already Know About CPD*. London: Learning and Skills Network.

Vizard, D. (2007) *How to Manage Behaviour in Further Education*. London: Paul Chapman.

Wallace, S. and Gravells, J. (2005) *Mentoring in Further Education*. Exeter: Learning Matters.

Watkins, C. (2011) *Managing Classroom Behaviour*. London: Association of Teachers and Lecturers (ATL). www.atl.org.uk/Images/Managing%20classroom%20behaviour%20-%20 2011.pdf.

Weeden, P., Winter, J. and Broadfoot, P. (2002) *Assessment: What's in it for Schools?* London: Routledge Falmer.

Wells, G. (1986) *The Meaning Makers*. London: Hodder and Stoughton.

Wenger, E. (1998) *Communities of Practice: Learning, Meaning and Identity*. Cambridge: Cambridge University Press.

Whalley, J., Welch, T. and Williamson, L. (2006) *E-learning in FE*. London: Continuum.

Whitehead, A. N. (1932) *The Aims of Education*. London: Williams and Norgate.

Wolf, A. (1995) *Competence-Based Assessment*. Maidenhead: Open University Press.

Wolvin, A. (1984) Meeting the communication needs of the adult learner, *Communication Education*, 33: 267–271.

Woolfolk, A., Hughes, M. and Walkup, V. (2008) *Psychology in Education*. Harlow: Pearson Education.

Wragg, E. (1984) *Classroom Teaching Skills*. London: Routledge.

Wright, A.-M., Sina, A.-J., Colquhoun, S., Speare, J. and Partridge, T. (2006) *FE Lecturer's Guide to Diversity and Inclusion*. London: Continuum.

# Index